BANDITS IN PRINT

THE WATER MARGIN AND THE TRANSFORMATIONS OF THE CHINESE NOVEL

SCOTT W. GREGORY

CORNELL EAST ASIA SERIES
An imprint of

CORNELL UNIVERSITY PRESS
Ithaca and London

Number 212 in the Cornell East Asia Series

First published 2023 by Cornell University Press

The open-access version of this book was made possible in part by an award from the James P. Geiss and Margaret Y. Hsu Foundation.

GEISS HSU
FOUNDATION

ISBN 9781501769191 (hardback)
ISBN 9781501769689 (paperback)
ISBN 9781501769207 (epub)
ISBN 9781501769214 (pdf)

Library of Congress Control Number: 2022030033

For Michelle, Phoebe, and Zoe

Contents

ILLUSTRATIONS

ACKNOWLEDGMENTS

This is a book that has taken longer than expected to write, interrupted as it was several times by events on the personal and the global scale. As the years went by, the list of people to whom I owe a debt of gratitude grew ever longer; acknowledging them all is a daunting task indeed. Some of these people have remained constant presences, while others may even have forgotten the reason for their inclusion by now. Nevertheless, I wish to mention them here.

This book grew out of the research I conducted while at Princeton University. I would like to convey special thanks to Andrew Plaks, whose work on the Ming novel set me on the path once I stumbled across it in the National Central Library in Taipei. I would also like to thank Anna Shields, who has been a mentor to me even when she was under absolutely no obligation to do so. I am also indebted to Benjamin Elman, Susan Naquin, Martin Kern, Stephen F. Teiser, Martin Heijdra, and Paize Keulemans at Princeton, and to Shang Wei of Columbia University, for their guidance and support. My fellow graduate students were also a source of inspiration: Wayne Soon, Ja Ian Chong, Mick Hunter, Nick Admussen, Zhiyi Yang, Bryan Lowe, Will Bridges, Yulia Frumer, Erin Brightwell, Margaret Ng, Jim Bonk, Maren Ehlers, Esther Klein, Ya Zuo, Chunmei Du, Brigid Vance, Mårten Söderblom Saarela, Mark Meulenbeld, Ori Sela, and April Hughes, to name but a few. Spending several years as part of this community was an immense privilege.

Portions of the dissertation were completed in Taipei, Taiwan, with generous support from the Chiang Ching-kuo Foundation, Academia Sinica, and the Center for Chinese Studies at the National Central Library. Ayling Wang, Siao-chen Hu, Chiung-yun Liu, and William Hsu were kind hosts during my stay in Taiwan.

I am grateful to my former colleagues at the National University of Singapore, Yung Sai-shing, Su Jui-lung Su, Ong Chang Woei, Koh Khee Heong, Xu Lanjun, Nico Volland, Ken Dean, and John DiMoia, for welcoming me to the Little Red Dot. At the University of Arizona,

I am grateful for the support I have received from my colleagues Albert Welter, Jiang Wu, Fabio Lanza, Kim Jones, Takashi Miura, Wenhao Diao, Maggie Camp, Nathaniel Smith (now of Ritsumeikan University), Kaoru Hayashi, Sunyoung Yang, and Heng Du (now of Wellesley University), and to Huiqiao Yao for assistance with tracking down errant references. I am also grateful for Dean A.-P. Durand's tireless advocacy for the humanities.

I presented material from this book at many conferences and meetings and benefited from comments and conversations with fellow panelists, discussants, chairs, and audience members. In particular, I would like to thank Will Hedberg, Xiaoqiao Ling, Maria Franca Sibau, Lucille Chia, Oki Yasushi, Robert Hegel, Yuanfei Wang, Katherine Alexander, Mengjun Li, Maram Epstein, Pat Sieber, Steve West, Tina Lu, David Rolston, Ariel Fox, and Yuming He. I am also very appreciative of the Society for Ming Studies regulars, especially Sarah Schneewind and Ihor Pidhainy, for introducing me to a friendly space within larger and more impersonal conferences. Ariel Fox and all of the participants in the Early Modern Online Workshop helped me maintain some sense of connection to a larger scholarly community as the pandemic forced us into isolation. Finally, the northern contingent of the greater Arizona *jianghu*, Will Hedberg, Xiaoqiao Ling, and Steve West, have been great hosts and occasional collaborators.

Material from chapter 1 appeared in an earlier form in the journal *East Asian Publishing and Society*. The editors have kindly granted permission to reprint some of that material here. I would like to thank my editor at Cornell University Press, Alexis Siemon, for shepherding this project through, and to the anonymous readers, whose feedback was invaluable. I would also like to thank the James P. Geiss and Margaret Y. Hsu Foundation for the generous funding that made it possible to publish this book in an open-access format.

Most of all, however, I wish to thank my wife Michelle and my daughters Phoebe and Zoe, for being by my side all of these years across continents, my father, Stephen, and my mother, Helen, who unfortunately did not get to see this book's completion. It is to them that this book and the labor behind it are dedicated.

Introduction
The Bandits' Reception

The traditional long-form novel, as developed in late Ming China, could be endlessly reshaped and repackaged. Its text could be freely altered. Commentaries could be added to its chapters, whether at their beginnings, at their ends, or even interpolated into the text itself, in order to assist less-experienced readers or to provide interpretations. Prefaces could be appended in order to orient readers' expectations and understandings from the outset. Illustrations could be added, whether to the chapters themselves or in a folio at the front of the work. Decisions about what shape the novel would take—its text, paratext, and physical form—were made by editors and publishers of print editions in anticipation of their target readerships' needs and desires. As such, the Ming novel was a genre intimately tied to the medium of print.

Shaping the Novel

The novel *The Water Margin* (*Shuihu zhuan*), which appears to have been first printed in the early sixteenth century, exemplifies the relations between the genre and the dynamic print culture of the era. It was among the earliest such works, and among the most influential. It appeared—and continues to appear—in a wide range of forms, for different readerships, with different implied meanings. It created a sensation among its earliest readers and was the inspiration for many works that followed. This book follows the transformations of the Ming novel genre in print by tracing print editions of *The Water Margin*, a pathbreaking example.

The process by which a novel such as *The Water Margin* could be reshaped by editor-publishers is perhaps best illustrated by a note included in the front matter of a commercial edition printed by the Fujian publisher Yu Xiangdou, one of the most renowned such editor-publishers of the Ming. In the note, Yu distinguished his edition of the novel from the many others available on the market. He warned potential customers of the many shortcomings of his competitors' editions: many of them were only partially illustrated, or their texts lacked *shi* poems and *ci* lyrics and were therefore less suitable for recitation aloud. They were printed from woodblocks that had worn with age, creating images and text that were indistinct and difficult to make out. Only the edition of his own Shuangfeng tang publishing house, Yu declared, was fully illustrated and featured commentary in its margins. Yu went on to note that he had edited the text, removing all impediments to leisurely browsing and ensuring that all of the characters used were correct. "From front to back," he concluded, "in all twenty volumes of the book, there is not a single mistake in a single sentence. Gentlemen customers can recognize the mark of the Shuangfeng tang house."

It is apparent that, in shaping his edition, Yu took into account his potential readership. He calculated that they demanded texts that were clearly printed and easy to read, with illustrations and a mix of prose and verse of various kinds. He recognized that they had heard of *The Water Margin* before, and that they did not want to miss out on any of the features that the competition offered in their own editions. With these factors in mind, he crafted an edition of the novel and had it carved on wooden blocks. He, or his Shuangfeng tang firm, would have had to estimate the number of copies that the market could bear, purchase paper accordingly, and turn the visions into material reality through print. Since printers of novels in the Ming used woodblocks rather than moveable type, the calculations did not need to be exact; there was no need to tear down the page layout and recover the font after a run. An edition's woodblocks could be kept indefinitely—or at least until they became blunt and blurry through repeated stamping. They could also be rented out or sold to other printing establishments, perhaps in different geographical areas, to further defray costs.

Other than the expectations and desires of their readerships, Ming editor-publishers like Yu were unimpeded in their ability to repackage and reshape the novel at will. In terms of legality, it almost goes without saying that there was no formal copyright system in place that would have prevented editor-publishers from altering the texts of novels as they saw fit. If anything, it was they and not any authors who could claim legal rights to the texts of their editions; there was a precedent of woodblock imprints containing warnings against unauthorized copying, and at least one publisher, as this book will show, made indignant assertions that his editing work was a form of intellectual labor from which he was entitled to profit. There are some parallels here with the development of the copyright system in Europe, wherein it was publishers who claimed that authors held the natural rights to their creations, and that those rights were transferred to them. Titles would be recorded in a central registry so that the publishers could prove that they held the rights to their texts and pursue action against "pirates" who appropriated them unlawfully. Despite the similarities between these claims of some publishers in the Ming and those in the Europe, the former did not enter claims of ownership in a registry or conceive of an exclusive right to a text.[1]

Moreover, an editor-publisher reshaping a novel for publication would not have felt any compulsion to be true to an author's "original" text. The names of novelists were shadowy at best, and even when a name was closely associated with a work, that name rarely held much significance for how the novel was understood. In the case of *The Water Margin*, authorship was attributed to two names, Luo Guanzhong and Shi Nai'an, usually in some combination as author and editor or compiler. Yet next to nothing is known about either man, and the existing sources seem to indicate that they lived long before known editions of *The Water Margin* began to appear in the sixteenth century. The earliest available sources claim that Luo Guanzhong was a loner who took the sobriquet "Wanderer of the Lakes and Seas" (*Huhai sanren*) and lived sometime around the time of the Yuan-Ming transition. Various accounts claim he was from either Taiyuan, Qiantang, or Dongyuan. In addition to *The Water Margin*, Luo Guanzhong was also credited with the authorship of *Romance of the Three Kingdoms* and a handful of other works, including *Record of the Sui and Tang* (*Sui Tang zhizhuan*), *The Three Sui Quash the Demons* (*San Sui pingyao zhuan*), *History of the Remnant Tang and Five Dynasties* (*Can Tang wudai shi*), and *The Rouge Chamber* (*Fenzhuang lou*). However, judging from the various commentaries, prefaces, and other writings, readers do not seem to have taken these works to form a consistent oeuvre, whether stylistically or thematically. As for Shi Nai'an, almost nothing is known of him; claims that he lived in the late Yuan or that he was a native of Qiantang appear to be based merely on the assumption that he worked in tandem with Luo.[2] Whatever the case, editor-publishers would hardly have had to worry about someone like Luo Guanzhong or Shi Nai'an lodging a complaint about their treatment of their work. Nor, more important, would they have to worry about their readerships expecting a work to conform to a particular authorial style known from that author's other works.

Finally, an editor-publisher would also not have felt any obligation to maintain fidelity to the moral character of an author. More culturally privileged forms of writing such as shi poetry were tightly bound to their authorial figures; there was an underlying assumption that, by reading the poem, one came to know its author. This close association would discourage overt textual meddling. With the nascent long-form novel genre of the Ming dynasty, there was no such hermeneutic of character to prevent editorial tampering.

In sum, the Ming novel was a highly flexible genre that could be reshaped endlessly in print by editor-publishers. Editor-publishers would shape editions with an eye to their anticipated readerships, not to an author or any other original stakeholder. Editor-publishers were free to modify a novel, add to it, or cut from it to suit the needs and desires of that readership, whether the goal was to express membership in a certain group, to create profit, to use it to circulate ideas or police interpretations, or any combination thereof.

Editions

In the case of *The Water Margin*, the differences between editions were far from simple or cosmetic ones. Rather, they struck to the very heart of the work's significance. *The Water Margin* is in essence a collection of intertwined stories telling of men such as Lu Zhishen, the "tattooed monk" who caused havoc in a monastery with his drunken brawling, or Wu Song, who battled a tiger to the death with only his bare hands. There is Song Jiang, the minor official who goes on the run after killing his adulterous wife and who becomes an underworld leader. And there is Li Kui, the "Black Whirlwind," whose exaggerated fits of blind rage lend a comic edge to the proceedings. The novel moves from one story to the next, at times weaving them together as the men cross paths, and in the denouement they all gather in the Hall of Loyalty and Righteousness in a lair beyond the watery marshes of the title. Yet through paratextual materials such as prefaces, "how-to-read" essays, and intertextual commentaries, the editions suggest to their readers widely disparate interpretations of the meaning of these intertwined tales. Some treat the rebellious content cautiously, while others unapologetically glorify these outlaws and suggest that they are paragons of virtue in an age of corruption.

The sheer variety of editions of *The Water Margin* that appeared in the Ming demonstrates this flexibility of the novel. In addition to the competing editions, now lost, of which Yu Xiangdou complained in the 1590s, there were others that had appeared at least fifty years earlier. Those editions, the earliest known, were not the products of for-profit publishers like Yu, but rather of the elite world around the Jiajing court. Both the Censorate bureau and the Marquis of Wuding, Guo Xun, produced editions. Another edition, published in the 1580s, purported to be based on the Wuding edition and featured a preface signed Tiandu waichen, believed to be a pen name of Wang Daokun. Within a decade after Yu Xiangdou's edition, multiple editions featuring commentaries attributed to the noted iconoclast Li Zhi appeared in the marketplace. Then, on the eve of the Ming's collapse, Jin Shengtan produced his severely truncated and reworked edition. A fragment of yet another edition, believed to be from the Jiajing or even the Zhengde reign and simply called *Record of the Loyal and Righteous* (*Zhongyi zhuan*), was discovered in the collection of the Shanghai Municipal Library in 1975. The main texts of the various editions are divided into two major recensions, the so-called simple recensions (*jianben*) and full recensions (*fanben*). These differ in both style and content, with the former narrating more episodes but in simpler language, and the latter narrating fewer events but using a more elaborate prose style.

These editions vary to such an extent that one might even ask whether it makes sense to speak of "the" *Water Margin* as a distinct novel at all, instead of simply regarding it as a family of related story cycles. But, in spite of the range of shapes that the novel took, there is still a commonality that sets it apart from the other narratives that relate stories of some of the same protagonists. The various editions of the novel all share a general outline of plot. The plot opens with an arrogant official of the Song Dynasty releasing thirty-six Heavenly Spirits (*Tiangang*) and seventy-two Earthly Demons (*Disha*) from a sealed chamber in a cave, despite all warnings. From there, the focus moves to the individual characters who will eventually become members of the band of outlaws. The novel follows them as they run into one another, in Andrew Plaks's words, "billiard-ball" style, and several standout episodes and characters such as those mentioned above emerge.[3] This action coalesces in the triumphant gathering of the fully formed band under their leader Song Jiang in their mountain stronghold, which they christen the Hall of Loyalty and Righteousness (*Zhongyi tang*).

What happens after this climactic event depends again on the edition. The edition that was most widely read throughout the Qing Dynasty (1644–1911), the Jin Shengtan edition, ends here on an ambiguous note: after the banquet, the character Lu Junyi has a dream in which his fellow outlaws are executed by government troops. He awakes to see the words "Great peace under Heaven" (*Tianxia taiping*) before his eyes. In other editions, the banquet scene is followed by the band's acceptance of an offer of amnesty from the imperial authorities. From there, they embark on a number of campaigns on behalf of the Song. In the simple-recension editions, the targets of those campaigns are the Liao kingdom and the rebels Tian Hu, Wang Qing, and Fang La. The full-recension editions, on the other hand, omit the Tian Hu and Wang Qing campaigns. In all, the band gradually dissolves, with members either dispersing or dying off in sickness or battle.

It is this intertwining of tales that defines the *Water Margin* as a novel and sets it apart from other related narratives, such as dramas, oral storytellers' tales, and historiographical works that feature some of the same characters or events. There are at least thirty-nine dramas featuring "Water Margin" characters, for example, that predate known editions of the novel.[4] But these are based on single incidents and characters, typically Li Kui or Wu Song, rather than the "billiard-ball" action, climactic gathering, and dispersal seen in the novel. There are records of oral storytellers performing tales of these outlaws as early as the Southern Song. Of course, the precise details of these performances are lost to time due to the transient nature of that medium, but from continuing oral performance traditions, we can surmise that these too focused on single events or characters, such as the well-known story of Wu Song fighting a tiger. Moreover, performers in such traditions are not beholden to a set script; rather, they tend to weave set piece building blocks into extemporaneous performances.[5] The historiographical sources, meanwhile, provide only the briefest outline of *The Water Margin's* story. The historical Song Jiang is mentioned three times in the dynastic history of the Song: once in the record of Huizong's reign, once in the biography of the official Hou Meng, and once in the biography of Zhang Shuye, the governor who was assigned to subdue him. Hou Meng's biography includes a memorial by Hou in which he notes Song Jiang's skills in leading a band of thirty-six men and suggests that he be granted official amnesty so his talents could be used in pursuit of Fang La.[6] The *Fragments of the Xuanhe Era* (*Xuanhe yishi*), an "unofficial history" (*waishi*) of the collapse of the Northern Song, also features a brief account of Song Jiang and his band of thirty-six men.[7]

This is to say that when printed editions of *The Water Margin* appeared in the early sixteenth century, some of the stories they contained may have been old, but the form they took—gathered and intertwined—was new. Even *Three Kingdoms*, the other early novel alongside which *The Water Margin* was frequently published, was ultimately still bound to the general contours of official historiography.[8] With *The Water Margin*, fragments of narrative were captured and woven together through print; there are no records of it circulating in manuscript form beforehand. As chapters below will show, this quality of interwovenness was striking and novel to even the elite circles who read the earliest known editions. And subsequent editor-publishers continued to modify the novel to suit their own readerships. *The Water Margin* was a pioneer of the genre, and other works of vernacular fiction followed in the path it cut. Under its influence, editor-publishers of the Ming repurposed and repackaged other similar story cycles, turning them into "novels" as well.

Variation and Print

Variation is, of course, not unique to the late imperial novel genre. In fact, it is to be found among even the most basic building blocks of Chinese texts, the characters themselves. It has even been suggested that variation was so prevalent in early texts that the notion of a "correct" character with multiple "variant" forms should be called into question. Imre Galambos has argued that, in the face of a growing corpus of unearthed texts, variation that was once explained away as local forms, changes in writing over time, or scribal error can now be better understood as being representative of a high degree of tolerance among scribes and readers alike for orthographical difference. He suggests that chatters in the pre-Han period existed in a "'cloud' of potential forms."[9] Pre-Han readers, he continues, may not have even noticed the variation among instances of any given word, as they would have been more focused on sound and lexical meaning than graphical form.

To extend Galambos's metaphor, not only characters but the texts they comprise could said to exist as a "cloud of potential forms." This extends even to the most privileged literary genre in traditional China, shi poetry. As mentioned above, shi poetry was unlike the Ming novel in that it was closely associated with its authors rather than murky authorial figures such as Luo Guanzhong and Shi Nai'an. In the Confucian tradition, poems were considered to be an expression of their authors' "aims," and one could judge the character of a writer by reading that writer's poetry.[10] Yet this close association between author and work in the genre could paradoxically encourage rather than discourage variation: one could always claim to better understand, or better "know the tone," of a poet and thereby be best suited to select the "correct" character among variants—or even subtly alter the text oneself according to one's own image of the poet.

Perhaps the most famous example of this sort of correction comes in a line from Tao Yuanming's "On Drinking #5," which reads, "I see South Mountain in the distance" (youran jian Nanshan). No less an "editor" than the Song dynasty master Su Shi castigated "vulgar" editions that had "gaze" (wang) rather than "see" (jian) in the line and thereby turned Tao's "casual effortlessness" into an overeager, conscious act.[11] Su's justification for his choice, then, was the direct opposite of Yu Xiangdou's for his alterations of The Water Margin seen above: Su claims to understand deeply the character or intention of the author and bases his claims accordingly, whereas Yu pointed only to his potential readers' desires.

The hermeneutic paradox that the poet is known through the poem and the poem is interpreted through the understanding of the poet does not seem to have bothered traditional readers. In many cases, we can see the image of a poet develop through time and trace how the interpretation of the poetry changes accordingly. Just as Su Shi read Tao Yuanming as the embodiment of natural spontaneity, successive generations of readers made Du Fu into the embodiment of humaneness and morally impeccable loyalty, Li Bai into the unfettered genius, and so on.[12]

The usual culprit for this sort of textual change is usually the manuscript medium, which is held in contrast with the presumably stabilizing force of print. In her study of Tao Yuanming, in which she also discusses "On Drinking #5," Xiaofei Tian notes that the stability of the received texts readers are now accustomed to reading is largely an illusion, and "just underneath the smooth, fixed surface of a modern printed edition is a chaotic and unstable world" full of variants found in traditional manuscript copies.[13] In cases where a word in a poem varies across editions, modern editors have deemed one to be "correct" and either relegated the other possibilities to the footnotes or ignored them entirely. Texts, as has been frequently pointed out, are susceptible to change each time they are copied, and this is especially the case when they are copied by hand, one at a time. Scribal error is surely a factor, as is meddling on the part of a scribe wishing to improve on a text. But again, there is an underlying assumption that an error or variant stands in contrast with a "correct" or ideal version. Christopher Nugent has recently challenged this assumption, positing that textual variation in poetry is not merely evidence of frequent scribal error, but a consequence of a cultural understanding that copyists played an active role in textual creation. Authors, Nugent argues, were not the final authority in their own texts as they circulated in the world.[14]

Print, by contrast, carries connotations of textual stability, increased authorial presence, and a fixed moment of creation—though these qualities often prove illusory. The Confucian Classics, which served as the basis for the civil examinations, are a case in point. As Susan Cherniack discusses in a pioneering article, the Classics were first set to woodblocks by the Directorate of Education (*Guozi jian*) in the Later Tang for distribution purposes, in the hopes that the medium would have the same "petrifying effect" on the texts that inscribing them on stone stelae had had in the past.[15] The officially sanctioned woodblock imprint editions would then serve as models for hand copying, just as stelae had served for the making of rubbings. Cherniack notes that under the print culture of the Song, however, "it became abundantly clear, through the exploitation of printing's potential for allowing endless adjustments and revisions, that printed texts lacked the finality of texts engraved in stone."[16] More recently, Suyoung Son has demonstrated how, in the Qing dynasty, print could be a social, "collective process" among a "coterie" of literati. Publishers might actively solicit comments, corrections, and additions to a printed edition from a network of participants, and no one involved would expect any two copies of the "final" product to be identical.[17]

The textual stability ascribed to print has the power to consolidate the image of an author as well. The Shakespeare scholar David Scott Kastan, for example, has shown the role of print in transforming a playwright to "virtually the iconic name for authorship itself."[18] Kastan reminds us that, as a playwright, Shakespeare of course wrote his plays for the stage. They were by definition performed collectively by the actors of the theater, and fidelity to the script was not a concern. Yet when the plays were gathered together in the First Folio, they were advertised by its editors as being presented in their ideal form, as conceived by Shakespeare himself.[19] Moreover, bundled together, a perception of his voice emerged, and the plays became the written oeuvre of "Shakespeare." Despite the simple fact of these texts' provenance, traditional editors and scholars spent much energy on uncovering the "original" texts of these works. Newer branches of Shakespeare studies, meanwhile, have emphasized that the material incarnations of texts are important, and are more than merely the "accidental and vehicular" means by which an idealized and disembodied text is transmitted.[20]

With the reified image of the author comes an illusion of a singular moment of creation, the imagined point when that author set brush to paper and created a text. Yet as the Roger Chartier has put it, "Authors do not write 'books,' not even their own books."[21] Even, Chartier notes, in an instance where there is an identifiable, empirical author who is strongly associated with a text, such as Cervantes and *Don Quixote*, this still does not mean that there was a single, original version of the text disembodied from, but captured in, its printed form. Any number of intermediary processes, whether editorial, mechanical, or even legal in nature, might come between the act of writing and the printed edition. The "text" only exists in its material manifestations.[22]

A Phenomenon of Print

As Yu's note about his competitors' editions makes clear, variation in Ming novels like *The Water Margin* was different from the types of variation seen in poetry and manuscript. It occurred in print, but print did not stabilize the text, nor did it transform the shadowy Luo Guanzhong and Shi Nai'an into "authors" in the strong sense of the word, with an oeuvre, as it did with Shakespeare. It did not even firmly fix the moment of the novel's creation in time, as the yawning gap between those purported authors' eras and the earliest known editions of *The Water Margin* attest. With no strong presence of an author, no assumption that the work expresses the author's aims, and no textually fluid manuscript transmission process, editor-publishers held the power to reshape *The Water Margin* as they saw fit. Their guiding purpose was to meet the needs and expectations of their anticipated readerships. They would speculate as to those particular needs, have their visions set to woodblocks, and print books for those readerships. The variation of *The Water Margin* is a phenomenon of print.

By treating *The Water Margin* as a phenomenon of print, this book sidesteps several thorny problems that have plagued studies in the past. First, it avoids the question of authorship, not by solving it once and for all but by rendering it moot. As we have seen, even if the attribution to Luo Guanzhong and/or Shi Nai'an is accurate, these men would have lived more than a century before the appearance of printed editions in the record in the early sixteenth century. The earliest known printed editions, which appeared in the period of time I call "before the fire" in this book, were then followed by a steady stream of new editions and comments about the work—what has been called "*Water Margin* fever."[23] Earlier editions, whether manuscript or print, would not likely have had the same impact either in their time or afterward.

Second, by treating *The Water Margin* as a phenomenon of print, we sidestep the question of the literary merit of vernacular fiction. Studies of this complex of genres often assume that they were of "low" status, "despised" by the literati for its "vulgar" language. In this study, I suspend such literary judgments, instead returning particular editions to the circumstances in which they were produced. This includes other works printed by their publishers, cutting across generic lines we might otherwise impose on them. Rather than considering a work such as *The Water Margin* as the product of a particular genre, we can think of it as one of many literal products of a particular publishing agency of some kind, in particular social, historical, and literary contexts. This book will also take into account, to the extent possible, specific readerships and how they read the novel.

Finally, this approach considers a work like *The Water Margin* not as a single idealized work that is substantiated in various forms but as a series of reshaped works. By doing so, the relations between not only the work itself and other works of the genre, or the genre and other genres, but also between the work and other instantiations of itself come to the fore. Here, we must modify the concept of the reception of a work. Reception theory, as outlined by figures such as Hans Robert Jauss, places individual works of literature into a "literary series," in which each successive work can "solve formal and moral problems" presented by the previous and pose new ones for the next.[24] In the case of the late Ming novel, with its varying editions and textual fluidity, it is necessary to move away from the "work" and toward the "edition" to better conceive of the "literary series" into which it is to be inserted. That literary series will oftentimes contain previous editions of the same work, and subsequent editions will attempt to solve the formal and moral problems presented by previous editions.

Chapter Outline

This study is divided into two main parts, with an interlude in-between. The first section focuses on the early, elite editions of *The Water Margin* that were printed by and circulated among the elite of the Jiajing court during the period "before the fire." Chapter 1 is concerned with an edition printed by Guo Xun, Marquis of Wuding, a military figure of hereditary rank whose ancestors had taken part in the founding of the Ming. Chapter 2 deals with an edition printed by the Ming Censorate, the dynasty's highest oversight body. Neither of these editions survives, precluding textual analysis. However, the purpose of this study is to reconstitute the field around these two missing editions and to reconstruct the social environment in which they were created. What did it mean to print and publish *The Water Margin* in this early era, long before the publishing boom of the late sixteenth century? What sorts of other books were "adjacent" to it, and what were their genres? Toward whom were the printing projects of Guo and the Censorate oriented? These chapters turn to historical records; bibliographies; "casual jottings," or *biji*; and other such materials in order to answer these questions.

The interlude, Chapter 3, turns from the early publishers of *The Water Margin* to one of its earliest known readers, the literatus and playwright Li Kaixian. It will demonstrate how Li Kaixian and his extended social circles bring together the two publishing entities of the first section. It will also attempt to deduce what *The Water Margin* meant to Li both before and after his exile through a reading of his casual writings and one of his dramatic works. Additionally, it will contrast these activities with the gradual emergence of a more commercially oriented mode of novel creation, as personified by Li Kaixian's near-contemporary, the printer Xiong Damu.

The second section follows *The Water Margin* as it was transformed by the dynamic commercial publishing industry of the late Ming, in the period "after the fire," as *Water Margin* editions began to answer the Jaussian "formal and moral problems" posed by other editions of itself. Chapter 4 follows *The Water Margin* as commercial editor-publishers adapted it for the tastes of their particular readerships. In particular, they added prefaces, commentaries, and other forms of paratext with particular points of view, often satirizing the social order and flirting with "outlaw" values. These include the aforementioned Shuangfeng tang edition of Yu Xiangdou and the slightly later Rongyu tang edition featuring commentary (spuriously) attributed to the renowned icono-clast Li Zhuowu. This chapter suggests that the voices of these added materials were distinct enough that they could be considered "charac-ters" themselves, rivaling the characters in the novel in terms of their presences.

Chapter 5 then looks to the edition of Jin Shengtan, which eclipsed all others upon its appearance in the waning years of the Ming. Jin ap-peared to be both inspired and outraged by the Li Zhuowu edition, and staged his own radical intervention in the novel. He made drastic changes to its text and appended to it several prefaces and an elaborate commentary. Because of their close attention to the surface of the text, these paratextual materials have frequently been mined by scholars for insights into the aesthetics of the traditional Chinese novel. However, this chapter will argue that such "literary" qualities of Jin's commentary have been overemphasized at the expense of his own original thought, which engages in the discourse of values surrounding previous editions of *The Water Margin*.

The conclusion returns to the legacy of *The Water Margin* in its various incarnations, and to the traditional novel genre to which they belong. It also discusses implications of treating the novel as a phenomenon of print for the study of the genre.

CHAPTER 1

"Falsifying a Biography Brought Him Power"

The "Wuding Editions" of Guo Xun

       In May 1541, a fire destroyed the newly constructed ancestral temple of the Jiajing emperor. In the aftermath of this fire, a dozen officials were found culpable and removed from office, banished, or jailed. They included Guo Xun, a military figure and holder of hereditary rank; Wang Tingxiang, a member of the Former Seven Masters literary clique and head of the prestigious and powerful Censorate agency; and Li Kaixian, the renowned poet-dramatist and member of the Eight Talents of the Jiajing Era.[1] Guo was imprisoned on a number of charges and died in jail soon after. Wang was stripped of his status and sent home to Yifeng, Henan, where he died just three years later. Li was also removed from office and sent home to Zhangqiu, Shandong, where he remained until his death in 1568.

Before the Fire

These men's departure from life at court in Beijing serves as an important milestone in the development of vernacular fiction, as they represented nodes in a network formed around the novel *The Water Margin*: Guo Xun had printed one of the earliest known editions of the work, as had the Censorate, of which Wang Tingxiang was head. Li Kaixian, meanwhile, was an early *Water Margin* admirer and an advocate of its prose style. Moreover, as these chapters will show, these men had ties loose and strong with one another both directly and through other literary associations.

As high-ranking officials and influential men of letters, Guo, Wang, and Li were at the center of the Jiajing political and literary worlds. Yet the book they admired, *The Water Margin*, was a tale of outlaws at the margins of society. Many of its most celebrated protagonists, such as Lin Chong, Song Jiang, or Lu Zhishen, are minor officials or military officers who are forced from their positions by corrupt superiors or other unjust circumstances and left with no choice but to take refuge on Mount Liang, where they form an underground brotherhood with one another. What was it about this novel of society's margins that appealed to these men at the center? Of what sort of literary activities was it a part, and how were these men involved with it? This chapter attempts to answer these questions by reconstructing the reading and publishing practices surrounding *The Water Margin* in this early stage of its existence as a printed phenomenon and tracing the networks in which it was the nexus. This provides a view of *The Water Margin*—and of vernacular fiction—at an early stage of its development as a printed phenomenon.

The novel as a genre only truly flourished decades after the temple fire of 1541 resulted in these three men leaving the capital; *The Water Margin* would be widely reprinted around the turn of the seventeenth century in a variety of forms by commercial publishers of Fujian and the Jiangnan region, the likes of whom were renowned for their "promiscuous" editing practices.[2] Such printers famously catered to a growing class of literate non-elite, among whom this and other works of vernacular fiction were particular favorites. In that competitive and commercialized environment, *The Water Margin* would be given new meanings through printers' and commentators' addition of paratextual materials. By the end of the Ming, there would even be real-life bandits modeling their personae on the characters of *The Water Margin*, taking their nicknames from the book and flocking to the areas depicted in it. In this time before the fire, by contrast, no editions of *The Water Margin* or any other work of vernacular fiction were to be found among the woodblock imprints put up for sale by the booksellers in the northern capital. There were a handful of commercial printers in the capital during the time of the tenure of Guo, Wang, and Li in the capital, but fiction was not among their wares. The lower-end outfits among them published cheap popular song collections and chantefables, while the higher-end ones focused on classics, Tang literary anthologies, and the like.[3] *The Water Margin* we find before the temple fire of 1541 inhabited a social world that was quite different from the one in which its genre would eventually flourish. It is that world before the fire that is the subject of the first section of this book.

Reading the "Wuding Edition"

The edition of *The Water Margin* printed by Guo Xun is known as the "Wuding edition," after Guo's inherited title, the Marquis of Wuding. An entry for a Wuding edition of *The Water Margin* is listed in the Baowen tang catalogue of the Ming bibliophile Chao Li's collection, as is one for a Wuding edition of *Romance of the Three Kingdoms*.[4] Though the Wuding marquisate was hereditary and Xun was not the only member of the Guo clan to hold it, his personal involvement in the creation of the Wuding edition of *The Water Margin* can be seen in other sources as well: A preface to a later edition of the novel, signed "Tiandu waichen" and tentatively dated to 1589, describes Guo Xun as having edited and printed a fine edition in the Jiajing era (1522–67).[5] The late Ming gossip Shen Defu describes the text of a contemporary fine edition of *The Water Margin* printed in Xin'an as being based on one transmitted by Guo Xun's family. This is most likely in reference to the "Tiandu waichen" preface edition.

Despite the Tiandu waichen preface's statement that Guo merely edited and printed an edition of *The Water Margin*, some scholars have speculated that he actually had a hand in the novel's creation. Most influentially, the modern scholar Dai Bufan wrote of his "suspicion" that either Guo or someone in his employ was the author of the novel. Dai noted that Guo's edition appears to have been the earliest one printed, and that no full-length version of *The Water Margin* existed before it in any form. Furthermore, Dai noted, there is no mention of Shi Nai'an, the novel's reputed author, before Guo's time despite the fact that Shi allegedly lived well before Guo. Dai dismissed the claims in the Tiandu waichen preface that Guo merely edited the text as simply a tactic to dissociate the novel from the by-then infamous Guo. Another scholar, Zhang Guoguang, pointed to the depiction of Daoist elements in the novel as further evidence of Guo's involvement; Daoism was a shared interest between Guo and the Jiajing emperor, with whom he curried favor. Zhang concluded that Guo had a retainer create *The Water Margin* no earlier than the early 1530s.[6] More recently, Yuan Shishuo has challenged these arguments on textual and historical grounds, including geographical inconsistencies and the apparent ideological discrepancy of Guo, a figure of power, having a hand in the creation of a work depicting violent rebellion. Ultimately, however, he concedes that it is impossible to ascertain whether or not Guo was involved in the novel's creation.[7]

No positively identified exemplar of an original Wuding *Water Margin* survives. The pioneering scholar of vernacular fiction Zheng Zhenduo claimed to have been in possession of a five-chapter fragment of the edition, though that claim has not been widely accepted.[8] Other claims have been refuted by Y. W. Ma.[9] Judging from the comments by Tiandu waichen and Shen Defu, however, we can assume that the Wuding *Water Margin* was a finely printed edition. The preface to the Tiandu waichen edition claims that its text is a reconstruction of the Wuding edition, and that Guo had based his edition on an even earlier one-hundred-chapter edition by the mysterious Luo Guanzhong. According to the preface, Guo excised introductory stories that prefaced that earlier edition's chapters. However, there is no corroborating evidence for these claims about the text of the edition, so the precise shape of the contents of the Wuding *Water Margin* remains a mystery.

How, then, can we understand the significance of a book that no longer exists? Without a text, attempting a "close reading" of "the" *Water Margin* in order to ascertain its appeal to Guo and his Jiajing court coterie is an impossible task. After all, as the following chapters will discuss at length, *The Water Margin's* text appeared in many guises and was invested with new meanings at every turn. However, the lack of an exemplar of the Wuding *Water Margin* and the lingering questions concerning its filiation does not completely prevent us from gauging its meaning in the context of its era. We can create a sort of reading of this nonextant book by reassembling its social, historical, and literary circumstances around its publication, including both literary and material factors, and through them, decode the literary tastes that shaped them. To turn again to the terms of Jauss and reception theory, we can uncover the "objectifiable system of expectations" in which a work such as the Wuding *Water Margin* appears "in the historical moment of its appearance," fitting it into the "pre-understanding of the genre" and "the form and themes of already familiar works."[10] It is this objectifiable system that arose in the historical moment of the appearance of the Wuding *Water Margin* that is to be uncovered in the following discussion.

A point of comparison from contemporary America is to be found in the work of Janice Radway on the Book-of-the-Month Club. Radway describes the organization, which continues to select a book each month for its subscribers, as "a club that uses sophisticated marketing techniques to sell not only individual books but the very idea of taste itself."[11] Like the Book-of-the-Month Club's editorial team, Guo Xun also "marketed" to particular targeted audience by selecting certain books for publication according to specific ideas of taste. This chapter will explore Guo's overall printing project and the place of *The Water Margin* within it in order to contextualize the novel historically and aesthetically, and to consider that realm of taste to which Guo aimed his publications.

Where Guo differed from the Book-of-the-Month Club, of course, was in that Guo was not a publisher working within a capitalist social framework in order to make monetary profit. Rather, as this chapter will illustrate, he published in order to burnish the social reputation of himself and his ancestral lineage. This goal was not directly profit-oriented, though he was granted ever-increasing salaries by the court as he advanced in rank. To borrow from the terminology of Pierre Bourdieu, Guo sought to gain cultural capital by staking out positions in a semiautonomous field of cultural production, and this capital was not immediately reducible to monetary terms.[12] However, again, this terminology must be adapted to the circumstances of the era and genre of the Wuding *Water Margin*: as with the Book-of-the-Month Club, Guo staked out his position in the field of cultural production through the selecting and publishing of texts rather than through writing them. *The Water Margin* and other early works of vernacular fiction did not at the time, and would not until the mid-seventeenth century, be invested by readers with a strong assumption of authorial presence. Only with the rise of strongly opinionated *pingdian* commentators such as Jin Shengtan would readers begin, paradoxically, to be pointed to the "intentions" of fiction "authors" such as Shi Nai'an or Luo Guanzhong. In the early years before even the Jiajing ancestral temple fire, the "authors" of these works were much less well-known—and of less importance—than their publishers.

Guo and Print

In addition to *The Water Margin*, Guo printed a number of other books. Through his publishing activity he was able to enter into literary debates of his time and to craft for himself a literary persona without so much as lifting a brush, let alone participating in the civil examination system. The image that Guo crafted was one of a learned military man, a "Confucian-general" (*Ru jiang*), whose literary activities were a demonstration of his own personal virtue. He did this through the texts he chose to publish and through the prefaces for them that he commissioned from colleagues and well-known literati of the day. In these texts and prefaces, he burnished his credentials as the scion of a family with roots in the founding of the Ming dynasty, and as a cultured man with access to a variety of books that he was willing to make more widely available through recarving and reprinting. The latter activity also demonstrates his connections with interested literati. Like the commercial publishing houses would be later in the century, he was led in his choices of material by anticipating or speculating on what sorts of books his intended audiences would desire. Yet rather than the urban nouveau riche, his audiences were elite members of the official class. It was for these audiences that he presented his Confucian-general persona. He used print to cement his social standing, to establish his virtue, and to project himself as a man of culture. Accordingly, Guo's publishing must be understood in the context of his own life and position.

"Crafty, Deceitful, and Quite Involved in Books"

Despite his best efforts at crafting a persona for himself, Guo quite literally went down in history as a conniving character who took advantage of his position and his relationships for personal gain. In the words of a biographical sketch of Guo Xun in the *Ming History*, included under the biography of the first Marquis of Wuding, Guo Ying, Xun was "crafty, deceitful, and quite involved in books" (*Xun jiexia you zhishu, po she shushi*).[13] The sketch goes on to detail his roles in several Jiajing-era scandals, beginning with none other than the Great Rites Controversy that engulfed the court immediately after the Jiajing Emperor took the throne. Guo was an early supporter of the newly installed emperor's position that his biological father should be posthumously named an emperor and placed in the imperial ancestral hall. Because of this support, Guo won the lasting favor of the emperor and, realizing that he had this powerful backing, "often put on airs" (*Xun huchong, po jiaozi*). The description of Guo goes on to detail his corruption, and how each time he was punished, his political capital outlasted that of his accusers and he was eventually reinstated. Though he suffered setbacks, he continued to climb the social ladder until the very end.

The *Ming History* also details Guo's relationships with two supposed magicians. The first, Li Fuda, was accused of being a shape-shifting fugitive from the law, and Guo intervened on his behalf to the consternation of the officials who were on his trail.[14] Li claimed that he could turn an elixir into silver and gold. The second, Duan Chaoyong, claimed that he could turn silver and gold into eating utensils that would grant their users long life. Guo introduced Duan to the emperor himself, and the emperor was pleased with Guo's "loyalty" for doing so. Unsurprisingly, Duan was found to be a charlatan.

The biographical sketch lists the ups and downs of Guo's career: officials accused him of taking bribes, of illegally running shops throughout the capital and extorting citizens, and of having a relative in the notorious Eastern Depot (*Dongchang*) torture people on his private orders. Yet each time Guo would meet punishment or demotion, he would end up being reinstated and climbing to an even higher rung on the social ladder.

The height of Guo Xun's power came in 1539, when he requested of the emperor that his ancestor Guo Ying be installed in the imperial ancestral hall. Despite objections of court officials, the emperor granted his wishes. Perhaps the Jiajing emperor was particularly sympathetic to Guo's filial display due to his own position in regard to his biological father being installed in the imperial ancestral hall; the following year, the Jiajing emperor's father was installed in the ancestral hall as a posthumous emperor. That year, the emperor also conveyed upon Guo Xun the title of Duke of Yi (*Yiguo gong*) and the prestigious merit title Grand Preceptor (*taishi*).

This peak of Guo's power did not last long, however. According to the entry, court officials continued to bring up accusations against Guo, and eventually even his personal relationship with the emperor could not save him. When accused of shirking his duties, Guo haughtily countered the charges by questioning the need to trouble the emperor with pardoning him. The emperor was offended by Guo's arrogant assumption of his own immunity and put Guo in the prison of the Brocade Guard (*Jinyi wei*) in the autumn of 1541. The emperor was still reluctant to allow Guo to be executed, despite the continuing charges against him. Guo died in prison the following year. The dynastic history does not say if he was executed or if he died of natural causes while in prison. The entry ends with a note that, of all of the officials of inherited rank since the founding of the Ming, none took part in governance; only Xun, with his imperial favor, engaged in such corruption and eventually brought about his own downfall.

With this end, the biographical sketch of Guo Xun in the *Ming History* never provides any details about his "involvement in books." It does, however, go into extensive detail about his "crafty and deceitful" nature. Was it the intention of the *Ming History's* compilers to insinuate a connection between the former and the latter without delving into the particulars of the matter? Did the compilers simply find the titles and contents of Guo's books too trivial to mention compared to the seriousness of his alleged crimes and currying for favor? Whatever the case, the involvement in books must be reconstituted by other means. Several exemplars of his imprints survive; others, including his printings of vernacular novels, are only known through bibliographical records or other forms of writing. Together, these sources can be used to reconstitute Guo Xun's printing project. That printing project, in turn, represents an opening into the early life in print of *The Water Margin* and the vernacular novel genre. Proceeding chronologically, we will look at his editions of private clan histories, classics of Tang poetry and prose, and *qu* art-song collections. Since the circumstances surrounding his imprints of novels are less well-documented and their place in the chronology less certain, discussion of them will be saved for last.

A Family History in Print

Although the *Ming History* remains silent on the details of Guo's publishing, he possessed or published enough books to warrant a catalogue of them: Gao Ru's *Baichuan Catalogue of Books* (*Baichuan shuzhi*) lists a single-volume catalogue of Guo's books named *A Record of the Village of Books* (*Shuzhuang ji*). That catalogue is no longer extant. Most of the books discussed below save for the novels are still extant and held in various library collections.

The known editions published by Guo roughly correspond to certain periods of his life, suggesting that he used publishing for different purposes at different times. First came his private clan histories, which appear to be intended to shore up his social reputation. These were followed by his editions of Tang literature, which were explicitly targeted at court officials and apparently intended to burnish Guo's cultural capital. The *qu* song anthology and related rhyme manuals, which came slightly later, suggest a role for Guo as not only a connoisseur but an active participant in literary production. Finally, according to late-Ming rumor, he used vernacular fiction to win for himself his promotion from the rank of marquis to that of duke.

Guo came on the power of publishing early in his official career, using it to announce his status as the worthy descendant of an illustrious ancestor, Guo Ying. Ying had been an early follower and bodyguard of the Ming's founder, Zhu Yuanzhang, and later served as a military commander. Ying's greatest accomplishment was in the Battle of Poyang Lake against Zhu Yuanzhang's enemy Chen Youliang. Zhu credited Guo Ying with firing the shot that killed Chen Youliang. He conferred the Wuding marquisate on Ying in 1384. Xun sought to portray himself as the latest in a direct and unbroken line that could be traced back to the dynastic founding. The *Ming History*, however, tells a different story of the transmission of the Wuding marquisate. Between the time of its original bestowal upon Ying and its eventual inheritance by Guo Xun in 1508, its transmission was punctuated by disputes between two branches of the family. One branch descended from Ying's eldest son, Zhen, while the other descended from another son, Ming. Ming's daughter had become the favored consort of the Hongxi emperor, and the emperor granted the marquisate to Ming's son, the consort's brother. Zhen, however, had his own ties to the imperial family: he had married a daughter of Zhu Yuanzhang, the Yongjia princess, and the princess requested that their offspring be granted the marquisate. Yet when Ming's son passed away, Ming's grandson, Cong, contested the transfer of the marquisate to Zhen's branch. The court terminated the transmission of the marquisate altogether and gave equal ranks to each side as a concession. Later, the marquisate was revived when the next generation in the Zhen branch received it by imperial favor. Cong contested it again, this time unsuccessfully. Yet when the marquisate was to be passed down again, Cong contested it for the third time, saying that its inheritor was illegitimate. Once again, the transmission was brought to an end.

That purportedly illegitimate inheritor was Guo Liang, Xun's father. Liang lobbied for the marquisate several times, only to land in prison and be pardoned each time. Finally, the Guo clan collectively requested that the court settle the matter once and for all by selecting one of Ying's descendants as the rightful heir of the Wuding marquisate. The court determined that Liang, as the descendant of the lineage of Ying's eldest son, was the proper heir to the title, and Liang became the Marquis of Wuding in 1502.

Liang died only a few years later, in 1507, and the Wuding marquisate was conferred upon Xun on April 28, 1508. In the twelfth month of
that year, the emperor placed him in charge of the imperial guards, and
in the following year he was appointed to a series of military ranks. In
1510, he was granted the title of Grand Guardian (*taibao*), and in the following year, he was appointed by the emperor to be the Grand Defender
(*zhenshou*) of the Guangdong-Guangxi region.

The Generational Compendium of the Three Families

The earliest known Guo imprint, titled *The Generational Compendium of
the Three Families* (*Sanjia shidian*), is a collective biography of Guo Xun's
ancestor Guo Ying; his comrades-in-arms Xu Da and Mu Ying; and
their respective descendants. In the account of the Guo family history,
the troubles encountered in the transmission of the Wuding marquisate are left unmentioned. Yet more than the particulars of the accounts
of family history, it is the grouping of the descendants of Guo, Xu, and
Mu as the "Three Families" that is of importance. Guo Xun's ancestor
Ying had been posthumously granted the title Duke of Ying (*Yingguo
gong*) by Zhu Yuanzhang, the dynasty's founder, while Xu Da and Mu
Ying were both made princes. Guo Xun seems to intentionally conflate
his own ancestor's prestige with that of his higher-ranked associates by
placing them together.

Indeed, the Qing-era compilers of the *Complete Library of the Four Treasuries* (*Siku quanshu*) expressed their doubts about the appropriateness
of the "Three Families" grouping. They also remarked that the *Generational Compendium* is little more than unembellished excerpts from dynastic veritable records and histories. They provided a description of
the work in the catalogue (*zongmu*), but saw no need to include the text
itself in the collection.

The prefaces to the *Generational Compendium* are dated 1515, just
seven years after Guo Xun was granted the Wuding marquisate. Each
preface praises Guo Xun's merit and portrays him as a worthy successor to his ancestor. They are by three men Guo knew from his time in
the Guangdong-Guangxi region: the famed official and military leader
Yang Yiqing; Zhou Nan; and Chen Jin; the latter two being Censorate
officials as well as Guo Xun's colleagues in the military administration
of Guangdong and Guangxi.

Yang Yiqing's preface is dated the first month of the tenth year of
the Zhengde reign (1515). Anticipating objections such as those that

were later made by the *Four Treasuries* editors, Yang notes that of the scores of noble titles granted at the founding of the dynasty, only a very few remained in the current generation. The majority, he writes, ceased transmission after their holders committed offenses of some sort, and it is a credit to the virtues of these three particular families that their titles had continued to be passed down. He lists the civil and martial accomplishments of Xu Da, Mu Ying, and Guo Ying, but points out that while they were great military leaders they never reveled in killing. Their descendants inherited their humaneness and wisdom in governing, and that quality makes them sagely officials of the court.

Yang concludes the preface with remarks about the power of print to spread word of the virtues of Guo Xun and the scions of the Xu and Mu families. Yang also states that Guo's act of compiling the *Generational Compendium* is evidence that he has inherited his illustrious ancestor's considerable talents. It is the book, then, that bridges the generations.

Zhou Nan, the author of the second preface, was Supreme Commander of Military Affairs for the Guangdong-Guangxi region, with concurrent appointment as Grand Coordinator (*xunfu*) Censor-in-Chief of the Right. Zhou writes of the importance of worthy ministers to the endeavor of a leader and continues on to the particular case of the service of Xu Da, Mu Ying, and Guo Ying under Zhu Yuanzhang. Notably, he avoids using Ying's formal ducal title, instead referring to him as "Lord" or "Duke" Wuding Guo Ying (*Wuding Guo gong Ying*) in order to emphasize the title that Guo Xun inherited. He also avoids the usage of Xu and Mu's princely titles.

Like Yang Yiqing, Zhou Nan also notes the rarity of the unbroken transmission of inherited titles from the founding of the dynasty to the present day (again eliding the disputes into which the Wuding marquisate's transmission fell) and the virtues of the three families that are the subject of the text at hand, calling them cause for commemoration. Also like Yang Yiqing, Zhou Nan presents Guo Xun as a talented military leader who, due to his competence in governing, had the leisure time to engage in literary pursuits.

The author of the third preface, Chen Jin, was Censor-in-Chief of the Left and also held several military appointments in the Guangdong-Guangxi region. He also points out the rarity of noble titles being transmitted for over more than one hundred years, pointing out that of six dukes and eighteen marquises, the three families are all that remain.[15] Like Zhou Nan, he obscures the differences in the three ancestors' ranks.

Chen is unique in that he writes of knowing all three of the direct ancestors of Xu, Mu, and Guo. He writes that he was willing to pen a preface because he knew of the virtue and filial piety of the three descendants, and of Guo Xun in particular.

A Collection Nurturing and Celebrating Meritorious Service

Around the same time Guo Xun was assembling the *Generational Compendium of the Three Families*, during his tenure in the Guangdong-Guangxi area, he was also collating *A Collection Nurturing and Celebrating Meritorious Service* (*Yuqing xunyi ji*), a collection of family documents. These documents, which include not only his direct ancestral line but his extended clan as well, are broader in scope than the biographical outlines given in the *Generational Compendium*. This work features correspondence between Zhu Yuanzhang and the Guo clan, and the imperial orders granting Guo Ying and his descendants their titles. It also includes documents concerning the sons, daughters, and granddaughters of Ying who intermarried with the family of the Ming's founding emperor, as well as subsequent generations of the family who held prestigious official and noble positions, and their wives and extended families. Additionally, it includes documents pertaining to Guo Ying's elder brother, Guo Xing, who fought alongside him.

The *Meritorious Service* collection is dated 1516, though it was compiled in some form earlier. Guo Xun's father Liang (1454–1507) is credited in the edition with "respectfully collating and recording (*dunshou jilu*)" its documents, while Xun himself is credited with its publishing (*kanxing*) (figure 1.1) By 1516, Guo Liang had already been dead for nine years. Guo's father Liang likely assembled it originally as part of his campaign to revive the Wuding marquisate, and Xun printed it in order to spread word of his legitimacy and reputation.

In this social campaign, Guo Xun enlisted Fei Hong (1468–1535), Wang Zan, and Zhan Ruoshui (1466–1560), all prominent figures, to contribute prefaces to the print edition of the collection. Fei Hong's preface describes how Guo Xun's father Liang had put the collection together, and emphasizes the ties between the Guo clan and the imperial household. It remarks that the documents in the collection illustrate the closeness between them, and it enumerates the marquises, earls, and other titles conferred on members of the extended Guo clan. It then suggests that Xun had the volume printed in order to preserve his ancestors' worthy legacy.

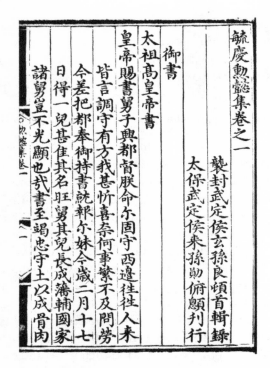

FIGURE 1.1. Guo Xun's *Collection Celebrating and Nurturing Meritorious Service* (1516).
Source: Princeton University Microform, 26.

When the Fei Hong preface returns to the subject of Xun and his father Liang, it deems them to be worthy inheritors of their clan's tradition and enumerates the positive moral values that that tradition represents. It then turns to the cultural pursuits of the father and son, noting that their love of books, learning, and the sages are literary rather than martial achievements. These moral and cultural values, it continues, complement one another; the former are preserved and transmitted by the latter, and the collection itself is testament to their loyalty and filiality. Moreover, it declares, one who realizes that the civil and the martial are dependent on one another and has mastered both can be known as a "Confucian general." The Grand Guardian, Guo Xun, is a man of such talent and stature, it concludes.

Wang Zan's preface follows along very similar lines. It declares that the collection was first put together by Guo Liang and then expanded and printed by Xun, and he enumerates the ranks of members of the Guo clan. Recalling the rhetorical strategy of the *Generational Compendium* prefaces, it also remarks on the relative rarity of a rank being passed down from the beginning of the dynasty to the present day. It also makes explicit reference to the *Generational Compendium* and Guo's act of compiling it.

Zhan Ruoshui's preface differs from the other two in that it focuses on the merit of Guo Xun himself, rather than his lineage. It explains the meaning of the work in terms of its title, creatively interpreting the first two characters, *yuqing*, as referring to Guo Xun's family and its second two, *xunyi*, as Guo's ancestors. It goes on to say that the "collection" (*ji*) of the title refers to its collection of "eight praise-worthy merits" (*ba yi*). These are humaneness toward others, filiality, respect for family, reverence toward ancestors, veneration of one's ruler, maintaining proper family relations, recognizing worthies, and managing political affairs. Zhan places these in a chain, reminiscent of that of the *Great Learning*, with each step being a prerequisite for the one that follows. Guo Xun, Zhan claims, has brought this chain of merits to realization and is therefore a credit to his family lineage and the dynasty.

Gao Ru's *Baichuan Catalogue of Books* lists an additional title associated with Guo Xun and his family, *The Family Biographies of Messrs. Guo* (*Guo shi jia zhuan*). It is described as consisting of four *juan* and relating the biographies of Guo Xun and his relative, Guo Deng, the Earl of Dingxiang. It is no longer extant.

Guo and the Circulation of Literature

The image that Guo Xun fashioned for himself through his early clan histories was that of a virtuous and talented scion of a prominent family, a "Confucian general" whose involvement in publishing was an illustration of his own positive qualities. In their contents and their prefaces, the editions that followed these histories aimed to further burnish his literary reputation. During and soon after his tenure in Guangdong and Guangxi, Guo Xun printed three anthologies of Tang prose and poetry: *A Literary Anthology of Yuan Jie* (*Yuan Cishan wenji*) in 1517, *A Poetry Anthology of Bai Juyi* (*Bai Xiangshan shiji*) in 1517, and *A Literary Anthology of Bai Juyi* (*Bai Letian wenji*) in 1519. These feature prefaces praising Guo's taste and depicting him as interacting with literati peers in acts of circulating books.

Yuan Jie (719–792) was a renowned moralist known for his critiques of the corruption of his era. His most well-known essay, "On Begging," which is included in Guo's anthology, compares a beggar acquaintance favorably with officials who engage in "begging" of another, less scrupulous kind. Also included in the anthology is Yuan's preface to his own "Anthology from a Box" (*Qiezhong ji*), in which Yuan collected writings by "friends on the periphery of official life."[16] Yuan praises them for their authentically moral voices and freedom from conventional standards.

Guo's anthology of Yuan Jie's prose features another preface from Zhan Ruoshui, which draws on Yuan Jie's moral image in representing Guo himself. Zhan writes of how he came across an edition of Yuan Jie's writings while traveling in the capital, and how he was struck by the unadorned simplicity of Yuan's prose. He remarks that the writings of the "greats of the Tang" like Yuan Jie have long been a civilizing force in the world, and that the current generation must do its part in passing on this cultural legacy.

In words that echo Fei Hong's "Confucian general," Zhan refers to Guo as a "military man who loves literature" (*wu er haowen*). He explains how he gave Guo the edition of Yuan Jie's literary anthology, and that it were as if Yuan and Guo had some "tacit understanding" (*ruo you qi*) from across the ages. Zhan claims that Guo read Yuan Jie, remarked that he was a figure who stood up boldly against the corruption of his times, and lamented that there were not a hundred such men in the present to critique current literary customs. Zhan then says that Guo ordered new woodblocks based on the edition to be carved and requested that Zhan pen an explanation of Guo's vision of it.[17]

The prefaces to the collections of the poetry and prose of Bai Juyi depict Guo Xun as an active participant in the circulation and exchange of imprints as well. The poetry collection features a preface, dated 1517, by Chen Jin, who had previously contributed a preface to the *Generational Compendium*. It describes Guo as having received the poetry edition from one "Principal Gentleman Shi" (*zhenglang Shi jun*). By contrast, the preface to the prose collection—dated 1519 and written by Wang Zan, who had contributed a preface to the *Meritorious Service* collection—describes Guo as reprinting a rare edition from his father's collection in response to the demand of court officials, who wanted to pair it with the more readily available poetry collection of Bai Juyi. By the time of the latter edition, Guo had returned from Guangdong-Guangxi to the capital. He had entered new social circles, and his presentational strategy had changed: Guo presented himself as having better access to rare editions than the literati themselves.

Back in the Capital

Guo Xun's appointment in the Guangdong-Guangxi region came to an end in the eighth month of the twelfth year of the Zhengde reign (1517), when he was recalled to Beijing in order to take up his former position as commander of training the Division of the Three Thousand. He was also jointly appointed commissioner-in-chief of the Left Chief Military Commission, a commission of the highest rank.

It was here, in 1519, that Guo published his collection of Bai Juyi's prose. He followed this with a philological work called *Rhymes of Poetry, Explicated* (*Shiyun shiyi*), which is dated 1520. If the prose collection suggests that Guo interacted with literati as a source of rare editions, *Rhymes of Poetry* suggests his participation in circles of literary creation. The work is a rhyming dictionary for use in the composition of poetry, with 10,260 words organized into 106 rhyme categories. Each word is provided a definition of typically six or less characters in length. Its original compilation is credited to "The Old Man of the Snowy Cliffs East of the River" (*Jiangdong xueya laoren*). More notably, however, the definitions are credited to Guanxi Xiuranzi (Figure 1.2). This name, it will be shown below, is associated with a 1522 edition of the *Romance of the Three Kingdoms* often considered to be the first print version of that novel.

Rhymes of Poetry, Explicated also features a preface by Yang Yiying, a native of Nanhai, Guangdong.[18] In that preface, dated 1520, Yang Yiying points out that Guo has already published the *Generational Compendium* and the Bai Juyi poetry collection, and says Guo has followed them with the current volume, which is to aid in the composition of poetry. He also echoes earlier prefaces in remarking that, since the dynastic founding, the Guo family has always "placed emphasis on literature in the same manner as Confucian officials" (*zhuyi wenmo yu Rujia chen tong*).[19]

In the following year, a series of events began that would alter the course of Guo Xun's career for the rest of his life. Born without rank, he had already in his lifetime been awarded the previously defunct Wuding marquisate and been granted the honorary title of Grand Defender. He had also risen through the military ranks and held an important post in the capital region. However, his rise in power was only in its beginning stages. On April 19, 1521, the Zhengde emperor passed away after a prolonged illness, leaving no direct heir. Faced with the prospect of an

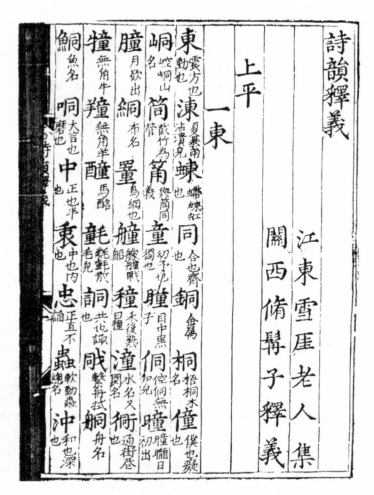

FIGURE 1.2. *Rhymes of Poetry, Explicated* (1520), with definitions by Xiuranzi.
Source: Reprinted in Ning Jifu, *Hanyu yunshu shi, Mingdai juan*, 6.

insurgency due to the power vacuum, the chief Grand Secretary, Yang Tinghe, engineered the installment of the Hongzhi emperor's younger brother's son, the Zhengde emperor's cousin, as the new emperor. Yang's intentions were to have the new emperor-to-be adopted into the main imperial line as the Hongzhi emperor's son and the Zhengde emperor's younger brother, and have him treat his biological father as his uncle. Yang saw precedents to his plan in the succession of the Han throne from the emperor Chengdi to his nephew, the Prince of Dingtao, and in that of the Song emperor Renzong to a distant relative.

The newly installed Jiajing emperor was not pleased with this plan, and a crisis began to brew. The emperor sought instead to have his biological father posthumously entered into the imperial lineage as an emperor, a plan that many officials saw as a serious breach of ritual protocol. In the fall of the same year, a student sitting the metropolitan examinations, Zhang Cong (1475–1539), argued that the precedents were not valid and eventually found himself in direct conflict with Yang Tinghe. This was the beginning of the Great Rites Controversy (*Da Liyi*), which rippled through officialdom.

According to the account of the Great Rites Controversy in the unofficial historiographical record *Complete Events of the Ming Dynasty* (*Mingshi jishi benmo*), Guo Xun opened his home to Zhang Cong and another ally taking the emperor's side, Gui E (?–1531), early in the controversy. There they could meet without fear of Yang Tinghe's men. Guo, the account says, took delight in their planning and "pledged allegiance as an assistant from the inside" (*yuewei neizhu*). The controversy came to a head in the seventh month (August 1524). The emperor ordered the Ministry of Rites to carry out his plans. A large crowd of officials protested against his actions, and the emperor ordered the Directorate of Ceremonial (*Silijian*) to move against them. Over 180 officials were beaten, and seventeen died of their injuries. The rest were banished. In the ninth month, Guo Xun and sixty-three other officials memorialized in support of the emperor's actions, praising his filial piety. Could Guo have empathized with the new emperor due to his own experiences with the inheritance of the Wuding marquisate?

The Jiajing emperor remembered Guo Xun's early support, and rewarded him for it. Other officials, however, resented Guo's activism and favor. Guo's life from this point on would be marked by a series of promotions and impeachments, eventually culminating in his death in prison.

According to the *Ming History*, Guo's first promotion under the Jiajing emperor came early in his reign, as the Great Rites Controversy was brewing. Guo Xun was put in command of the Integrated Divisions (*tuanying*) protecting the capital region. The first year of the Jiajing reign also saw the publication of the *Three Kingdoms* edition with the Xiuranzi preface, a topic to which I will return later in this chapter in order to discuss it in relation to Guo Xun.

The first scandal to envelop Guo Xun was the case of Li Fuda, as mentioned in the biographical sketch from the *Ming History* cited above. The incident occurred in 1526. An inspector in Shanxi named Ma Lu arrested a man he asserted to be Li Fuda, a fugitive and member of the messianic White Lotus Society, living under a different name. One of the sons of this "Li Fuda" was under the patronage of Guo Xun in the capital, making alchemical elixirs for him. Guo came to the defense of this alleged Li Fuda on behalf of the son, and in return, Ma Lu drew up charges of treason against Guo Xun. Other censors and inspectors added to the charges against Guo, but Guo justified himself to the emperor by saying the accusers simply retained a grudge against him for his support of the emperor in the Great Rites Controversy and were colluding against him. Zhang Cong and Gui E, to whom Guo Xun had pledged to serve as an "assistant from the inside" in the original flare-up of the Great Rites Controversy, were at this time Left Censor-in-Chief and minister of justice, respectively, and were involved in the investigation. They determined that this particular Li Fuda was not the fugitive the authorities had been looking for. The man was released, and Guo Xun was cleared of charges. In a turnaround, it was Ma Lu who ended up being banished, and a purge of the officials who had accused Guo commenced. In the words of James Geiss, "At [the emperor's] behest, [his advisors] dismissed the charges against the accused and initiated an investigation of those officials at court who had supported the indictment. Ten officials were beaten to death and over forty were banished to frontier posts. When it was over, the Censorate and the ministries had been purged of officials who had associated with Yang T'ing-ho and the Hanlin clique."[20] Yang Tinghe was deposed in 1528, and instated in his place was another ally of Guo Xun's: Yang Yiqing, who had contributed a preface to Guo's *Generational Compendium* in 1515. Zhang Cong and Gui E had moved to bring Yang in to counter the authority of Grand Secretary Fei Hong, whom they had seen as an obstacle to their power. Remarkably, in these maneuverings, Guo's connections run to all sides. Not only was Guo an "assistant from the inside" to Zhang and Gui, he had ties to both Fei Hong and Yang Yiqing from his days in the Guangdong-Guangxi region. Yang, it will be remembered, had contributed a preface to Guo's *Generational Compendium*, and Fei had contributed one to Guo's *Meritorious Service* collection of documents.

However, whatever goodwill Guo might have had with Yang Yiqing from his days in the Guangdong-Guangxi region did not last long. As the *Ming History* account of Guo's life relates, Yang Yiqing turned against Guo, and when bribery charges were leveled against Guo in 1529, he was stripped of his position in the Integrated Divisions and his Grand Defender rank. Relations between Yang Yiqing and Zhang Cong also soured, and in 1529 Zhang was briefly sent away from the capital. Yet by late 1530, Zhang was back as senior secretary and Yang was out of his position. By 1531, Guo was reinstated with the Integrated Divisions.

Ballads of Harmonious Peace

The year of his reinstatement in the Integrated Divisions, 1531, also marked the year of Guo's publication of the *Ballads of Harmonious Peace* (*Yongxi yuefu*) collection.[21] *Ballads of Harmonious Peace* is considered one of the three most important collection of *qu* arias of the Yuan and Ming dynasties, alongside *A New Voice for a Flourishing Age* (*Shengshi xinsheng*) and *Selected Beauties from the Forest of Lyrics* (*Cilin zhaiyan*). It is also notable for including all of the arias from the *Record of the Western Chamber*, in textually identical form to the 1498 edition of the latter, the earliest known edition of that text. Guo Xun himself is credited with the compilation of *Ballads of Harmonious Peace*.

In this time of rapidly shifting allegiances, after the shakeup of the Great Rites Controversy and soon after Guo's reinstatement, Guo used the publication of *Ballads of Harmonious Peace* as a vehicle to advertise both his talents and his close relationship with the emperor. A preface by Wang Yan explains that Guo was able to take advantage of the peaceful times to collect lyrics and arias, and that Guo had them printed so that they might spread more widely. Wang explains that Guo showed him the collection and, upon reading it, he felt transported to the "court of the sagely Shun of antiquity" (*ru zuo Yu ting*). At the same time, he frets that the unsophisticated might not be equipped to appreciate the treasures on offer in the volume—a preemptive defense against allegations of the *qu* aria genre's impropriety.

Indeed, the preface continues on to say that the arias included in the volume are themselves the result of the current era of peace and good governance. It explains the title of the anthology by claiming that the first two words, *yong* and *xi*, both mean "peace" and refer to the era of harmonious peace under the legendary sage-rulers Yao and Shun. There were capable ministers such as Yu and Houji below, institutions were strong, and people responded to governance. Songs praising the tranquility of the times were sung throughout the land. Songs, it points out, were a necessary part of a harmonious peace; without them, such a peace cannot be enjoyed and this is not a true peace.

From this point on, the preface turns to Guo Xun and the present day. Guo, it claims, proclaims the flourishing of harmonious peace and enjoys its blessings. Moreover, he shares it with the world through the present anthology of songs, thereby spreading peace. "Harmonious peace," the preface says, is not relegated to the distant past of Yao and Shun but present in the current age, and the songs of the present are testimony to that fact. The preface makes note of Guo's elite status and his relationship with the emperor, and says he dedicated his leisure time to collating this collection of songs proclaiming peace and good governance. The preface is dated 1531.

The language in the preface concerning Guo's social status was not mere boasting. Guo was among the Jiajing emperor's elite inner circles. This can be seen in the fact that, in the eleventh month of the same year, the Jiajing emperor began a series of Daoist ceremonies to ensure an heir, and Guo Xun took part in them. Guo Xun's old ally Zhan Ruoshui, who had written a preface for Guo's *Meritorious Service* collection, served as one of the guiding officials of the ceremonies, and Guo Xun himself was one of five civil and military officials who took turns conducting them. In the following years, Guo's alliance with the Jiajing emperor continued to be strong. Guo rose even further in rank, receiving in 1536 the merit title Left Pillar of the State (*zuo zhuguo*).

The Wuding Novels

Unlike the editions discussed above, no exemplar of a Guo imprint of a novel has been positively identified; they are known through bibliographical entries and other such written records. Nor is there a positive dating for any of the novels with which he is associated as printer, editor, or writer. Yet according to late-Ming gossip, his involvement with one such work, *The Record of the Heroes and Martyrs* (*Yinglie zhuan*), came in the last years of his life, a few years after the publication of *Ballads of a Harmonious Peace*. Rumor had it that Guo wrote *Heroes and Martyrs* in imitation of *The Water Margin* and *Romance of the Three Kingdoms*, and circulated it as part of a plot to win a promotion in rank for himself.

Yet before turning to the *Heroes and Martyrs*, let us first examine Guo's involvement with its two better-known masterwork cousins. The Baowen tang bibliographic catalogue of the Ming collector Chao Li (js. 1541) lists "Wuding editions" of both *The Water Margin* and *Romance of the Three Kingdoms* under the category of "Masters; miscellaneous" (*ziza*).[22]

Though no exemplar of the Wuding edition *Water Margin* survives, the Tiandu waichen preface edition mentioned above, tentatively dated to 1589, claims to be based on it. Tiandu waichen is believed to be a pen name of Wang Daokun (1525–93).[23] In the preface, Tiandu waichen complains of the treatment of *The Water Margin* at the hands of "village pedants," who have ruined it with poor editing and the addition of extraneous material, and claims that the present edition is a reconstruction of Guo Xun's edition. Shen Defu also makes reference to a contemporary fine edition of *The Water Margin* printed in Xin'an, which he identifies as the version transmitted by Guo Xun's family (*qijia suochuan*): the Tiandu waichen preface edition is likely the edition to which he refers.[24]

As for *Romance of the Three Kingdoms*, there is a fine edition that features prefaces dated 1494 and 1522. This edition is frequently believed to be the first printed edition of the novel due to comments in the prefaces. The first preface makes reference to the production of manuscript copies of the novel, saying that once it was completed, scholars and aficionados "contended with one another to copy it" (*zheng xiang tenglu*). The later preface, by contrast, discusses the novel in terms of printing. It notes the rarity of fine editions, and suggests that committing the novel to the medium of the woodblock imprint will ensure its wide dissemination and longevity.[25]

This 1522 edition of *Romance of the Three Kingdoms* is often referred to as the "Censorate edition" since it is known that the Censorate printed an edition of *Romance of the Three Kingdoms* and this particular edition bears similarities to other "official printings" of the era.[26] However, the 1522 preface is signed Xiuranzi; that name, it will be recalled, was credited with providing the definitions for Guo Xun's 1520 edition of *Rhymes of Poetry, Explicated*. To my knowledge, the name "Xiuranzi" does not appear anywhere outside of these two editions, which appeared within two years of one another. It seems likely, then, that this Xiuranzi was someone within the employ of Guo Xun, and that what has been identified as the Censorate edition of *Romance of the Three Kingdoms* is in fact the Wuding edition. Another possibility is that the Censorate edition and the Wuding edition were one and the same, products of some sort of cooperation between Guo and that agency. As the following chapter will show, the printing outputs of Guo and the Censorate share several titles in common, including both *The Water Margin* and *Romance of the Three Kingdoms* as well as titles associated with Guo personally. If the 1522 *Romance of the Three Kingdoms* edition with the Xiuranzi preface is in fact the product of Guo Xun, that would place its publication shortly after Guo's return to the capital, the moment when he was ingratiating himself with the literati of the court through publishing.

The lesser-known novel *Record of the Heroes and Martyrs* is the third such work associated with Guo Xun. Gossip around the *Record of the Heroes and Martyrs* discusses openly what the biographical sketch in the *Ming History* only hinted at—that Guo's "crafty and deceitful" nature was indeed directly tied to his "involvement with books," and he created *Record of the Heroes and Martyrs* as part of a plot to win personal gain. Specifically, the claim was that Guo made (presumably, had underlings write on his behalf) *Record of the Heroes and Martyrs* in imitation of *Three Kingdoms* and *The Water Margin* in order to elevate the position of his ancestor Guo Ying, the first Marquis of Wuding. A fictionalized account of the founding of the Ming could credit Ying with the capture of Zhang Shicheng and the slaying of Chen Youliang, rivals of the dynastic founder. Guo is claimed to have undertaken the plan in 1537, with the goal of having Ying installed in the imperial hall. A work called *Words on the Present* (*Jinyan*) by Guo's younger contemporary, Zheng Xiao (1499–1566), is the first record of this claim. Zheng claims that *Record of the Heroes and Martyrs* was read in the emperor's quarters and moved those who heard it (*chuanshuo gongjin, dongren tingwen*).

Decades later, Shen Defu repeated these claims, with further details added. Shen calls the alleged plot a "marvelous plan" (*qiji*), and places it within the context of Guo's early support of the Jiajing emperor in the Great Rites Controversy and the subsequent favor Guo received from him. Guo allegedly sought to exploit their relationship in an attempt to have his own rank raised from marquis to duke. Shen claims that Guo personally wrote the novel to equate Ying's achievements in battle with those of Chang Yuchun and Xu Da, both of whom were made princes. Since at the time no one knew who fired the arrow that killed Chen Youliang, Shen claims, Guo credited the act to Ying. Guo then had the officials in charge of storytelling recite the story for the emperor daily and claim that it was an "old edition" that had been passed down.

In Shen's telling, the plan worked. Thinking that the discrepancy between the rank bestowed upon Ying and those of other founders was a pity, the emperor granted Xun the title of Duke of Yi. Shen ends his account with a striking statement about the power of narrative: "Thus, falsifying a biography brought him power" (*weizao jizhuan yu youli yan*). He also notes that this vernacular book is still in circulation.

As described, *Heroes and Martyrs* is indeed a vernacular-style recounting of the founding of the Ming under its Grand Progenitor, Taizu, and his loyal followers, written in a semiclassical style reminiscent of *Three Kingdoms*. It even borrows several plot devices from *Three Kingdoms* and

The Water Margin. It begins with portentous omens occurring in the palace of the Yuan emperor, indicating that that dynastic house has lost its legitimacy, and ends with the full consolidation of the newly founded Ming dynasty's territory. Guo Xun's exalted ancestor, Guo Ying, plays a small yet crucial part, most notably for his part in the Battle of Poyang Lake. In the scene, Taizu (as Zhu Yuanzhang is anachronistically called throughout the novel, even before the Ming is founded) engages the forces of his key rival Chen Youliang on the waters in a great naval battle. Taizu's chief adviser, Liu Ji, divines the shifting of the winds and sets the enemy armada ablaze as arrows rain down upon Taizu's forces. In the barrage, Guo Ying, is hit; he pulls the arrow from his arm, mounts it on his bow and fires it back toward the enemy forces. Incredibly, the arrow strikes Chen Youliang himself directly in the eye with such force that it exits the back of his skull, killing him instantly. Later, Taizu inspects his troops and wants to know who fired this miraculous shot that brought the battle to a conclusion. Guo Ying refrains from taking credit for his deed. It is only when a comrade in arms shows Ying's wound to Taizu that he is recognized for his merit. Taizu asks Ying if the account is true, and Ying only responds, "It was brought about by the might of heaven and the calculations of the spirits; what merit is it of your subject?" (*Tianwei shensuan suozhi, chen hegong yi*). Taizu then rewards him for his deed and for his humility. Taizu is greatly pleased and states, "Guo Ying's single arrow has surpassed 100,000 troops— how could his merit be matched?" (*Guo Ying yijian sheng shiwan shi, qigong he kedang ye?*)."

With its burning ships and sage adviser, the scene has obvious parallels to the critical Battle at Red Cliff in the *Romance of the Three Kingdoms*, and to Liu Bei's sagely adviser Zhuge Liang in that novel. The depiction of Guo Ying's martial courage also calls to mind the fierce fighters of *The Water Margin*. The similarities were not lost upon the compiler or compilers of *Record of the Heroes and Martyrs*, either; when Liu Ji explains his plan to burn the enemy fleet, Taizu remarks that Liu is Zhuge Liang reborn. If those parallels between the two battle scenes were not obvious enough, the earliest-known recension of *Heroes and Martyrs* draws them out explicitly through verse scattered throughout the scene, such as the following:

The ingenious calculations in his breast startle ghosts and spirits,
With one fire he is able to incinerate a million troops.
Marquis Han [Xin], vanquisher of Chu, now appears again,
Through Liu [Ji], Zhuge [Liang] lives once again.

Another reads:

> Blazing fire in the west burns the soldiers of [Chen Youliang's]
> impostor Han soldiers,
> The mysterious machinations and ingenious calculations startle
> ghosts and spirits,
> At that moment, what use was the Red Cliff,
> In the struggle rule over the land was decided?

In *Heroes and Martyrs*, the history of the current dynasty was recast in the style of the nascent novel genre, and Guo Xun's ancestor Ying was transformed into a hero against a backdrop in the style of *Romance of the Three Kingdoms*' Battle of Red Cliff.

Although gossip-mongers such as Shen Defu cast suspicion on Guo and his "marvelous plan," accusing him of opportunistically playing up the role of his ancestor Ying in the founding of the dynasty by crediting him with this miraculous shot, this version of events had in actuality long been part of Guo family lore. The account found in the *Generational Compendium of the Three Families*, from 1515, is similar. It credits Ying with battling Chen Youliang's "impostor Han" forces at Poyang Lake for days on end despite an old wound that hadn't healed. The Ming forces burned enemy ships at the mouth of a tributary river, it says, and then Chen Youliang was struck and killed by a stray arrow: "There was word that this was Ying's accomplishment. His Majesty asked about it, and Ying said, 'It was the might of heaven and the calculations of the spirits; what power is it of your subject?' His Majesty rewarded him heavily."

Guo Ying's response here closely echoes the one shown later in the fictionalized *Heroes and Martyrs*, though expressed here in more "literary" language than in the novel. This suggests that either Guo's plan to win merit by "falsifying records" had been long in the making, or Guo sincerely believed all along that his ancestor played this important role in the founding of the dynasty.

Whether a cynical plot or a reflection of a sincere belief, Guo received the promotions he sought. Ying was installed in the imperial ancestral hall in 1537, and Guo was granted the prestige title of Grand Preceptor (*taishi*) in 1538. Then, in 1539, he was granted the title Duke of Yi. But his success was not long-lived. In the following year, he introduced another magician, Duan Chaoyong, to the emperor. Duan claimed to be able to make eating utensils that would grant the user immortality.

For introducing Duan, the emperor granted Guo yet another raise in salary. When Duan was exposed as a fraud, the ensuing controversy enveloped Guo as well. A flurry of charges was leveled at Guo, and this time he could not escape. Further accusations claimed that Guo had been abusing his power by mistreating officers, unrightfully claiming land, using government transportation for personal purposes, and running a network of shops.

The charges were sent to the Censorate for investigation, but the Censorate took no action against Guo. A persistent supervising secretary from the Ministry of Justice's Office of Scrutiny memorialized to the court, saying that no action had been taken by the Censorate for more than forty days, and the emperor demanded Guo explain himself. Guo's haughty response was that there was no need to investigate him and trouble the emperor with yet another pardon. The emperor had finally reached his limit, and Guo was imprisoned in the fall of 1541.

The reluctance of the Censorate to investigate Guo Xun was likely due in part to the censor-in-chief, Wang Tingxiang. Wang had been serving as censor-in-chief from 1533, and was concurrently made civilian director of the Integrated Divisions, of which Guo Xun was head, early in 1534. When the emperor lost patience with Guo, Wang Tingxiang was implicated as well. Wang was stripped of his position and ordered to leave the capital for his native place.

At the same time as these accusations were coming against Guo, the newly constructed imperial ancestral hall was destroyed in a fire, and the emperor ordered relevant officials to submit reviews of their own conduct. Wang Tingxiang had narrowly escaped punishment for the time being, but twelve officials, including Li Kaixian, were dismissed. When Guo was brought in for questioning, Shen Defu claims that his publishing activities nearly saved him. The Jiajing emperor ordered leniency because of his allyship in the Great Rites Controversy and his publication of a book called *Record of the Great Harmony* (*Taihe zhuan*). Shen adds that he does not know what Guo's "*Record of Great Harmony*" was, though he mentions the *Proper Sounds of Great Harmony* (*Taihe zhengyin pu*) as a possibility. Yet Guo's release was not to be: Guo Xun died in prison in the tenth month of the twenty-first year of the Jiajing reign (November 1542), more than a year after he was jailed.

Ultimately, it cannot be known for certain whether the allegations about Guo's creation of the *Heroes and Martyrs* are true; there simply is not enough evidence. Twenty-first century readers accustomed to thinking of vernacular fiction as a phenomenon of popular culture might even be tempted to dismiss the entire story of Guo's gaining power through "falsifying a biography" as absurd on its face: Would a high-ranking military official who moved in such elite circles be involved in the creation of a work of vernacular fiction—and a second-rate one at that? Would it really be possible for such a work of fiction to be presented to the emperor, and would the emperor be so moved by it that he would grant a promotion in rank? That is to say, would it be possible for novels to circulate in these circles and wield this level of influence within them?

Yet Guo's history of publishing demonstrates that the story is not as far-fetched as it might seem: He had a long history of using publishing to craft for himself a persona of a "Confucian general," a "military man who loves literature" from a long and unbroken line of distinguished men. He positioned himself among elite circles of the court by making imprints of works old and new available to them, and further advertised that position by obtaining prefaces from prominent men of the day. As a member of a military family, he did not go through the rigorous training for the civil service examinations and lacked the shared background of the literati. Yet he was educated, and he was able to find points of common interest between himself and his literati peers. These points included the nascent vernacular fiction genre. It is against this backdrop that the earliest print editions of vernacular fiction novels—including *The Water Margin*—appeared.

It might be objected that *Record of the Heroes and Martyrs* is no match by any standard, in the Ming or in the present day, for the "classic" works *The Water Margin* and *Romance of the Three Kingdoms*; if Guo were involved in it as well, then why does it lack the literariness of the latter two works?

Like *Three Kingdoms*, *Heroes and Martyrs* is tied to history. Yet whereas *Three Kingdoms* depicts the long and drawn-out collapse of the Han dynasty, *Heroes and Martyrs* depicts a dynasty at its inception. Over the long term, it is perhaps due precisely to the fact that *Heroes and Martyrs* depicts a founding rather than a collapse that it did not become a perennial favorite and cultural touchstone the way that *Three Kingdoms* did: for the most part, the Ming novel is a genre of the aesthetic of decline, whether it be of a dynasty or a household. As opposed to the drama genre, with its convention of the *tuanyuan* reunion for the ending, the most cherished of the traditional novels see their main protagonists fade away well before the book has ended. From the standpoint of one who is familiar with those masterworks, the subject matter of

Heroes and Martyrs—the successful founding of a dynasty—might seem a poor match for this particular genre. Further complicating matters for this novel is the fact that the dynastic founding that it depicts is that of the Ming itself, the very same dynasty in which it was written and published. Since for a Ming reader the end result of its action is the current state of affairs, *Heroes and Martyrs* is a novel doomed by both its subject matter and the timing of its initial publication to end in triumph.

Yet during the lifetime of Guo Xun, the novel was still a nascent genre without the conventions it would later develop. It would be more than a decade before commercial editions of vernacular fiction would appear as the handiwork of the well-known for-profit printer Xiong Damu, who would begin cutting and pasting historiographical works together into long historical-fiction narratives in the 1550s. It would be several decades more before the genre would truly come to fruition, spurred along by the late-sixteenth-century "printing boom" and thriving commercial publishers such as Yu Xiangdou—a time when the reputation of the genre would be altered further by the association with eccentrics such as Li Zhuowu, whose names were listed (often spuriously) as authors of commentaries on novels. This was an era, the time before the fire, when novels moved among elites.

CHAPTER 2

"One Freshly Slaughtered Pig, Two Flagons of Jinhua Wine . . . and a Small Book"

The Censorate Edition

The Wuding edition was not the only early edition of *The Water Margin* to move in elite circles; there are also records of an edition printed by the Ming Censorate bureau (*Ducha yuan*). The Censorate was the Ming's equivalent of the Tribunal of Censors (*Yushi tai*) of preceding dynasties, and like the Tribunal of Censors, it was a powerful bureau tasked with investigating the workings of the entire administration. The Censorate was, in fact, even more powerful than its predecessors, having been restructured by the founding emperor early in the history of the Ming and granted the ability to report directly to the emperor about any administrative abuses.

The Censorate *Water Margin*

Later scholars have often looked askance at the notion of such an important administrative body printing something as apparently frivolous as *The Water Margin*. In the subsequent Qing dynasty, in particular, scholars pointed to the Censorate *Water Margin* as being emblematic of the lack of seriousness in the Ming that led to the dynasty's eventual downfall. More recently, others have even suggested that such a powerful agency printing such a "commercial" work meant that the rampant profiteering environment of the late Ming era had penetrated even the highest levels of the dynastic administration. Yet as the previous chapter has shown, in the era of the Wuding edition, printed, long-form vernacular fiction was at an earlier stage of development and had yet to take on such associations with the marketplace or commercial printing. As this chapter will show, the Censorate edition was most likely created around the same time as the Wuding edition, and most likely circulated in similar circles as well. What, then, was the point of the Censorate *Water Margin*? Why did such a high and powerful agency print this work of vernacular fiction? For a hint about possible answers to this question, we first turn to the *Jin Ping Mei*, a work of fiction that, coincidentally, is a spin-off of *The Water Margin*. Somewhat ironically, this work of fiction serves as a reminder that a book is often more than its text.

"One Freshly Slaughtered Pig, Two Flagons of Jinhua Wine . . . and a Small Book"

No character in late imperial literature better understands the economy of the gift and the bribe than Ximen Qing, the dissolute protagonist of the late Ming novel *Jin Ping Mei*. Ximen is a master of *guanxi*, the art of making social connections and plying them in order to get what one wants. Giving and receiving gifts is a critical element of that art: one must know the right amount to give in the circumstances, and how much to reciprocate when given a gift. As Sophie Volpp has pointed out, Ximen Qing devotes an entire room, a literati-style "study," to the storage of gifts, which he catalogues in detail.[1]

We see this art of giving and receiving in a series of exchanges beginning in chapter 47 of the novel. The episode begins when a young servant boy named Miao Qing, who is on the lam after playing a role in his master's murder, enlists Ximen Qing's assistance in his attempt to evade the authorities.[2] Miao bribes Ximen Qing's lover Wang Liu'er into setting up a meeting for him, giving her fifty taels of silver and two silk outfits. She is thrilled with this unexpected windfall, and reports to Ximen Qing about the matter. Ximen Qing, however, scoffs at the petty amount Miao has offered her. In light of the severity of the crime and the witnesses who will testify against Miao, Ximen sees that a much larger sum would be necessary. He advises her to return the gift to Miao Qing immediately, and she does so.

In a panic, Miao quickly sells off all of his ill-gotten gain in order to raise the funds for a proper "gift." He doubles his introduction fee to

Wang Liu'er and comes up with no less than a thousand taels for Ximen Qing himself. Additionally, he prepares small amounts of cash for all of the servants in Ximen Qing's household. With the meeting set, he conceals the thousand taels in wine containers and discreetly delivers them to Ximen Qing along with a roast pig. Now, with the proper pay-off in hand, Ximen Qing is ready to do business with Miao. He discusses Miao's case with his colleague Judicial Commissioner Xia and splits the thousand taels with him. Together Ximen and Xia manage to get Miao Qing off the hook for the murder.

However, another servant of the murdered man files a complaint about this miscarriage of justice, and now it is Ximen Qing and Xia's turn to use the art of gift-giving to extricate themselves from a bad situation. They bring gifts to the house of the powerful court official Cai Jing, and Cai Jing's people in turn find a way to bury the complaint against them. The investigating official sees what has happened, and files a memorial against Cai Jing. Cai concocts reasons to have the investigating official removed from office and replaced.

In the midst of all of this bribing of officials, Ximen Qing and Xia gain inside knowledge of a way to profit by manipulating a salt-voucher exchange program that is soon to be implemented. In order to do so, they need to establish *guanxi* with the salt-control censor. It just so happens that the new salt-control censor is traveling with the replacement investigating official, so Ximen Qing and Xia jump at the chance to get in good with him to further their scheme. They ask the salt-control censor to bring the new investigating official along on a visit to the Ximen household, and he agrees to do so. Just days after the replacement takes up his duties, the two officials set out together by boat.

When the two officials arrive at Ximen Qing's residence, they follow protocol and exchange gifts in the reception hall. The censor, Cai Yun, orders his retainers to present the following: "Two bolts of Huzhou silk, a literary collection (*wenji*), four bags of tender-leaf tea, and an inkstone from Duanqi."[3]

Ximen Qing is only functionally literate; previously we have seen him struggle to read official documents. But these gifts, tokens of a luxurious lifestyle, are readily accepted. The other official, meanwhile, presents only his visiting card. Ximen Qing provides them with a lavish banquet. Though the new official returns to his boat early, the salt control official takes up Ximen Qing's offer to stay at his residence. Ximen Qing gets him to agree to help in the manipulation of the voucher system, and then provides singing girls to accompany him for the night.

Later, when the newly appointed official returns to the Ximen household, he brings another set of gifts to Ximen Qing, which Ximen Qing's servants record on a card for him. The card reads: "One freshly slaughtered pig, two flagons of Jinhua wine, four hundred sheets of official-quality stationery, and a small book (*xiaoshu yibu*)."[4]

This story, with all of its exchanges of gifts and bribes, demonstrates how books consist of more than the texts that they bear on their pages. Like slaughtered pigs, flagons of wine, Duanqi inkstones, and taels of silver, books are physical objects, and like these other physical objects, they can be objects of exchange. When officials arrive, in both cases they come bearing books as gifts—even when the recipient is a semi-literate man like Ximen Qing, who is seen in those same chapters calling for help to read complex official documents. More straightforward quid pro quo bribery on the other hand is done more transparently, by means of the commodities silver and silk. Books are signifiers of taste. When given as a gift, a book is a token of a shared culture between the giver and the recipient. Even if the recipient is not a literatus himself, the presented book is an acknowledgement of symbolic acceptance within that shared culture.

Lu Rong's Lament: Officials Bearing Gifts

Though the *Jin Ping Mei* is, of course, a work of fiction, it is rich with description of the late Ming milieu. Craig Clunas has remarked that it is "almost a crash-course in Ming civilization" and that it is "generally held to reflect the social conditions and attitudes in the decades immediately preceding its probable first publication in 1617."[5] This verisimilitude extends to the presentation of books as gifts, a common practice in the era. By the mid-Ming, it was such a widespread practice among officials that literati lamented the unequal distribution it created despite the abundance of imprints, as well as the tastes that it propagated. Lu Rong (1436–94) made such a complaint. He remarked that, by his era, woodblock printing had become widespread but the quality and distribution of books remained mixed. "Useless and contemptible" books abounded and scholars' studies were becoming superficial; high officials printed books by the hundred and gave them back and forth as gifts, but rustic scholars of remote areas could not get even a glimpse of them.[6]

The officials bearing books as gifts in the novel are agents of the Song dynasty's Tribunal of Censors, a powerful and prestigious central oversight agency that was charged with conducting both regular and ad hoc investigations into the conduct of the bureaucracy. Censorial bodies had been part of dynastic administrations as early as the Qin, when one of the "Three Dukes" who administered the central government was titled censor-in-chief (*yushi dafu*). The Former Han saw the creation of the Tribunal of Censors as a bureaucratic agency, and that agency set the pattern followed by successive dynasties.

The Ming Censorate, the successor to the Tribunal of Censors of previous dynasties, had been reorganized by the founding emperor in the wake of the Hu Weiyong affair. The emperor accused the official Hu Weiyong of plotting a coup and purged the administration of his suspected faction. In the aftermath, the emperor restructured the Censorate so that it could report directly to him.

The *Ming History* defines the roles played by the agency. It says that censors-in-chief were charged with "conducting investigations into officials of all ranks, looking into grievances, supervising the circuits, and acting as the eyes and ears of the emperor." Such investigations could be part of regular inspections or ad hoc. The Censorate could investigate corruption and false reports, and assist with important interrogations. It was charged with overseeing several important administrative bodies in the two capitals, Nanjing and Beijing. It was also charged with miscellaneous tasks involving military discipline and the patrol of transportation infrastructure. In major cases, censors could memorialize to the court; in minor ones, they could settle matters themselves on the spot.[7]

Needless to say, publishing was not among the main duties of this elite agency. However, it is easy to imagine circumstances where books and other physical objects marking taste would come into play in the course of censors' duties—just as the censors in the *Jin Ping Mei* presented Ximen Qing with a "literary collection" of an unnamed author and a "miniature book" upon their visit to his household.

When books are considered in this way, as physical items that could be presented as a signifier of presumed shared membership in a certain class or of shared tastes, it is less surprising to learn that the Ming Censorate was a major publisher of woodblock imprint books. According to the catalogue of official imprints called *Imprints Old and New* (*Gujin shuke*), compiled sometime in the mid-sixteenth century by an official named Zhou Hongzu (fl. 1559), the Censorate published thirty-three titles in all. That number is higher than those for any other agency save the court itself and the Imperial Academies of Beijing and Nanjing.

Somewhat more surprising, however, are some of the titles on the list of the Censorate's publications: listed among them are both *The Water Margin* and *Romance of the Three Kingdoms*.[8]

If a censor were to present a copy of *The Water Margin* as a gift, what would that say about the presumed relationship between presenter and recipient? Would a work of fiction be seen as one of those "useless and contemptible" books complained about by Lu Rong, or would it have signified something more rarefied? Would it signify membership in a world of elite connoisseurship, like the censors' gifts of small books and literary collections to Ximen Qing, or would it be base pandering, like Miao Qing's silk and silver? To answer these questions, we must look at the other titles on the list.

The Censorate List

The complete list of Censorate publications in the *Imprints Old and New* are as follows:[9]

1. *Records of the Grand Historian (Shi ji)*
2. *Selections of Literature (Wenxuan)*
3. *Discourses of a Recluse (Qianfu lun)*
4. *Collected Commentaries on the Poetry of Du Fu (Du shi jijie)*
5. *Expanded Record of a Forest of Poems (Shilin guangji)*
6. *The Poetry of Su Shi, with Notes of Numerous Commentators (Qianjia zhu Su Shi)*
7. *A New Voice for a Flourishing Age (Shengshi xinsheng)*
8. *Remnant Sounds of Great Antiquity (Taigu yiyin)*
9. *Sounds of the Tang (Tang yin)*
10. *The Wondrous Secret Sourcebook of the Emaciated Immortal (Quxian shenqi mipu)*
11. *Subtle Meanings of the Jade Machinations (Yuji weiyi)*
12. *Poetic Couplets, Arranged by Rhyme (Shidui yayun)*
13. *The Direct Commentaries on the Military Classics (Wujing zhijie)*
14. *The Classic of Filial Piety, with Arranged Commentaries (Xiaojing zhushu)*
15. *A Record Suiting the Emotions (Shiqing lu)*
16. *The Great Compendium of Calculations (Suanfa daquan)*
17. *A Primer of Qin Harmonies (Qinyun qimeng)*
18. *Romance of the Three Kingdoms (Sanguo zhi yanyi)*
19. *The Water Margin (Shuihu zhuan)*

20. *The Precious Essentials of a Thousand in Gold (Qianjin baoyao)*
21. *Ballads of Great Peace (Taiping yuefu)*
22. *On Realizing Truth (Wuzhen pian)*
23. *Ocean of Jade Voices* [?] *(Yuyin haipian)*
24. *The Calendar of the Seven Governances (Qi zheng lu)*
25. *A Collection Nurturing and Celebrating Meritorious Service (Yuqing xunyi ji)*
26. *Ballads for a Harmonious Peace (Yongxi yuefu)*
27. *The Classic of the Rotten Axe Handle (Lanke jing)*
28. *Dark Machinations of Myriad Transformations (Wanhua xuanji)*
29. *Illustrated Oceanic [Mirror] for Measuring [Circles]* [?] *(Pitu cehai)*
30. *Rhymes of the Central Plains (Zhongyuan yinyun)*
31. *Token for the Agreement of the Three (Cantong qi)*
32. *Collected Works of Mr. Wang (Tingxiang) (Wang shi cangji)*
33. *Collected Works of Du Yangang (Du Yangang ji)*

It would be safe to assume that, as an imprint created by an official agency, a Ming "Censorate edition" of *The Water Margin* would be of high quality.[10] Unfortunately, however, there is no extant copy of the Censorate *Water Margin* or, for that matter, any other Ming Censorate publication. The only edition that has been claimed as one of the Censorate publications is a 1522 edition of *Romance of the Three Kingdoms* held in the Shanghai Library and widely available in facsimile reprint. However, that edition features no colophons or other markings identifying it as such; the identification is based on its date and the quality of its print, which is assumed to be consistent with official imprints.[11]

As mentioned in the previous chapter, this 1522 edition of *Romance of the Three Kingdoms* is frequently assumed to be the first printed edition of that novel due to comments in its two prefaces.[12]

The name Xiuranzi, it will be recalled from the last chapter, has also appeared in connection with Guo Xun: Guo's edition of the rhyme manual *Rhymes of Poetry Explained* featured word definitions credited to this figure. That rhyme manual was also published around the same time as this edition of *Romance of the Three Kingdoms*. The Xiuranzi pseudonym does not, to the best of my knowledge, appear in any other known text or imprint, suggesting some connection between this particular edition of *Romance of the Three Kingdoms* and Guo; Xiuranzi might have been someone in Guo's employ. Furthermore, it will be seen below that Guo and his Wuding editions have further commonalities with the Censorate and its publications, both in terms of personal connections and in shared imprint titles. Though it cannot be confirmed that this particular edition of *Romance of the Three Kingdoms* is the Censorate edition, it undoubtedly originated in these overlapping circles.

Literary Censors

In addition to *The Water Margin* and *Romance of the Three Kingdoms*, there are a number of others listed among these thirty-three titles that a serious-minded scholar such as Lu Rong might have found "useless and contemptible," and the "orthodox" classics of old he longed for are almost entirely absent. Yet several books may have served social purposes, including literary collections of censors themselves. These are the *Collected Works of Mr. Wang* (*Wang shi cangji*) and the *Collected Works of Du Yangang* (*Du Yangang ji*), the literary collections of censors Wang Tingxiang (1474–1544) and Du Nan, respectively. The list of titles also includes evidence of connections with Guo Xun: in addition to *The Water Margin* and the *Romance of the Three Kingdoms*, the Censorate titles also include the collection of Guo family documents *A Collection Nurturing and Celebrating Meritorious Service* and the *qu* song anthology purportedly edited by Guo, *Ballads for a Harmonious Peace*. These titles reflect actual social relationships between these men: Wang Tingxiang and Du Nan were colleagues, and each of their literary collections features a preface written by the other.[13] Furthermore, Guo Xun worked closely with Wang Tingxiang as the military and civilian directors, respectively, of the Integrated Divisions guarding the capital.

Wang Tingxiang, a major intellectual figure of the mid-Ming whose achievements touched on literature, music, philosophy, and governance, was appointed to the post of vice censor-in-chief in 1527 and was promoted to censor-in-chief in 1533.[14] The following year, he was made civilian director of the Integrated Divisions, the military director of which was Guo Xun. Like Guo, Wang came to power in the wake of the Great Rites Controversy, in which he had also been an early supporter of the Jiajing emperor's effort to have his biological father posthumously named an emperor. When Guo was placed in prison in 1541, the emperor turned on Wang Tingxiang as well, declaring that he was part of Guo's faction. Wang was dismissed from office and sent home as a commoner. He died just three years later.

Wang had passed the imperial examination in 1502 and, upon entering officialdom in the capital, had enmeshed himself in the literary circles loosely surrounding the influential Li Mengyang, including He

Jingming and Cui Xian. Wang and others at the core of this group came to be known as the Former Seven Masters in literary history, known for advocating an "archaist" style and holding up the prose of the Qin and Han and poetry of the Tang as literary models. The Former Seven Masters are Wang, Li Mengyang, He Jingming, Bian Gong, Xu Zhenqing, Kang Hai, and Wang Jiusi.[15]

As the title implies, *The Collected Works of Mr. Wang* is an anthology of Wang Tingxiang's writings, including poetry and prose of a variety of genres. It features prefaces by Tang Long and Li Yinghong in addition to that by Du Nan mentioned above. All of the prefaces are dated 1536, placing its publication within the period when Wang was censor-in-chief and working alongside Guo Xun as civilian director of the Integrated Divisions in Beijing. *The Collected Works of Du Yangang* refers to Du Nan's literary name. It features a preface by Wang Tingxiang, signed the previous year (1535), an earlier one by Cui Xian signed 1531, an undated preface by the poet Gao Shusi (1501–37), and another one by Li Yinghong signed 1535.[16]

Sanqu Art-Song on the Censorate List

Another group of titles on the Censorate list that also suggests social uses, in both the circumstances of their production and their intended function, are titles related to *sanqu* art songs. The list includes three major Ming sanqu collections, as well as a philological work designed to aid in the composition of sanqu. The target readership of the Censorate likely was interested in both the reading and writing of sanqu. The qu as a genre does not hold the esteem of the privileged shi poetry form in regular circles. However it is precisely that lack of esteem that has made the genre attractive in several situations. Engaging in such nonserious writing was, for example, a way for Ming princes to display what Wilt Idema has referred to in one case as "a conspicuous display" of a "lack of political ambition."[17] It was also, conversely, a way for disaffected former officials to express their dissatisfaction in an artistically open manner and build communities around themselves with like-minded individuals.[18] But the existence of these editions among the publications of both Guo Xun and the Censorate—along with the social ties between Guo and the censors—suggests that such works did circulate in precisely those circles.

Prefaces to these books demonstrate how they could be taken as both politicized and yet neutral at the same time; they trace the roots of the genre to the songs of the people (hence the *"yuefu"*/"ballads" of the titles), claim that they are worthy and morally upright, and claim that these qualities arise from the "peace" that comes with good governance.

The first collection is *Ballads of Harmonious Peace*, the sanqu collection purportedly edited by Guo Xun himself that was discussed in the previous chapter. The presence of this title on the Censorate list along with *A Collection Nurturing and Celebrating Meritorious Service*, *The Water Margin*, and *Romance of the Three Kingdoms*, as well as the involvement of Xiuranzi in both the 1522 *Three Kingdoms* edition and Guo's *Rhymes of Poetry Explained*, further underscores the social ties between Guo, the Censorate, and Censor-in-Chief Wang Tingxiang. In light of this working relationship between Guo and Wang, it is conceivable that the Wuding editions and Censorate editions of all of these shared titles were printed from the same blocks or even were some sort of joint venture between the marquis and the bureau. However, barring the unearthing of further evidence, this conjecture is ultimately unprovable.

Whatever the case, the preface to *Ballads* discussed in the previous chapter positions it as a product of a populace at peace due to the good governance of Guo Xun during his tenure in the Guangdong-Guangxi region. It can easily be imagined that *Ballads* could carry similar connotations as the product of a government agency.

The second collection, *A New Voice for a Flourishing Age*, is an anonymously compiled collection of sanqu (poetically referred to as *"yuefu"* in the preface) arias in the northern style. A copy of this title with a preface from the twelfth year of the Zhengde reign (1517) is possibly an exemplar of the Censorate edition, dating to within five years of the "Xiuranzi" *Three Kingdoms* edition discussed above.[19] Like that edition of *Three Kingdoms*, the 1517 copy of *A New Voice* features no publisher's colophon or other identifying marks. In 1525, *A New Voice* was largely superseded by *Splendor Plucked from the Forest of Lyrics* (*Cilin zhaiyan*), a version of the collection greatly expanded and retitled by Zhang Lu. There is, however, a 1525 edition of *A New Voice* that features the Zhang Lu preface from *Splendor Plucked from the Forest of Lyrics*. That edition is credited to "Mr. Zhang of Jintai"; it is unclear whether "Mr. Zhang" is Zhang Lu himself, or if a commercial publisher named Mr. Zhang of Jintai obtained and modified the blocks of the newer collection's preface, adding it to an edition of *A New Voice*.[20] We will return to "Mr. Zhang" and other Jintai publishers below.

The 1517 preface to *A New Voice* works the sanqu songs of the collection into a long genealogy of "ballads" (*yuefu*) reaching back to the

Han dynasty. It vouches for their literary worthiness by claiming that they employ classical poetic techniques, and assures the reader of their respectable provenance. It also claims to consist of works that are both popular yet written by poets, and that the collection's organization by rhyme scheme facilitates the writing of matching lyrics without errors of rhyme or meter.[21]

The third collection, *Ballads of Great Peace,* is considerably older, having been originally compiled by Yang Chaoying in 1351. Yang had previously produced another edition of sanqu titled *White Snow, Sunny Spring* (*Yangchun baixue,* ca. 1324). These two works were among the first printed collections of sanqu songs, contributing to the textualization what was once an orally transmitted genre.[22]

A 1351 preface to *Ballads of Great Peace* makes claims about the genre similar to the ones seen in *Ballads for Harmonious Peace* and *A New Voice* above. It claims that the roots of the ballad as a genre are in the *Classic of Poetry*, and that it and other forms of sung verse are in actuality no different from pentasyllabic shi poetry. It vouches for the respectability of the genre and claims that it retains the legacy of being sung aloud that shi poetry no longer has. It also vouches for the orthodox lineage and literary worth of the songs within the collection, which is organized by keys and modes.[23]

The final work related to sanqu and the social ramifications of the genre is *Rhymes of the Central Plains.* Rather than a collection of songs, however, *Rhymes of the Central Plains* is a phonological work. Compiled by Zhou Deqing in 1324, *Rhymes of the Central Plains* was a major breakthrough in rhyme books in that it greatly simplified the categories of rhymes found in earlier works such as the Song-era *Expanded Rhymes* (*Guangyun*), and made rhymes conform to contemporary spoken pronunciations from the north. Because of these innovations, it could be consulted in the process of composing northern-style qu lyrics.[24] Also included with the work is the compiler Zhou Deqing's "Ten Rules for Composing Song Lyrics" (*zuoci shifa*), a guide to writing sanqu. Along with the *Proper Sounds of Great Harmony* (*Taihe zhengyin pu*) and the aforementioned *Ballads of Great Peace, Rhymes of the Central Plain* played an important role in the creation of a canonical rhyme scheme for sanqu song lyrics.[25]

Shared Tastes Reflected

Taken as a group, these books—three major anthologies of sanqu songs, arranged by rhyme, and a rhyme dictionary organized by northern pronunciation—suggest that the Censorate titles were intended for those who by personal interest or social circumstance wrote sanqu song lyrics. Prefaces to these works suggest literati involvement in, and justification of, a genre that was not as privileged as shi poetry. What might be deemed a lowly genre was fashioned into an authentic voice of a well-governed age, as reflected in their very titles.

In addition to these collections of sanqu, there are also five collections of classical poetry, including three anthologies and two single-poet collections. The anthologies are *The Expanded Forest of Poems*, *Sounds of the Tang*, and *Poetic Couplets Arranged by Rhyme*. The collections are of the works of Du Fu and Su Shi. *The Expanded Forest of Poems* was compiled by the late Song/early Yuan poet Cai Zhengsun and consists of 671 poems of the Jin, Tang, and Song he deemed "popular and widely read" (*kuaizhi renkou*)—a phrase also found, perhaps coincidentally, in the preface to *A New Voice* above.[26] A reprint dating to 1497, the tenth year of the Hongzhi reign, features a preface by a censor, Zhang Nai, raising the possibility of the Censorate's involvement. However, once again, the edition contains no colophon or other marking definitively identifying it as such.[27]

Sounds of the Tang, meanwhile, was an influential Yuan-era collection of Tang poetry compiled by Yang Shihong between 1335 and 1344.[28] *Poetic Couplets Indexed by Rhyme*, compiled in 1453 by Geng Chun (fl. 1432), consists of poems in regulated verse and is organized by shared rhyme.[29] Similar to how the works discussed previously would assist in the composition of sanqu lyrics, this work would inspire writers composing regulated verse.

A handful of classical prose titles are also included on the Censorate list. These are *The Records of the Grand Historian*, *Selections of Literature*, commentary editions of a collection of strategy manuals and the *Classic of Filial Piety*, and *Discourses of a Recluse*.

In addition to these literary titles, there are several other Censorate publications related to what might be called leisure activities, broadly defined. There are, for example, three handbooks for playing the qin: *Remnant Sounds of Great Antiquity*, *The Wondrous Secret Sourcebook of the Emaciated Immortal*, and *A Primer of Qin Harmonies*. Again, there are no identified exemplars of these Censorate editions, but it can be presumed that they were fine editions. Ming-era qin handbooks such as these employed a specialized form of musical notation called "abbreviated notation" (*jianzipu*), in which several characters and symbols are printed together in a cluster telling the reader how to play the instrument. This specialized system required precise block carving and printing in order for the book to remain useful to players: mistakes would hinder players' ability to interpret the score (*dapu*). For this reason, many Ming qin handbooks are lavishly produced editions.

The *Secret Sourcebook*, one of the most important qin handbooks of the Ming, was such a lavish edition.[30] It was originally published by Zhu Quan, Prince of Ning, and bears a preface dated to 1425. *Remnant Sounds* was also originally published by Zhu Quan; in a preface dated 1413, he claims that his edition is based on a work originally from the Song that had been annotated and expanded by Yuan Junzhe in the early Ming. Extant Ming editions feature intricate diagrams of fingering positions and various types of qin.[31]

Also related to cultured leisure activities are two chess manuals, the first of which is *A Record Suiting the Emotions*. An extant edition held in the Peking University library features a preface dated the third year of the Jiajing era (1525), and no publisher's information.[32] The second is *The Classic of the Rotten Axe Handle*, the title of which refers to the legend of Wang Zhi of the Jin (265–420) era. Wang Zhi encountered two immortal boys while cutting firewood and watched them play a round of chess. By the time they were finished, Wang's axe handle had rotted away and a century had passed. An edition of this manual had also been printed by Zhu Quan.

In addition to these, other titles on the Censorate list deal with diverse subjects such as medicine (*Subtle Meanings of the Jade Machinations* and *The Precious Essentials of a Thousand in Gold*) and Daoism and alchemy (*On Realizing Truth* and *Token for the Agreement of the Three*). Others are more difficult to positively identify: The *Great Compendium of Calculations*, for example, appears to refer to the *Jiuzhang bilei suanfa daquan*, a 1450 mathematical work that includes mnemonic formulae for performing calculations on an abacus. Less clear are *Dark Machinations of Myriad Transformations*, *The Calendar of the Seven Governances*, *Illustrated Oceanic [Mirror] for Measuring [Circles]*, and *Ocean of Jade Voices*. Judging solely from the title and the other works on the list, the first is likely another Daoist work. *The Calendar of the Seven Governances* presumably is a calendrical system based on the "Seven Governances" (*qi zheng*), that is, the sun, the moon, and the five planets. The third, *Illustrated Oceanic [Mirror] for Measuring [Circles]*, is most likely an illustrated (*pitu*) edition of the *Ceyuan haijing*, abbreviated to *cehai*. The *Ceyuan haijing* is another mathematical work by Li Ye; it is the earliest surviving work describing the "heavenly element [i.e., variable] notation" (*tianyuan shu*) methodology for solving algebraic equations. As for the *Ocean of Jade Voices*, there are several character books (*zishu*) from the Ming with "*haipian*" in the title, and this is likely a variation on them.

Comparison with the Market

Such "leisurely" books might have been just the type that provoked Lu Rong's complaint about the flood of "useless" books. But it is easy to imagine titles such as these being presented to Ximen Qing along with a freshly slaughtered pig, two flagons of wine, and four hundred sheets of official-quality stationery. If the fictional censor Cai Yun could present literary collections as gifts, perhaps an actual Ming censor might present the collected works of Wang Tingxiang or Du Nan. With such gifts, one could show recognition of the recipient as a peer with similar leisure interests and social connections. Not to mention, in such circumstances, presenting a more "scholarly" title would demonstrate the perception of deficiency in the recipient's education; it would signal exclusion rather than inclusion.

We have seen above how the Censorate list shares several titles with the list of Guo Xun's Wuding editions; assuming that a Censorate *Water Margin* appeared during this period—the period in which Guo and Wang Tingxiang served together as directors of the Integrated Divisions, and around the time of the Xiuranzi editions of *Three Kingdoms* and *Rhymes of Poetry Explained*—what would it mean as a gift? What sort of physical object would it be, and what significance would it hold? With no positively identified exemplars of Censorate editions, and only a handful of possible candidates of them, how can we estimate the quality of such editions? The best candidate is the 1522 *Three Kingdoms* edition, with the preface by Xiuranzi, that is widely assumed to be the first printed edition of that work. It is finely carved, and would likely be prized by collectors and "aficionados." A contemporary edition of *The Water Margin*, whether printed by Guo or the Censorate, would most likely have been of similar quality.

In addition to the similarities with Guo Xun's publishing output, there are also even more similarities between the list of Censorate publications and titles put out by the higher-end commercial firms in contemporary Beijing's book market. But even those firms had yet, to our knowledge, to print an edition of *The Water Margin* or, for that matter, any other work of long-form vernacular fiction.

Printing for Profit in Beijing

Let us imagine the Censorate's place in the "publishing space" of sixteenth-century Beijing. Beijing was known neither for the quality nor the quantity of its commercial publishing output in the Ming dynasty, paling in comparison to southern locales such as Nanjing, Hangzhou, and Jianyang on either count. As the dynasty's primary capital, it was of course home to many literate people and connoisseurs of books. Yet the majority of those people were from elsewhere and likely obtained the bulk of their libraries in their places of origin. It might also be that, as a trading hub, Beijing saw enough of an inflow of books from elsewhere to render local publishing at least partially redundant. The late Ming bibliophile and scholar Hu Yinglin (1551–1602) suggested that it was the high price of paper in the north that hindered the book trade there. As for quality of editions, he rated those from Suzhou and Changzhou as the best, followed by those from Jinling and Hangzhou. He rated Fujian imprints as the worst. The situation had been the same, he claimed, since the Song dynasty, though in recent times Huzhou and She County had produced fine imprints that rival those of Suzhou and Changzhou in price. Sichuan imprints were rare. The imprints of Beijing did not even warrant a mention in Hu's ranking.[33]

The Ming writer Xie Zhaozhe (1567–1624) wrote a similar ranking of imprints of various areas; of imprints from the Song dynasty, he ranked those of Hangzhou as the finest, though he notes that recent imprints from the region do not live up to the name. Sichuan imprints followed, and Fujian imprints were the lowest in quality. Of the present, he wrote, imprints from Jinling, Xin'an, and Wuxing were not inferior to Song-dynasty imprints in quality of craftsmanship. Once again, Beijing is absent from the discussion altogether.[34]

With the level of prestige granted to books printed in the south, it is likely that rich and powerful residents of Beijing preferred them over locally printed books.[35] Lower-end consumers, on the other hand, might find locally produced books prohibitively expensive, especially in comparison with cheap Fujian imprints arriving through trade routes.

In terms of numbers, only thirteen book publishers are known to have been operating in Ming-era Beijing. By contrast, estimates place the number of Nanjing publishers at around one hundred for the dynasty.[36] Those for Suzhou vary more widely, with the highest at sixty-seven.[37] Various counts put the number for Jianyang between 67 and 129.[38] Jianyang County also encompasses the town Masha, the home of the notorious "Masha editions," a term which perhaps unfairly became synonymous with cheap, shoddy imprints.

These known publishers of Beijing varied widely in the types and quality of books that they sold, running the gamut from fine editions modeled after the most-prized Song imprints on the one hand to cheaply produced chapbooks on the other. Most of the titles on the list of Censorate publications were not available at either end of the spectrum, and those that were match the higher end more closely.

The greatest overlap between the Censorate titles and those of a commercial publisher is with one called Wang Liang of Jintai. A 1522 edition of *Selections of Literature* printed by Wang Liang features an advertisement for the firm's other wares (figure 2.1).[39] Fourteen titles are listed, and of those, all but one—the *Han Shi waizhuan*—are on the list of Censorate publications as well.[40] Furthermore, those thirteen titles are grouped together at the beginning of the Censorate list, interrupted only by *A New Voice for a Flourishing Age*, which appears in the seventh place. The advertisement features two lists of seven titles each, printed in horizontal rows. The first list is of prints from "facsimile recut" (*fanke*) blocks based on Song and Yuan editions, and the second list, printed directly underneath the first, is of books printed from "newly recarved" (*chongke*) versions of texts from "ancient woodblocks" (*guban*).[41] When read vertically rather than horizontally, however, more than half of the titles are even listed in the same order as on the Censorate list.

Beyond this list of wares, nothing is known about Wang Liang of Jintai outside of its name and location. The designation "Jintai," or "Golden Terrace," is found in the names of several Ming-era Beijing publishers. In addition to Wang Liang, there were Mr. Lu (*Lu shi*) of Jintai, Mr. Yan (*Yan shi*) of Jintai, Jintai House of Yue (*Yue jia*), and Mr. Feng (*Feng shi*) of Jintai. The name refers to an area in the north of the city, near Chaoyang Gate, where King Zhao of Yan supposedly heaped gold as a reward for any minister who could assist him in taking revenge upon the state of Qi. It was also one of the eight vistas of the city painted by the Yongle emperor's court artists after moving the capital there. These factors gave the place name a cultural connotation of "rewards due to men of talent and acumen."[42] Despite Jintai being located in the north of the city, near Chaoyang Gate, the Wang Liang advertisement lists that establishment's location as being "across from the first patrol watch office to the west and inside the Zhengyang Gate." This spot is near the center of the old city, near what is now Tian'anmen Square, rather than the geographical Jintai. The "Jintai"

金臺書鋪汪諒見居

正陽門內西第一巡警更鋪對門今將所刻古書目錄列于左及

家藏今古書籍不能悉載願市者覽焉

翻刻司馬遷正義解註史記一部　　　重刻名賢叢話詩林廣記一部

翻刻梁昭明解註文選一部　　　重刻韓詩外傳一部十卷韓嬰集

翻刻黃鶴解註杜詩一部全集　　　重刻潛夫論漢王符撰一部

翻刻千家註蘇詩一部　　　重刻太古遺音大全一部

翻刻解註唐音一部　　　重刻朧仙神奇秘譜一部

翻刻王機微義一部係醫書　　　重刻詩對押韻一部

翻刻武經直解一部劉寅進士註　　　重刻孝經註跋一冊

俱宋元板　　　俱古板

嘉靖元年十二月望日金臺汪諒古板校正新刊

FIGURE 2.1. Advertisement in Wang Liang of Jintai edition of *Selections of Literature* (1522).
Source: Reprinted in *Quan Ming fensheng fenxian keshu kao*, 1:12.

House of Yue was also in the vicinity of Wang Liang's establishment. This suggests that Beijing publishers used "Jintai" as a cultural rather than geographical signifier.

What is known, however, is that Wang Liang of Jintai imprints were admired by later collectors. The Qing-dynasty bibliophile Ding Bing (1832–99), for example, listed Wang Liang titles in the catalogue of his collection, *A Guide to the Collection of the Fine Edition Book Room* (*Shanben shushi cangshu zhi*). Ding owned a copy of the Wang Liang *Selections of Literature*, which he describes at length. After marveling at the many commentaries included in the edition, Ding compares it favorably to Song editions: "Could anything but an edition originally from the Song be like this?" He claims that Wang Liang obtained Song editions and had new blocks cut based on them. The carvers, he notes, knew nothing of the You Mao (1127–94) or Zhang Boyuan (fl. 1314–20) editions, implying that this edition predated them.[43] Ding also identifies Wang Liang as the one who set up shop inside the Zhengyang Gate, across from the patrol watch office.[44]

Ding's catalogue also has an entry for a Wang Liang edition of Du Fu's poetry called *A Collection of a Thousand Commentaries to the Poetry of Du Fu, Separated by Category, in Twenty Volumes* (*Ji qianjia zhu fenlei Du Gongbu shi ershi juan*), which Ding (mistakenly) believed to be a facsimile reprint of a Yuan-dynasty edition. He writes that it does not differ in the number of lines and character count from the Yuan edition, but that its brush strokes are slightly thicker. He notes that many discarded official documents were used in its printing, lending it a strong air of antiquity (*duo guqu*). He also notes that Wang Liang also published the Ke Weixong edition of *Records of the Grand Historian* and the "Mr. Zhang" edition of *Selections of Literature*.[45]

The similarity between the Censorate and Wang Liang imprints raises the possibility of some sort of connection between the two entities. Ding's reference to discarded official documents used in printing further fuels speculation. Yet ultimately there is no concrete evidence proving the connection. Furthermore, it seems unlikely that the Censorate simply entered the book trade as a money-making strategy. What is clear is that the two had similar audiences in mind, and that those audiences were connoisseurs. Wang Liang of Jintai was among the most highly regarded publishers of Ming Beijing, and no other commercial bookseller of the era shared so many titles in common with the Censorate.[46]

Narratives for Sale

Wang Liang of Jintai, it should be noted, did not feature *The Water Margin* or any other such long-form vernacular novels among its wares. Nor does any of the other commercial publishers active in Beijing at the time. The closest works to the novel genre that were possibly available commercially were, arguably, those found in a cache of seventeen volumes in an unearthed tomb in greater Shanghai's Jiading district in 1967. Six of these seventeen volumes bear the mark of a Yongshun tang either on their title page or at the end, and one of them reads, "Newly printed in Beijing."[47] Several bear dates between the seventh and fourteenth years of the Chenghua reign (that is, between 1471 and 1478). On this limited evidence, it is widely assumed that Yongshun tang was active in Beijing during that period and printed all of these volumes; however, there are no other records of this establishment or its existence in Beijing. It is possible that Yongshun tang was actually based in the south, closer to where the exemplars were found, and that the "Beijing" edition was a reference to a Beijing branch of the establishment, some sort of marketing ruse, or the product of another firm altogether.

In any case, even if all of these, including the unmarked volumes, were printed commercially by Yongshun tang in Beijing, they are still a far cry from what printed works like *The Water Margin* must have been. First, their contents are much shorter: they consist of twelve single-volume chante-fables (*shuochang cihua*) mixing prose and verse; a four-volume chante-fable telling the story of Hua Guan Suo, and one single-volume legend (*chuanqi*). As will be shown in the following chapter, the length and complexity of *The Water Margin,* with its intertwining storylines, are features that were particularly admired among its elite readership. Second, the Yongshun tang imprints are rather crudely carved, in both their print and the illustrations that they bear in top registers or some verso sides.

Also somewhat related to the novel genre, though also cruder in form and content, was an erotic novella called *Pleasing Vignettes of Concentrated Love* (*Zhongqing liji*) published by the aforementioned Mr. Yan of Jintai in the sixteenth year of the Hongzhi reign, or 1503. Richard Wang notes that this edition was the earliest of the classical novella genre, though he notes, "From an intertextual perspective, Ming novellas and vernacular fiction of the same time frame do not seem to have had mutual influence."[48]

One other commercially printed work of narrative of note is an illustrated edition of *Record of the Western Chamber* (*Xixiang ji*) printed by another Jintai publisher, the aforementioned Jintai House of Yue, in 1498. This edition, the earliest extant, is finely carved and lavishly illustrated. While the Censorate (or, for that matter, Guo Xun) did not publish an edition of *Record of the Western Chamber* itself, all of the songs from the drama are contained within *Ballads for a Harmonious Peace*, the collection published by both the Censorate and Guo Xun.

All of these examples date to the Chenghua (1465–87) or Hongzhi (1488–1505) reigns, slightly earlier than Jintai Wang Liang's output and, presumably, the Censorate titles that match them as well.

Irony of Physicality

This chapter began with an episode from *Jin Ping Mei* about censors exchanging gifts with the protagonist Ximen Qing—a reminder that, in addition to being an instantiation of a text, the book is also a physical object with its own social life. As the above discussion has suggested, this role of the physical book was most likely the primary one in the actual Censorate publications. It is, then, somewhat ironic that no surviving exemplar of a Censorate edition has been positively identified as such.

Even without exemplars, however, our view of the publishing space has given us an insight into what these books might have represented. First, it is apparent from their overlap that the Censorate editions and the Wuding editions targeted similar audiences. It can also be said that these overlapping titles are the ones that were the rarest—and therefore, the ones with the most cultural capital—among the Censorate titles. That is to say, the works of fiction, the sanqu art song anthologies, and the personal works of the men involved, despite the connotations that the novel and qu genres would have later with "popular" audiences due to their "vernacular" language and sometimes crude subject matter, were likely the most highly valued by this particular audience. This is also true of the several "leisurely" Censorate titles related to Ming princes. Then there are the more readily available titles, which overlap with those sold by the Jintai Wang Liang establishment. These are of more conventional tastes, including Tang poetry and *Records of the Grand Historian*. Yet as the fine Wang Liang editions, prized by later collectors, show, these were also likely to be targeted at elite audiences. Chantefables, song pamphlets, and other such materials found on the "lower" end of the Ming Beijing publishing spectrum are found neither on the Censorate list nor Guo Xun's—despite the fact that, from a later, "literary" perspective, such materials might be seen as closer to the "vernacular" of the novel.

One of the pioneers of the modern study of the Chinese book, Ye Dehui (1864–1927), heaped scorn on the official imprints of the Ming. He singled out the Censorate in particular. With "upstanding supervisory agencies" like the Censorate printing "frivolous and preposterous" (*qing dan*) books such as *The Water Margin, Romance of the Three Kingdoms*, Daoist texts, and sanqu collections, he scoffs, "it is no wonder that books like the Five Classics, the Four Books, and *The Great Compendium on Nature and Coherence (Xingli daquan)* were the exclusive affair of the eunuch-run Directorate of the Ceremonial!"[49]

Other scholars have followed suit, assuming that the Censorate was making commercially driven publishing decisions to target larger audiences, or that it was shirking its solemn duties and printing simple entertainments.[50] In fact, such titles were more likely prized fine editions.

During the era in which censors such as Wang Tingxiang and Du Nan were active in the capital, and in which Wang Tingxiang worked with Guo Xun as directors of the Integrated Divisions, an edition of *The Water Margin* would have been regarded as a novelty—even more so than a lavish printed edition of a classic printed by the finest of Beijing publishers. For it to come into one's possession, one would most likely have had to be a member of the social circles in which these men and their literary collections moved. Though the Censorate was an institution tasked with maintaining order and *The Water Margin* is a book of banditry and disorder, such an edition does not necessarily signify the corruption or creeping commercialization of the Ming. It was rather, alongside the other books printed by the Censorate, a token of connoisseurship.

CHAPTER 3

After the Fire

Li Kaixian, The Precious Sword, *and the "Xiong Damu Mode"*

As the previous chapters have shown, in the years before the 1541 fire in the imperial ancestral temple, *The Water Margin* was printed in the elite circles around the Jiajing court. Guo Xun and the Censorate printed the first known editions of the novel along with other titles signifying a certain type of leisure, including interests in sanqu art songs, poetry, and chess. They also printed titles of concern to their own circles, such as personal literary collections and family histories. As for novels, *The Water Margin* was accompanied on these lists by *Romance of the Three Kingdoms*, but none of the other such works that would proliferate as commercial printers saw opportunities in the nascent genre. The imprints created by these two entities—and the significant number of titles printed by both—suggest that they were created for consumption among similar audiences, or even the same specific audience. *The Water Margin*, along with these other printed titles, was an accoutrement of a certain lifestyle.

For a view of how those editions of *The Water Margin* might have been consumed at this early stage of its life in print, we must turn to the poet, dramatist, and official Li Kaixian (1502–68).[1] Not only did Li exemplify many of the leisurely traits seen reflected in the imprints of Guo Xun and the Censorate, he also moved in their same extended social circles. Moreover, among his writings are the first known critical remarks on *The Water Margin*. He wrote of how the novel was read and admired by his literati coterie in the capital. Later, after being removed from office, he recast an episode from *The Water Margin* into a drama that provides further hints as to what the novel might have meant to him. That drama, *Record of the Precious Sword* (*Baojian ji*), then played a role in reshaping the novel genre that had inspired it in the first place.

Before the Fire: "A Book about a Single Event"

As was the case with Guo Xun and the censor Wang Tingxiang, Li Kaixian's career also came to an end in the wake of the 1541 ancestral temple fire. Relevant high officials were expected to tender what were to be pro forma resignations expressing culpability. Only a dozen such resignations were actually accepted, and Li's was among them. He was removed from office and exiled to his native place, Zhangqiu, in Shandong. He remained there until his death in 1568.

He had had an exemplary career, having passed the palace examinations in 1529 and steadily rising through the ranks of officialdom before finally being appointed vice minister of the Court of Imperial Sacrifices in 1540. He and five other members of his palace examination cohort, along with two from the previous one of 1526, would go down in the annals of Ming literary history as the Eight Talents of the Jiajing Era" (*Jiajing ba caizi*). During the course of his official duties, Li also formed important friendships with Kang Hai and Wang Jiusi, older men who would later be remembered along with Censor Wang Tingxiang as constituents of the Former Seven Masters (*Qian qizi*).

These two groups are often placed in opposition to one another in literary histories of the Ming, with the Seven Masters representing "Archaism" and the Eight Talents advocating pure expression. But whatever the theories they advocated for the composition of prose and *shi* poetry, men affiliated with both groups shared an interest with Li Kaixian in *The Water Margin*. In a collection of broad-ranging critical remarks on songs of the Yuan and Ming called *Banter on Lyrics* (*Cixue*), Li writes,

> Cui Xian, Xiong Guo, Tang Shunzhi, Wang Shenzhong, and Chen Shu say that *The Water Margin* is filled with minute details and numerous veins that link up, and that only the *Records of the Grand Historian* surpasses this book. Moreover, since ancient times there has never before been a book about a single event in twenty volumes (*ce*). One who would fault it for its treacherous banditry and

deception knows nothing of methods for narrating events or of the subtleties of the study of history.[2]

Xiong, Tang, and Chen passed the palace examinations and entered official life along with Li in 1529; Wang had passed in 1526. All were Li's fellow members of the Eight Talents of the Jiajing. Cui Xian, a generation older, had passed the examination in 1505 and been active in the extended circles around the influential literary figure and official Li Mengyang and the Seven Masters. As Cui died in 1541, the period in which this group could have read and discussed *The Water Margin* in the capital spans from 1529 to 1541, their years before the fire.

In these comments, it is notable that it is the literary craft of the novel that Li singles out as the object of his group's admiration. The terms in which he does so are entirely divorced from concerns about archaist literary patterns for imitation or spontaneous expression: Sima Qian's *Records of the Grand Historian*, a Han work written in elegant and economical classical prose, could not be more different from *The Water Margin* in its style. What Li's coterie praise is the novel's richness of detail and intricacy of plot—a plot that consists of strands, or "veins," that run separately and join up with one another in time.[3]

This intricacy is directly related to the very length of the novel, another feature that Li points out in his comment. The fact that he praises it for relating with its plot a single "event" suggests that he and his literati acquaintances read the novel in its entirety as an integral whole. And while Li does not mention how or where they obtained their copies of the work, the comment further suggests that they read it in a standardized form, with standardized divisions into fascicles, that is more consistent with print than manuscript form. A long work could of course still be transmitted in manuscript form, but print facilitates transmission in complete form. Contrast, for example, how decades later literati famously would write to one another asking to copy portions of the *Jin Ping Mei* that they did not yet possess.[4] Li Kaixian's emphasis here, by contrast, is on the whole of the work, and how its most admirable qualities are inherent to its overall structure.

Where might Li Kaixian and his literati acquaintances have obtained copies of such a printed edition of *The Water Margin*? Printed long-form fiction was indeed a new phenomenon at that time: Li Kaixian's career in the capital began in 1529, just seven years after the Xiuranzi edition of *Romance of the Three Kingdoms* was printed, and ended in 1541, along with those of Guo Xun and Wang Tingxiang. Though there is no conclusive evidence to confirm, it, circumstantial evidence placing Li Kaixian in the same extended circles as key figures in the production of *Water Margin* editions, as well as the relative rarity of such editions in this period, makes it highly plausible that it was Guo's or the Censorate's imprint that they read.

Indeed, Li seems to have been the perfect target audience for the publications of Guo Xun and the Censorate. He was interested in cultivated leisure activities such as qu songs and chess, subjects of books that both the Censorate and Guo published. It will be remembered from the previous chapters that both Guo and the Censorate published the collection of qu purportedly collated by Guo himself, the *Ballads of Harmonious Peace*, and the Censorate published the qu collection *A New Voice for a Flourishing Age*. The Censorate also published an edition of *Rhymes of the Central Plain*, which Li cited as a canonical source of rules of composition.[5] The Censorate, it will also be recalled, published the chess manuals *A Record Suiting the Emotions* and *Classic of the Rotten Axe Handle*. Li moved in circles of elite literati, the type within which Guo would have wanted to consolidate his status as the rightful Marquis of Wuding through his publishing of clan histories. Li was highly educated and saw *The Water Margin* not as "base" or "crude" in subject matter and language but as a novel literary innovation that took advantage of the medium of print. He was, in other words, the model reader of *The Water Margin* in the time before the fire.

Li also had direct and indirect social ties with Wang Tingxiang, the Censorate, and Guo Xun. Cui Xian, it will be recalled from the previous chapter, knew Wang Tingxiang and joined him in contributing a preface for the literary collection of the Censor Du Nan, which was published by the Censorate. In Cui Xian, Li also had another indirect connection to Guo Xun by way of Zhan Ruoshui. Zhan, it will be remembered, wrote prefaces filled with praise for Guo and his ancestors. Cui wrote a preface for a work by Zhan titled *Reconciling Master Yang* (*Yang Zi zhezhong*), dated 1540. Zhan wrote a response to the preface, titled "On Reading Cui Houqu's [Xian's] Description of *Reconciling Master Yang*" (*Du Cui gong Houqu xu Yang Zi zhezhong*), also dated 1540. In it, Zhan praises Cui's literary and analytical abilities.[6]

From his exile in Zhangqiu, Li also reminisced about his social circles in the capital. He composed a series of five-character quatrain poems about fellow officials he had admired called "Poems for Sixty Masters" (*Liushi zi shi*). In the preface, Li remarks that since he entered officialdom in 1529, he had the good fortune to make the acquaintance of many "wise men, renowned officials, noble poets, and scholars." His acquaintances with great men varied in their degrees of closeness, he writes, but there were over a hundred whom he felt to be of the same mind. Now, in his rustic dwelling, he laments, he thinks back on them; half have already passed away, and the majority of them never realized their ambitions. He explains that in his illness he is unable to write lengthy poems about them, so he has written five-character quatrains for each.

> For some I raise single incidents, and for others I outline their lives, but for the most part I describe our feelings. In total there are sixty people, and the number of poems is the same. Reading through them in a quiet room is almost like seeing their faces and suddenly hearing their voices. People refer to playing chess as "sitting in reclusion," and to viewing landscape paintings as "journeying in recline"; these, then, could be called "calling on friends without going out of doors."[7]

Among the men Li included in this series were Wang Tingxiang, Du Nan, and Cui Xian. Their poems are as follows:

Wang Tingxiang

Alone he was able to maintain the discipline of the Censorate [(*Yushi*) *tai*]
With his venerable virtue, he truly was my exemplar.
He is gone but his renown lingers on,
Our tradition of learning, I have faith, was manifest in him.[8]

Du Nan

As soon as he fell ill, he left for the afterworld,
Of those who knew him, none did not grieve.
An imprint of his poems circulates beyond the Luo River—
A portrait of the deceased just as he was in life.[9]

Cui Xian

Houqu [Xian] was a man who'd attained the Way,
In study of classics, he'd become lost in thought.
When did he ever attempt at grand schemes?
His *Words of Huan* were not words of extravagance.[10]

The preface and the poems underscore the sense of community and shared values that Li felt with his literati acquaintances, including some, such as Wang Tingxiang, whom Li felt were similarly aggrieved. Li's writing also underscores the role of texts and their circulation in print in creating that community. Two of the three poems here mention printed literary collections, and in the case of Du Nan, a literary collection that was found on the list of Censorate publications. To Li and his literati coterie, the written word was a means of "calling on friends without going out of doors," allowing the author to transcend time and space in a very personal way. While *The Water Margin* is of course not a literary collection, these poems do illustrate the social role of print among these particular circles—the circles among which *The Water Margin* moved before the fire.

After the Fire I: A Return to the Margins

Before the fire that brought about the end of Li Kaixian's career, *The Water Margin* was something that could stimulate conversations among his literati peers even as they played down—perhaps coyly—its seemingly antiauthoritarian content. The novel was part of a shared culture of leisure. Afterward, even as he mourned the loss of those friendships from his exile, Li returned to the novel. Now, he rewrote an episode from it as a literati revenge fantasy in dramatic form, an alternate history in which a slandered official could be returned to his former glory through the force of his own character and will. This *chuanqi* drama, *Record of the Precious Sword*, was completed in 1547, some six years after Li's banishment.[11]

In chapters 7–10 of the novel, the righteous military instructor Lin Chong and his wife visit a temple. There, the wife catches the eye of the son of Gao Qiu, a corrupt official who is one of the novel's chief villains. Lin stops the younger Gao before he can make his move, so the Gaos plot Lin's demise. Gao Qiu has accomplices sell Lin a precious sword on the street, and then summons Lin to his residence asking to see it. When Lin brings the sword into the Gao residence's inner sanctum, guards catch him and claim he is plotting an assassination. Lin is arrested and sentenced to banishment in Cangzhou. When his jailers in Cangzhou attempt to kill him, Lin kills them and escapes to take refuge among the bandits of Mount Liang.

In the drama version of the story as rewritten by the exiled Li Kaixian, however, the wronged official gets his revenge: Lin Chong submits memorials against Gao Qiu and Tong Guan, another corrupt official at court, and is banished. With the bandits of Mount Liang, he leads attacks on those who have wronged him. The emperor eventually grants him amnesty, and both of the Gaos, father and son, are delivered to Lin Chong's camp. Before putting his bitter enemies to death, Lin Chong first berates them for their crimes:

> Now, Gao Qiu, you were originally a lowlife of the common classes, an average villager, who specialized in paying visits to superiors and roaming about the capital. You're illiterate, so you have learned to sing and play music in order to eke out a living. But a one-inch arrow is of no use, so you relied on playing ball as a path to promoting yourself. Now that you've managed to have a minister position bestowed upon you, you dare to usurp the power of the sovereign! You covet material goods and bring disaster upon the people. You envy your superiors and bring harm upon the administration. You upturn the affairs of state and dare to ruin the standards of official conduct.

> You've forced me into a position where:

>> Mother and son were separated until death;
>> Husband and wife were divided in life;
>> Older women were scattered along the way;
>> Female servants to carry grievances to their graves.

> You thought you'd found everlasting wealth and rank, but now I've caught you![12]

Lin Chong then breaks into song:

To the Tune "Decorous and Pretty"
Enjoying wealth and distinction,
The recipient of imperial favor;
Having risen from bleak poverty,
You occupy an exalted position.
Wielding the scales of power, your authority dominates the capital;
Relying on imperial favor, you endeavor to deceive our sovereign.
In total disregard of benevolence or righteousness.

To the Tune "Playing with a Brocade Ball"
You employ corvée labor to construct ponds,
You buy landed estates for your descendants.

In your every endeavor you explore only the means of insuring your own benefit;
In your treacherous greed, what do you care if Yue suffers while Qin prospers?
Those who curry favor with you reach instant distinction;
Those who offend you find that their lives are endangered.
Envious of the worthy and talented,
You prefer the intimacy of the petty minded.
Motivated only by personal grudges, you show total disregard for the public interest.
You keep the Emperor in his nine-gated palace entirely in the dark,
While allowing the people within the four seas to descend into chaos.
But, as the saying goes, Heaven's net only seems to be loose.

To the Tune of "The Lucky Graduate"

With your clever words, you seek to elicit the transient amusement of the ruler;
But do not exert loyal effort toward achieving harmony among the myriad states.
You only try to subvert the work of real heroes in order to deceive the world.
Vainly scratching an itch through the hide of your boot;
Exhibiting the same symptoms that you pretend to cure;
You show no concern whatever for Heavenly principle.

Lin Chong then compares Gao Qiu to "traitors of old" in song:

To the Tune "Playing with a Brocade Ball"

You have the heart of Zhao Gao of Qin, who pointed to a deer [and called it a horse];
And the design of Tu'an Gu in loosing his dog.
You would emulate Wang Mang of the Han Dynasty in your disloyal objectives,
And deserve the same fate as the traitor Dong Zhuo whose navel was set on fire.
Wherever you move, you are accompanied by pipes and strings;
When you go out the gate, you are protected by armed guards.
When you enter the court, the hundred officials are rigid with apprehension;

Relying on the ruler, you usurp the tiger's might in flaunting
your authority.
There are no few clients who abase themselves to cater to your
perfidious cabal;
But who is there willing to yield his sword to execute the
toadying villains,
Rather than letting them do as they please?
Your designation as a minister is not found beneath the golden
goblet;
But in the works of historians your faults will be duly enumerated.
What do you know of reconciling yin and yang or nurturing the
vital energy?
All you can do is betray the country and make packets with
foreign barbarians.
You have no right to the jade girdle and gold fish suspended
from your python robe;
Excepting emolument without achievement, you should be
ashamed to sleep and eat.
As long as power remains in your hands, people will be afraid of you;
But when catastrophe descends upon you, it will be too late to
repent.
All the bamboo on the southern hills would not suffice on which
to enumerate your crimes;
When the waves on the eastern ocean are completely dry your
stench of infamy will remain.
It will be perpetuated for a myriad years,
Forevermore introducing people to revile you.[13]

Lin Chong then declares that any further pronouncements would do
nothing but "sully my fine speech," and orders that they be executed.
The scene ends with a poem describing the sudden turnaround of
events, in which the words *water margin* are mentioned:

Furiously clutching a steel axe and leaving the water margin;
Suddenly heading for the capital with an imperial pardon.
If he didn't exact revenge clearly,
It'd be in vain that he was a hard man.[14]

In the remaining scenes of the play, Lin Chong is reinstated to his
official position and reunited with his wife. Just six years after his own

career came to a sudden end, Li Kaixian had turned the story of Lin Chong into one of a literati revenge fantasy. In the full-length novel version, Lin Chong never gets his revenge on Gao Qiu. Instead, he dies of illness in the final chapters of the book, still a member of Song Jiang's band. The band has been granted amnesty and taken up a campaign against Fang La on behalf of the imperial authorities, but this ending is still different from the play's reinstatement of Lin Chong at court and the happy reunion of his family. The latter is more fitting of drama genre convention, with its stock ending in the protagonists' reunion. Such generic features, along with Li Kaixian's growing interest in writing and circulating qu songs, are surely the reason why he chose the drama form for this new "literati" version of the story of Lin Chong.

Return to the Novel

Though Li Kaixian's *Record of the Precious Sword* took the form of a chuanqi drama rather than a novel, it still played a role in the development of the latter genre. This happened quite literally, as arias from the drama were interwoven verbatim into the novel *Jin Ping Mei*. The *Jin Ping Mei* is a famously intertextual novel, borrowing liberally from a wide variety of texts for a deliberate narrative effect and point of view. David Roy, for example, argued against earlier critics that the *Jin Ping Mei* was in fact a highly structured work, that this structure incorporated borrowed textual fragments, and that this structure was indicative of its author's cosmic worldview.[15] Shang Wei has suggested that the novel "participates in the process of recycling, representing, and reorganizing ready-made contemporary materials from the commercial print culture" to the extent that it is itself "an encyclopedia of sorts."[16] Katherine Carlitz, in a pathbreaking study, analyzed the rhetoric of the novel's quotational practices and argued that external sources are used in the novel for both conventional and ironic effect. Particularly notable, though, is the fact that, according to Carlitz, the *Jin Ping Mei* borrows more heavily from *Record of the Precious Sword* than any other drama. Furthermore, it incorporates these passages into the novel in a manner that suggests the novel's author approved of the image of Li Kaixian among his contemporaries as writing "to vent his frustration in song when denied the opportunity to act."[17]

The quoted material from *Record of the Precious Sword* found in the *Jin Ping Mei* includes the arias quoted above in which Lin Chong addresses his enemies, the Gaos. In the *Jin Ping Mei*, however, they are presented as songs performed at a banquet for a corrupt official, Zhu Mian.[18] Such a usage provides the opportunity for ironic slippage between diegetic music and extradiegetic commentary on the action of the plot. It would also undoubtedly act as a knowing wink to a late Ming reader already familiar with the play.

The work of Li Kaixian is so deeply imprinted on the *Jin Ping Mei* both in spirit and in its text that some twentieth-century scholars, such as Wu Xiaoling and Xu Shuofang, even proposed that Li had a hand in the authorship of the novel.[19] Though the authorship of the *Jin Ping Mei* has not been decisively resolved in favor of any particular candidate, the Li Kaixian theory has not proven to be entirely convincing. However, as the example of the arias condemning Gao Qiu show, something of Li Kaixian's "post-fire" attitude found its way back into the novel genre, whether he played any (conscious) part in the authorship of the *Jin Ping Mei* or not. The use of Li's material in the *Jin Ping Mei* is an example of the knowing literary irony and iconoclastic attitudes considered to be hallmarks of the novel genre. And with the widespread influence of the *Jin Ping Mei*, it spread further—first via manuscript among literati such as Yuan Hongdao and Dong Qichang in the late sixteenth century, and then later in commercially published print editions.

After the Fire II: Imitations in the Marketplace

In 1553, less than a decade after Li Kaixian completed his *Record of the Precious Sword*, another work inspired by *The Water Margin*, *Record of the Book of the Tang* (*Tang shu zhizhuan*), was published.[20] Despite the common source of inspiration, however, these two works could not have been more different: Whereas *Record of the Precious Sword* was a literati revenge fantasy in drama form, *Record of the Book of the Tang* was a straightforward fictionalized historical narrative retelling of the titular *Book of the Tang*. And whereas *Record of the Precious Sword* was created for circulation among the cultured elite, *Record of the Book of the Tang* was intended for sale on the commercial book market of Jianyang, Fujian—a locale, we have seen in the previous chapter, that had a reputation for producing low-quality imprints.

A preface to *Record of the Book of the Tang* by Li Danian, the "Jiangnan Wanderer" (*Jiangnan sanren*), explains the influence of *The Water Margin* on this work. The Jiangnan Wanderer says that a certain Master Xiong Zhonggu collated the work and presented it to him. After reading it through, the Jiangnan Wanderer says, he was concerned that some might fault the book for throwing orthodox historiography into disarray and say it is not worthy of being circulated in the world. In preempting such objections, he invokes *The Water Margin*:

> Though it is simply my opinion, books in the marketplace that imitate *Record of the Three Kingdoms* [*sic*] and *The Water Margin* are not necessarily unacceptable. Moreover, the poems, lyrics, and official communiques in *cihua* are quite in accordance with literary principles, and allowing everyman poets to peruse them will naturally lead to them obtaining some joy and admiration. How could we take them all as absurd and ignore them?[21]

It is uncertain precisely to which imitators of *Romance of the Three Kingdoms* and *The Water Margin* the Jiangnan Wanderer refers, but these remarks indicate that by this time the novel genre was becoming a phenomenon of commercial print. Publishers had realized that there was potential for profit in printing vernacularized historical narratives.

The "Master" Xiong Zhonggu, or Xiong Damu, whom the Jiangnan Wanderer mentions was born into a clan that had been active in the Jianyang for-profit printing trade since the late Yuan. Details of Damu's life beyond what appears in prefaces are unclear; some sources give the unlikely dates of 1471 to 1576, which would mean he lived to the age of 105.[22] Despite his clan's long-standing involvement in the industry, he does not appear to have only acted as a proprietor of a publishing house himself; this edition of *Record of the Book of the Tang*, for example, was printed by the Qingjiang tang of the Yang family rather than one of the Xiong clan's establishments. Xiong Damu's name is also found in similar historical-narrative titles published by the Yang family's Qingbai tang. Xiong created similar narrative versions of the histories of the Han and Song dynasties, and he is also credited with annotating a book of morally exemplary tales called *Stories for Daily Observance* (*Riji gushi*).[23] This latter book was printed in 1542 by Zhongzheng tang, a house that some sources list as belonging to Xiong Damu. However, a lack of evidence prevents us from knowing the precise details of Xiong Damu's business dealings, including his relationship to Zhongzheng tang and the Yang family publishing houses.

Whatever the case with the financial arrangements of the business, Xiong sought to take advantage of the market opportunity presented by historical narrative fiction by creating more works along the lines of *The Water Margin* and *Romance of the Three Kingdoms*. In order to do so, he combined both official and unofficial historiographical records into unified narratives. In a preface to a historical narrative called *Romance of the Restoration of the Great Song* (*Da Song zhongxing yanyi*) dated 1552, Xiong describes his editing method. He explains that he obtained and read a copy of *Record of Prince Wumu's Utmost Loyalty* (*Wumu wang jingzhong lu*) but found its format and language unclear for those "below the literati class" (*shidafu yixia*). He then describes how he was approached by one Master Yang Su, style name Yongquan, who asked him to elaborate on the text and turn it into a vernacular narrative so those of lesser learning might understand it. Xiong protested that he lacked the talents of historians like Ban Gu or Sima Qian, he says, but Yang insisted. Xiong then explains how he wove multiple sources into a single narrative, and justifies the inclusion of unofficial sources:

> I used the details from the biography of the Prince and consulted the *Outline of the Comprehensive Mirror* (*Tongjian gangmu*) for their meaning. There are places where the minor discourses and the biography are similar and there are places where they differ; I have included them all for reference. One might say that minor discourses should not be intermixed with official history. I wholeheartedly acknowledge this point. However, there are truths recorded in unofficial, outside histories that official histories do not provide. If a book records obvious and corroborated facts, then it cannot be taken as extraneous "unofficial" history.[24]

The preface then goes on to the example of the historical beauty Xi Shi, and how details of her life and death were preserved in "unofficial" histories and poetry rather than official histories.

The modern scholar Chen Dakang has referred to this method of creating a narrative out of historiographical fragments arranged against a master timeline as the "Xiong Damu mode" of editing and compiling. According to Chen, the works produced through the Xiong Damu mode played a critical role in the development of the novel genre, despite their relative artistic inadequacy in comparison to the masterworks that came before and after them. Inspired by the success of *The Water Margin* and *Romance of the Three Kingdoms*, Chen argues, Xiong Damu created his own historiographically based narratives. In a "chain reaction" of influence, these narratives then inspired yet more novels in the decades to come, culminating in the printing boom of the Wanli era—a time that would see the publication of the *Jin Ping Mei* and the full-length *Journey to the West*, among many others. That such works as Xiong's fictionalized versions of the histories of the Tang and Song do not live up to the heights of the evergreen masterworks that came before and after, Chen claims, can be explained by the relatively short gestation period they had in which to develop. *The Water Margin* and *Romance of the Three Kingdoms* had been gestating since the early Ming, he claims, whereas Xiong Damu's creations were his own handiwork.[25] This argument about the relative lack of literary quality perhaps relies too heavily on the assumption of the historicity of Luo Guanzhong. But overall, the notion that printed narratives in the Xiong Damu mode leading to a "chain reaction" of novels fits the general pattern of the known printed editions. That is to say, Xiong Damu appeared just after the fire that separated the era when printed fiction circulated among the elite and the era when it was widely printed for commercial sale.

For these narrative products of the Xiong Damu mode of editing, there are no records of reader interpretations equivalent to those of Li Kaixian and his earlier remarks about how he and his circles appreciated *The Water Margin*. Nevertheless, the prefaces discussed above make apparent some of the differences between the space occupied by editions of novels before and after the fire. Whereas Li Kaixian had remarked that his literati acquaintances had admired the intricate, sustained structure of *The Water Margin* and warned that those who might condemn it for its content were simply ignorant of the art of narrative, Xiong Damu and his partner the Jiangnan Wanderer felt the need to reassure their prospective readers that this particular narrative form of history was acceptable despite its lack of orthodox historiographical conventions. They also saw the need to vouch for the accuracy of their pieced-together narratives, claiming that the heterodox historiographies that were consulted retained information that the orthodox, more readily acceptable historiographical sources left out. This historicity seems to take precedence over holistic "literary" qualities such as those cited by Li Kaixian.

The chain reaction that began with *The Water Margin* and its fellow traveler *Romance of the Three Kingdoms* and then accelerated through the Xiong Damu mode of editing would come to a head decades later. Around the turn of the seventeenth century, commercial print exploded in the variety of editions printed, and editor-publishers such as Yu Xiangdou came to the fore. Yu, who will be one of the subjects of the next chapter, took a prominent position in his own editions, adding commentaries and other paratextual materials to guide readers who were certainly less confident in their own abilities than earlier literati connoisseurs of the burgeoning novel form such as Li Kaixian and his coterie.

As names such as Yu Xiangdou's came to prominence, Xiong Damu's became obscured. In the case of an edition of a novel called *The Record of the Northern and Southern Song* (*Nanbei Song zhizhuan*) printed by Yu, this obscuration was quite literal: Yu's preface mentions Xiong's name, but the character for "mu" in "Damu" is mistakenly carved as "ben," with the addition of an extra stroke at the bottom. Yu introduces "Master Daben" (*Daben xiansheng*) as a learned man from Jianyang who had read widely and was thoroughly knowledgeable about the history of the Song dynasty. "Master Daben," according to Yu, compiled the *Romance of the Northern and Southern Song* using clear language to aid people in their understanding, and he was diligent in his efforts.[26]

The obscuration of Xiong Damu was taken further by another trend in turn-of-the-seventeenth-century commercial publishing: the tendency of editor-publishers to credit, often spuriously, the collation or commentary of their editions to the names of renowned literati. In the case of this particular fictionalized edition of the history of the Northern and Southern Song, the first page of the main body of the text lists its compiler as the well-known figure Chen Jiru, despite the preface's nod toward Xiong Damu.

Another Yu Xiangdou publication, *The Complete Record of the Han* (*Quan Han zhizhuan*), published in 1588, retains signs of the Xiong Damu era. Again, this is quite literal in that the Yu edition claims to be a combination of Xiong's *Record of the Western Han* and *Record of the Eastern Han*, and even features a page that retains the mark of the Yang family's Qingbai tang mentioned above. A different Ming edition of the *Complete Record of the Han*, this one by Baohua lou, purports to have been revised (*dingzi*) by Yu's establishment Santai guan and commented on by another renowned literatus, Zhong Xing.

Many of these attributions of commentary or editing to renowned literary figures are dubious at best. In the cases of some late Ming editions, such as the *Record of the Sui and Tang* (*Sui Tang zhizhuan*), the purported commentator—in this case, Yang Shen—was long dead by the time the first edition was published. However, even though these accreditations may not be factual and at times border on the outlandish, they speak to the experience of readers of this genre. Whereas readers of novels in the Xiong Damu era were concerned with historicity and accuracy, and needed justification for the literariness of the novels they were reading, later readers once again (at least nominally) associated novels with certain types of literary personality. In a way, with their creative forgeries, the editor-publishers of the turn of the century created for their readers a commodified emulation of the world of the novel before the fire. At times, as the next chapter will show, they also included for their readers a taste of the critical sentiment of Li Kaixian's *Record of the Precious Sword*.

CHAPTER 4

Characters in the Margins

The Commercial Editions

Before the fire in the imperial ancestral hall, Li Kaixian and his coterie of officials at the Jiajing court remarked on the breakthrough literary qualities of *The Water Margin*. They praised it for the skill with which it wove narrative threads together into a complex whole and scoffed at those who would simply condemn it for the violence it depicts on its surface. Theirs was the era of the editions printed by Guo Xun and the Censorate—and it is likely that those editions are the ones they read. After the fire and Li Kaixian's subsequent dismissal from office, however, that very same violent aspect of the novel seemed to have appealed to Li as a symbol of potency. He recast an episode from the novel into his drama *Record of the Precious Sword*, in which the wronged official Lin Chong is able to have his revenge. The "literary" quality of *The Water Margin* was now coupled with a subversive air. Such a vision of *The Water Margin* would later be reabsorbed back into the novel genre when swathes of text from *The Precious Sword* were incorporated into the novel *Jin Ping Mei*—itself another work inspired by an episode from *The Water Margin*.

Literary, Subversive, and Commercial

Within a decade of the completion of Li's drama *Record of the Precious Sword, The Water Margin* served as an inspiration of another sort, when the for-profit editor-publisher Xiong Damu saw the commercial potential of *The Water Margin* and *Romance of the Three Kingdoms*. Xiong attempted to imitate the success of these two novels by creating works in a similar mode. Those works, according to the modern scholar Chen Dakang, inspired yet more such works, setting off a "chain reaction" of historical fiction narratives in the world of commercial print.

Though worlds apart in terms of their social and literary status, the Marquis of Wuding Guo Xun, the Censors of the Censorate, the literatus Li Kaixian, and the commercial editor-publisher Xiong Damu shared an interest in *The Water Margin*—even if the novel meant very different things to them from their stations, with their purposes, and even at different points in their lives. Broadly speaking, the disparate approaches to *The Water Margin* that we have seen these various figures take up to this point could be said to fall into three categories: the literary, the subversive, and the commercial. Borrowing from the contemporary theorist Sianne Ngai, we might even consider these three categories to be aesthetic in nature: Ngai has identified the aesthetic categories of our present moment of late-stage capitalism as "zany," "cute," and "interesting."[1] The zany is typified by the hyperactivity of production, the cute by power dynamics and helplessness, and the interesting by the ability to elicit informational connections. The literary, subversive, and commercial qualities ascribed to *The Water Margin* by the figures discussed so far are not as far-reaching as Ngai's analysis of the postmodern condition; they are used here to identify common trends in the world of print in the late Ming. However, like Ngai's aesthetic categories, they too are affective rather than intrinsic, and they are not mutually exclusive. These categories, in various combinations, would continue to chart the course for editions of *The Water Margin* as they proliferated in the rapid upsurge of commercial print activity seen at the end of the sixteenth century. Because of the reflexive nature of editing and publishing around the novel genre, an editor-publisher could discern one or more of these qualities in *The Water Margin* and, in shaping a new edition, amplify them in anticipation of a particular readership.

Though Ngai's "zany," "cute," and "interesting" may not find particular resonance with the late Ming world of print, another term used by her in another study would be right at home: the "gimmick." The gimmick, in Ngai's usage, is something that labors too hard to win our attention even as it cuts labor with time-saving tricks of dubious quality.[2] The term is even somewhat reminiscent of the criticisms of late-Ming imprints made by scholars of the succeeding Qing dynasty. Looking on the freewheeling editing practices of the late Ming, those serious-minded Qing scholars scorned such editions as *baifan*, or in Yuming He's felicitous translation, "hucksterish."[3] One did not know where one text ended and another began; heterogeneous sources were stitched together cut-and-paste style to create "new" works without any sort of scholarly acknowledgement of their sources. Such a lack of rigor, the Qing scholars declared, was indicative of the very fundamental frivolousness and decadence that caused the Ming dynasty to fall.

However, as He has argued in her study, such late Ming books show a sophistication of their own. They demand of their readers a kind of "conversancy" with books that is different from classical literacy. Books of jokes and drinking games, for example, cleverly recontextualized quotations from texts written in different linguistic registers. Drama miscellanies included multiple texts on the same page in order to facilitate browsing and allow readers to find whatever appealed to their own interests. The "demimonde fantasy" of a book like *The Classic of Whoring* (*Piaojing*) allowed readers to safely explore parts of society beyond their own experience.[4] In the context of the late Ming moment, the "frivolousness" of these commercially printed books was the same playful, fashionable, and even subversive quality that their readers appreciated.

When it came to late Ming editions of novels, one seemingly unscrupulous, "hucksterish" editing practice was the attribution of a work's compilation or authorship to renowned or even notorious literary figures who, in all likelihood, had nothing to do with the edition, presumably to add perceived value to the book as commodity for sale. Some such attributions extended to prefaces, running commentaries, and other such paratextual materials that were included in editions in order to distinguish them on the market from other, similar editions. These practices have something of the air of the gimmick, working to grab potential readers' attention with these well-known names and at the same time promising readers an interpretive shortcut, allowing those renowned figures to either shoulder part of the hermeneutical burden for them or to lend the edition an air of distinction.

Questions of the "authenticity" of these materials or the "truth" of their attributions aside, many of these commentaries lent such distinct voices to their parent texts that they could be considered "characters" themselves, emerging not from the narrative but from the paratext of the edition. And since the novel was a genre without a strong author figure in the first place, these "paratextual characters" were concerned more with accompanying the reader on the journey through the text than with explicating authorial intention. They had free rein to point out literary or subversive features to the reader, which added to the commercial appeal of the edition. By referring to these voices as "paratextual characters," we can also distinguish them from the empirical, historical figures with whom they often share names. Here, it is the qualities of those voices that is of concern, rather than their authenticity. These paratextual characters are not bound to any single work; many of them appear across works and even genres.

"Commercial"

If the aesthetic category of the commercial could be personified, it would surely be found in the figure of the renowned editor-publisher Yu Xiangdou (fl.1590s). Yu operated in an age of an abundance of books. His clan had been active in the Jianyang, Fujian, book trade for centuries, and he was of the eleventh generation of Yus in the profession. However, whereas most of his ancestors had only a handful of imprint titles each associated with their names, Xiangdou appears to have published more than seventy. A cousin of the same generation, Yu Zhangde, was similarly prolific, having published fifty-seven.[5]

Little is known about Yu Xiangdou outside of what can be gathered from the imprints that he published. Even the dates of his birth and death are unknown. Judging from the range of dates that appear in his imprints, however, it would appear that he enjoyed a long life and career. The earliest imprint bearing his name is a vernacularized historical narrative of the Han dynasty after the fashion of Xiong Damu; it bears the year 1588. The latest, meanwhile, bears the year 1637, almost half a century later. That is an outlier, however, and the majority of the imprints associated with Yu Xiangdou appeared by 1609. A preface to his edition of Sima Qian's classic *Records of the Grand Historian* indicates that he sat for the civil service examinations three times before giving up and devoting himself to the family business in 1591. The exams were held once every three years; assuming that he sat for three successive exams and that he began in early adulthood, he would likely have been born in the 1550s. Assuming again that the 1637 date indeed did fall within his lifetime, that would indicate that he lived into his eighties.[6]

Titles published by Yu run the gamut from *The Water Margin* and *Romance of the Three Kingdoms* to versions of the Confucian Four Books and the Five Classics, the official history of the Han, and the pre-Qin philosophers. He is best known, however, for books such as his encyclopedia for daily use and his editions of vernacular fiction. He seems to have made efforts to distinguish between his different product lines; he included a long list of classic titles in his *Records of the Grand Historian* edition, and noted in the preface that he "dared not" record there the titles of miscellaneous books unrelated to training for the civil service examination system.[7]

Those titles that he "dared not" record included at least twenty works that could be considered to fall under the rough category of "fiction." In addition to *The Water Margin, Romance of the Three Kingdoms,* and the 1588 edition of the fictionalized history of the Han mentioned above, Yu also printed an edition of the fictionalized account of the rise of the Ming associated with Guo Xun, *Record of the Heroes and Martyrs;* Xiong Damu–style historical fiction narratives of the Song and the Warring States; two compilations of court-case fiction; and Daoist-themed *Journey (youji)* stories to the East, West, and North, to complement a version of the more famous *Journey to the West.* Many of the historical works credit Yu's relative Yu Shaoyu as the author, with Xiangdou listed as an editor.

Many of these publications bear signs of Yu's reshaping to fit his readers' needs. With the court-case collections, for example, Yu Xiangdou appears to have taken previously existing court case records and reconfigured them into materials for pleasure reading by editing out technical legal details and augmenting their narrative qualities.[8] The cases are organized by category (*lei*) of crime or complaint. Each individual case and its judgment is referred to as an item (*ze*), the same term that was used in early editions of novels before the chapter, or *hui,* came to dominate.[9] In a preface to one of the collections, Yu differentiates his cases from tales of Judge Bao and other similar detectives, claiming that his, by contrast, are more true to life and do not depend on supernatural elements.[10]

Some twentieth-century scholars such as Sun Kaidi felt that the lack of "literary" qualities of these court-case fiction collections indicated that they were intended for more practical use; they speculated that perhaps such books were in fact guides to writing legal documents or handbooks for the instruction of legal principles.[11] Others suggested that the collections represent the "embryonic" stage of the detective fiction genre that flourished later, and that many of the cases are too "short and fragmentary to be called stories."[12] More recent scholarship by Lin Kuei-ju, Wu Junqing, and others suggests that, to the contrary, these books would be of little use for such purposes due to the editing process that the cases have undergone, and that they were meant for pleasure reading.[13] Furthermore, according to Wu, the legal principles on display in the court-case fiction are often incorrect and do not accord with actual Ming law. Both Lin and Wu suggest that Yu was reacting to market trends in the publishing field and positioning his collections against other available books. If they seem distant from what we might call "literature," then that is more likely due to assumptions about that categorization than the characteristics of the collections themselves.

Yu is also credited with having "compiled" (*bian*) the *Journey* books, presumably from previously existing sources, although the lines of filiation are not clear. Like the court-case collections, these too have been criticized by scholars for their less than literary qualities—especially in light of the fact that Yu's *Journey to the West* reads as a simplified and greatly shortened version of the classic novel of the same name. The entire four-book set might even appear to be an attempt to capitalize off of the fame of the well-known *Journey to the West*, and indeed the Monkey King himself makes an appearance in Yu's *Journey to the South*. However, in contrast with the court case fiction collections, it has been suggested that these were more than simple entertainment. The anthropologist Gary Seaman has suggested that these are in fact Daoist revelatory texts reworked into narrative form, and that *Journey to the North* in particular is a "mythic charter" of the deity Zhenwu, the Emperor of the Dark Heavens (*Xuantian shangdi*).[14] Seaman speculates that Yu Xiangdou pieced the narrative together from unknown religious revelation texts, a pattern that would match the general pattern of late Ming commercial publishing. Seaman even speculates that *Journey to the North* was based on none other than Guo Xun's *Record of the Great Harmony (Taihe zhuan)*, the mysterious text that Ming gossip credits with nearly saving Guo from prison. *Record of the Great Harmony*, according to Seaman, may have been a record of the Jiajing emperor's Daoist spirit writing activities. The name of the text may be in reference to the Wudang Mountains, the home of the former imperially supported Daoist institutions.[15] Could a shared interest in Daoism between Guo Xun and Yu Xiangdou have served as a conduit for textual transmission, and could such a conduit have carried not only *Journey to the North* but also *The Water Margin* from Guo to Yu? The prospect, while speculative and ultimately unprovable, remains intriguing.

Yu Xiangdou made his own presence known within many of these books, not only through the editing practices he was credited with but also through his appearance as a paratextual character within and across them. This character overlaps with, but can be differentiated from, the "empirical" Yu Xiangdou; he projects confidence, offers assistance to readers, and reassures them of their tastes. The character is not always explicitly named, but the voice is consistent.

Perhaps the best-known instance of the paratextual Yu appearing in one of Yu's imprints comes in pictorial form; an idealized portrait of him is included in his 1599 encyclopedia for daily use, *Orthodox Instructions for Ten Thousand Uses* (*Wanyong zhengzong*), in which he is seated at a desk with all of the accoutrements of a scholar, in a luxurious garden waited on by a cadre of attendants. In his classic study *The Confusions of Pleasure*, Timothy Brook described the portrait as the product of social aspirations of the merchant class to the traditionally respected, cultured "gentry" class.[16] In this reading, Yu's portrait borders on being a "gimmick," hinting at a labor-saving shortcut to the status of cultural elite that was in reality unobtainable. But should we assume that he is nothing but a "huckster," selling suspect goods behind a thin veneer of social respectability? Elsewhere, in other books, there are signs that the paratextual Yu—if not the empirical one as well—was sincere in his belief that his editing and commenting were intellectual endeavors worthy of monetary recompense. In a preface to *Journey to the East*, Yu declares that he has poured time and money into the editing of such works as *Journey to the South*, and that other, shameless publishers have unfairly pirated them in order to seek a profit.[17]

There is of course no small measure of self-interest in his remarks, as he was a for-profit printer. Yet it is important to note that, even in this justification, he makes no claim toward the originality of his creation. He has shaped his imprint through editing, and that is what he claims has granted him the rights to it. Yu's claim is, incidentally, somewhat reminiscent of some of the claims on which European copyright were later based. Booksellers claimed that authors, through the act of creation, held natural property rights over the works which they had brought into being through their intellectual labor. Booksellers then claimed that authors could transfer those property rights to them through sale.[18] In the case of late Ming publishers like Yu Xiangdou, it was simply that editing rather than authoring was seen as the main labor in creating a text for publication, and that Yu was claiming a moral entitlement rather than a legal property right. It would be easy to view Yu's posturing in prefaces and his portrait as crude sales gimmicks, but it seems probable that there is at least some measure of sincerity in his words and lifestyle; "commercial" does not necessarily equate to "cynical."

"Subversive"

Before we turn to Yu's edition of *The Water Margin*, let us return to the
second of the three major aesthetic categories of late Ming print culture: the subversive. If the commercial was personified by Yu Xiangdou, then the subversive could be said to be personified by Li Zhuowu.
Like Yu, Li also existed as both an empirical person and a paratextual
character. Also like Yu, Li was from Fujian and had a connection with
The Water Margin. But other than these shared qualities, it is difficult to
imagine two more different figures.

"Zhuowu" was the style name of Li Zhi. Li was born in Quanzhou,
Fujian, in 1527 and passed the provincial *juren* examination in 1552. He
held a number of minor appointments, each lasting only a few years,
before retiring in 1581. At that time, he left Yao'an, Yunnan, where he
had been serving as prefect, and traveled to Macheng, Huguang, where
he stayed with his friends the Geng brothers. His wife and only surviving
daughter were escorted back to Fujian by his son-in-law, and though his
wife pleaded for years for him to return to his home, he eventually shaved
his head—though not his "Confucian" beard—and began living as an un-
orthodox monk in an unlicensed temple of his own. There, he was free to
engage in disseminating his unconventional teachings.[19] His unconventional teachings and behavior led to charges of impropriety being levied
against him, and he famously committed suicide in captivity in 1602.

Commercial editor-publishers had taken note of Li Zhi's notoriety and, in attempts to capitalize on it, attached his style name "Li
Zhuowu" to their wares. More than one hundred editions, many of
which date to the latter half of the Wanli reign, list Li Zhuowu as an
author, compiler, or commentator, though many of them undoubtedly
had nothing to do with the actual Li Zhi.[20] "Li Zhuowu" had become
something of brand.[21] Yet, unlike Yu Xiangdou's, this brand was not
associated with any particular editor-publisher. It became something
of a "multiple-use name," along the lines of "Luther Blissett" or "Wu
Ming" of the late twentieth century, which could be used by anyone
but was associated with a particular style or voice.[22] Robert Hegel has
shown the consistency of the "Li Zhuowu" as a "performed character"
across commentaries for various novels, including editions not only of
The Water Margin, but also of *Romance of the Three Kingdoms* and *Journey
to the West* as well.[23] For these reasons, and following Hegel, I will distinguish between the empirical figure and the paratextual character here
by referring to them as "Li Zhi" and "Li Zhuowu," respectively.

This use of the Li Zhuowu name in such a manner is, of course, a "commercial" move bordering on the hucksterish gimmick. Commercial publishers were well aware that the subversive connotations of this notorious name would attract buyers' interest. Therefore, it should be emphasized again that the aesthetic qualities of the commercial and the subversive in the novel are neither dependent on nor mutually exclusive of one another. A commercially printed edition of a novel advertised as featuring Li Zhuowu commentary could be seen as both commercial and subversive. But the novel could provoke readers for reasons other than potential for profit: *Jin Ping Mei*, for example, was seen by Li Zhi's disciple Yuan Hongdao as an implied admonishment of the establishment at a time when it was circulating among literati in manuscript form.

Many of the titles associated with Li Zhuowu are works of vernacular fiction, most likely due to Li Zhi's longstanding association with *The Water Margin*. Most famously, Li Zhi mentioned *The Water Margin* in his best-known essay, "On the Childlike Mind" (*Tongxin shuo*), as an example of unmediated spontaneity that was the hallmark of the best writing, regardless of genre.[24] The empirical Li Zhi was also known to have written a preface and commentary to *The Water Margin*, which Yuan Hongdao's brother Zhongdao claimed to have seen in manuscript form while staying with Li Zhi in Macheng.[25]

"Literary": Combining the Commercial and the Subversive in *The Water Margin*

Having seen Yu Xiangdou and Li Zhuowu as paratextual characters embodying the aesthetic qualities of the commercial and the subversive, respectively, let us return to editions of *The Water Margin* in which they appear in order to accompany the reader through the text. The Yu Xiangdou edition, the full title of which is *Capital Edition of the Expanded, Fully Illustrated, and Corrected Thicket of Comments on the Record of the Water Margin* (*Jingben zengbu quanxiang jiaozheng Zhongyi Shuihu zhizhuan pinglin*) (hereafter, *Thicket of Comments*), was published in 1594. It is divided into 25 fascicles (*juan*) and 104 chapters, though only chapters one through thirty are numbered.[26] The pages of the novel proper are split into three registers: The bottom register, which takes up around two-thirds of the page, features the main body of the novel's text. The middle register of each page features an illustration, as touted in the full title of the edition, with a title usually of eight to ten characters in length split across the right- and left-hand sides. The top register, which is about one-third the size of the middle register, usually features a comment of some sort, usually one or two brief sentences "evaluating" (*ping*) a character or incident in the story or providing interpretive assistance. Occasionally, longer comments continue on to the following page.

"Li Zhuowu" commentary editions of *The Water Margin*, meanwhile, began to appear soon after his death in 1602 to capitalize on his literary notoriety and his well-known fondness for the novel. The first Li Zhuowu *Water Margin* edition was published by the Rongyu tang publishing house of Hangzhou sometime after his death, with a revised edition appearing in 1610.[27] The second was printed by the publisher Yuan Wuyai of Suzhou sometime after the first Rongyu tang iteration but before 1612, when it is mentioned in *Casual Records from Useless-Timber Studio (Shuzhai manlu)* by Xu Zichang.[28]

The Yuan Wuyai edition perhaps has the better claim to authenticity, as Yuan moved in the same circles as Li Zhi. Yuan Zhongdao also claimed that the Yuan Wuyai edition's "Li Zhuowu" commentary was the same one that he had seen Li Zhi working on in Macheng, although more than a decade had passed.[29] However, despite this possible evidence of authenticity, it is the "Li Zhuowu" of the Rongyu tang edition that is the better expression of Li Zhuowu as a subversive paratextual character.

The Rongyu tang edition is divided into one hundred fascicles, each containing one chapter. Each chapter is prefaced by two images, one for each part of the chapter's title couplet. The pages of text contain no illustrations; unlike the *Thicket of Comments*, they consist of a single register. There are intermittent comments in the upper margin of the page, between the lines of the text, and in half-size characters within the columns of text when there is sufficient space. Rolston suggests that this indicates that the commentary was more of an "afterthought" than an "integral part of the edition."[30] Each chapter also has a longer post-chapter comment, an element that Hegel has called "an innovation in novel criticism."[31]

Both the Yu *Thicket of Comments* and the Rongyu tang edition of *The Water Margin* contain prefaces by their respective paratextual characters. While these prefaces are very different, they both ascribe *The Water Margin* with a level of literariness. That is to say, they justify the worth of the book as an important piece of writing. However, their reasoning behind doing so differs, and in each case is intertwined with their perception of the book's commercial and subversive qualities.

The Yu preface to *Thicket of Comments* is printed over four pages in the front of the edition, with seven columns of twelve characters each. The characters of the preface are carved in a fine style imitative of brushwork, more ornate than those of the body of the novel's text. The preface is unsigned, but it is written in the voice of Yu Xiangdou, master of the Shuangfeng tang publishing house. In the upper register of three of the four pages is an advertisement, making its appeal to potential buyers.[32]

The novel is, of course, about outlaws—potentially subversive subject matter that even Li Kaixian felt the need to justify in his comments about it when it was read among the elite around the Jiajing court over half a century earlier. In the *Thicket of Comments* preface, the paratextual Yu justifies their actions in terms of the conventional values of loyalty and righteousness (*zhong yi*). He first provides conventional definitions attributed to "Confucian forefathers" (*xian Ru*): "loyalty" is "bringing the heart to full realization," and righteousness is "controlling the heart and acting in the correct manner." He proceeds to modify these definitions, giving them more of a social dimension: loyalty is "bringing one's heart to full realization on behalf of the country," and righteousness is "acting in the correct manner in accordance with the needs of the people."

Yu goes on to ascribe these social values to the band of outlaws in the novel, claiming that they were righteous heroes who rose up due to the lack of moral integrity of the Song dynasty, in which the novel is set. He then addresses the problem of the violence at the heart of the novel in a rhetorical move that surprisingly echoes Li Kaixian's earlier one, in a very different social context: He states that an "ignorant person" (*buzhizhe*) might say that the bandits of the novel were "thieves of the people" (*min zhi zei*) and "the pestilence of the nation" (*guo zhi du*). Yet whereas Li Kaixian initially defended the violence of the novel by pointing to the literary qualities with which it was depicted, Yu here remains on the mimetic level of the action of the story in his defense. He admits of the bandits that "originally, their minds were not necessarily humane," but that their actions were justified by the corrupt times in which they lived and the good deeds they performed. Due to these factors, Yu claims, the heroes fit the social values of loyalty and righteousness that he has set out.

Like Li Kaixian before him, Yu also compares *The Water Margin* to classic literature. Whereas Li compared it to Sima Qian's *Records of the Grand Historian*, Yu compares it to no less than the *Spring and Autumn Annals*, the compilation of which was traditionally attributed to Confucius.

Invoking the words of the Song-era exegete Hu Anguo, whose work on the *Spring and Autumn Annals* was a standard in the Ming, Yu says that that Confucian classic is said to be an "essential canon that transmits the mind beyond history" (*shiwai chuanxin zhi yaodian*). He goes on to claim that *The Water Margin* is similarly an "essential summary that depicts events beyond the chronicles' (*jiwai xushi zhi yaolan*). Yu closes by asking rhetorically, "How could one say that this is not a classic of the sages or a record of the worthies and thus dismiss it?" Whatever subversive quality the novel may have has been safely contained, and its literary status as a classic worthy of readers' attention is affirmed.

Meanwhile, in the upper register of the same pages, Yu makes a different type of "literary" pitch. Here, in a brief note titled "Discerning the *Water Margins*" (*Shuihu bian*), (Figure 4.1) he asserts the quality of his edition of the novel over the others on the market. The others, he claims, are only partially illustrated, rife with incorrect characters, and printed from old and indistinct blocks. His, by contrast, has been edited to remove anything that would hinder the reader's browsing; he touts that it is also fully illustrated and features evaluations. He has corrected all mistakes, he claims, though poems and lyrics with incorrect rhymes have been left in lest readers think it incomplete. Yu ends the note with an affirmation of the trustworthiness of the brand of his publishing house: "Gentlemen customers can recognize the mark of the Shuangfeng tang house."

Taken together, Yu's preface and "Discerning the *Water Margins*" note serve to minimize the potential subversiveness of the novel and reassure the reader of its worth as a commercial product. That worth is phrased in literary terms, comparing the novel to the classics in terms of its supposedly serious-minded morality, but its literariness is aimed at the reader. It has been edited with the convenience and approval of the reader in mind, rather than any notion of textual fidelity or authorial intent.

The Li Zhuowu preface takes up seventeen pages, with five columns of around nine characters each. As with the preface in *Thicket of Comments*, it too is in characters imitative of brushwork and finer than the characters of the body of the novel's text. It is signed in the name of Li Zhi and also lists the name of the carver, Sun Pu. It is dated midsummer, 1610.[33] This preface was likely written by the empirical Li Zhi, as it was collected in his *A Book to Burn* collection, which was published in his lifetime. The "On the Childlike Mind" essay, which mentions *The Water Margin*, was also included in the collection. The commentary in

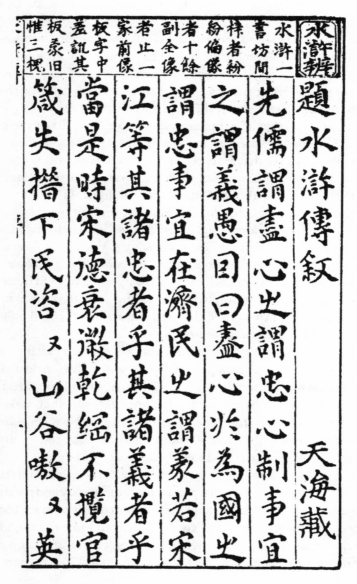

FIGURE 4.1. Yu Xiangdou edition, "Discerning the *Water Margins*."
Source: Reprinted from the Shanghai guji chubanshe edition of *Shuihu zhizhuan pinglin*, 1.

the Rongyu tang edition, however, is less likely to be an authentic work of Li Zhi. Nevertheless, for our purposes here, we will treat the preface and the commentary as the work of the same "Li Zhuowu" paratextual character.

Like the Yu Xiangdou preface, the Li Zhuowu preface also justifies the violence of *The Water Margin* on political and moral grounds. There is a critical difference, however: Whereas the Yu preface justified the action of the heroes of the novel as righteous rebellion against the corruption of the Song dynasty, the Li preface justifies the writing of the novel as an expression of righteous indignation. Li reaffirms the power of literary work to express anger; quoting Sima Qian's famous letter to Ren An, he states that Han Feizi's "Difficulties of Persuasion" and "Sorrow of Standing Alone" were sagely expressions of anger, and that only anger justified writing. Writing without anger, Li says, would be like shivering without being cold or moaning without being sick—"one could do it, but what sort of sight would it be?" On these grounds, the preface claims, the writing of *The Water Margin* was justified because it was an expression of its authors' anger. It claims that Shi Nai'an and Luo Guanzhong lived under the Yuan dynasty and harbored outrage at the weakness and corruption of the preceding Song that led to its fall. With the corrupt at the center, the loyal and righteous could only find their place at the margins of society.

Li Zhuowu singles out the eventual leader of the novel's band of outlaws, Song Jiang, as an exemplar of loyalty and righteousness. To Li, it is these exemplary moral qualities—and the incumbent threat to a society whose values have been turned upside down—that makes *The Water Margin* necessary. It was necessary to write, and it is necessary for those who have power to read. Without the book, Li states, loyalty and righteousness will be relegated to the margins of society.

Since the justification for writing is anger, and the anger is directed at social hierarchies, the Li Zhuowu preface fuses the literary and the subversive in a way that the Yu Xiangdou preface does not. It tempers the subversive by making its power implicit and contained while maintaining its potency. In some ways, it could even be said that it harnesses that potency in the name of the commercial—its power is its appeal and its necessity.

Evaluating the "Righteous Release"

Prefaces such as those discussed above shape expectations about the book before it is read—or, as the "Discerning the *Water Margins*" note suggests, even before it is purchased. Presumably, they would set the tone for the commentaries in the rest of their respective editions, serving to introduce the voice of the paratextual character who will accompany the reader on the journey through the book. Due to the sweeping scale of the novel genre, it would be difficult to compare those different possible journeys through *The Water Margin* side by side. However there are particularly telling scenes in which such differences come to light, illustrating how the literary, the subversive, and the commercial are negotiated within the commentary on the novel by the paratextual characters. Two such scenes involve the "righteous releases" (*yishi*) of Song Jiang.

The righteous release is a common plot device in the early modern Chinese novel in which situational and normative ethics clash: a captor allows personal obligations to a captive to take precedence over those of law and order, and releases the captive on the basis of their private relationship. Instances of the righteous release occur in the earliest works of the genre, including *Record of the Heroes and Martyrs* as discussed in previous chapters. The most famous righteous release is found in *Romance of the Three Kingdoms*, after the forces of Liu Bei have routed those of Cao Cao at the critical Battle of Red Cliff. Cao Cao and a small band of his men escape via the Huarong Trail, on which Zhuge Liang has installed Guan Yu to wait in ambush. In order to escape with his life, Cao Cao appeals to Guan's sentiments: Guan had previously surrendered to Cao and served him for a time under certain conditions. When Guan had escaped, he had killed five of Cao's commanders on the way. At Huarong Trail, Cao reminds Guan of the kindness he had received while in Cao's service, and of the lamentable fates of the five slain commanders. In what could be interpreted as an excessive sense of personal honor, Guan releases Cao, fully expecting to be put to death for betraying his mission. The incident occurs in chapter 50, a major structural turning point in the 120-chapter novel.[34]

In *The Water Margin*, the character Song Jiang—whom we have seen was treated as the embodiment of loyalty and righteousness by Li Zhuowu—is granted righteous release from captors twice, first from the hands of the law in chapter 22, and then from the hands of a gang of outlaws in chapter 32.[35]

The first righteous release, which occurs in chapter 22, requires a slightly complex backstory. When we first meet Song Jiang, in chapter 18, he is a minor official, a registrar, in Yuncheng, Shandong. Though he is a competent administrator in the local government, he is also a lover of the martial arts and a friend to the roving heroes of the "rivers and lakes" underworld. His generous support of those heroes has earned him the nickname "the Opportune Rain." The two worlds in which Song Jiang moves collide when an inspector arrives in Yuncheng on the trail of a suspect in the brazen robbery of gifts intended for the Grand Preceptor Cai Jing. Song Jiang invites the inspector out to discuss the case at a local teahouse and learns that the suspect is none other than his fellow denizen of the martial underworld, Chao Gai. Song Jiang tips Chao Gai off that the law is closing in on him, and the personal bond between the two men grows even stronger than before.

Song's close relationship with Chao Gai leads him into trouble. Song Jiang's wife, Yan Poxi, discovers a letter from Chao expressing his thanks and promising a gift of gold. Yan despises Song Jiang and has been having an affair with another minor official, Zhang Wenyuan. She threatens to expose Song unless he grants her freedom and gives her the gold mentioned in the letter. Song insists that he has not yet received the gold and flies into a rage, killing his wife. Yan's mother tricks Song Jiang, saying she will let the matter go as long as he pays for the funeral expenses. However, on their way to the coffin maker, Mother Yan grabs hold of Song Jiang and screams that he has killed her daughter. A crowd gathers, and a friend of Song Jiang's from the streets named Bullock Tang (Tang Niu'er) knocks Mother Yan aside. Song Jiang escapes her grasp and slips away. The official is now on the run.

The righteous release itself comes in chapter 22, which in the received edition is titled "Mother Yan causes an uproar in Yuncheng County; Zhu Tong righteously releases Song Gongming."[36] In the chapter, the county magistrate is reluctant to have Song Jiang arrested as they are on good terms with one another. Instead, he tries to bury the case by pinning it on Bullock Tang. It is only when Zhang Wenyuan insists on going after Song Jiang that two sergeants, Zhu Tong and Lei Heng, are dispatched to bring him in. However, despite their official appointments, Zhu Tong and Lei Heng also have ties with the martial underworld and are acquainted with Song Jiang through it. When they track Song Jiang down at the Song family compound, Zhu Tong throws the investigation off his trail and allows him to escape. Song Jiang then flees to the manor of another benefactor of the underworld, Chai Jin. There, he meets another of the novel's great heroes, Wu Song, and the focus of the narrative shifts once again.

The second righteous release of Song Jiang occurs ten chapters later, in chapter 32. The chapter is titled "Pilgrim Wu drunkenly beats Kong

Liang; the Brocade Tiger righteously releases Song Jiang."[37] This time, the righteous release comes not from the hands of the authorities with personal connections to Song Jiang but from those of minor bandits. He is on the run for the murder of his wife, heading to take shelter at a place called Windy Fort. While walking through a forest, he trips an alarm bell tied to a rope. Men who have been waiting in ambush seize him and drag him off to their lair. There, they tie him to a pillar and discuss their plan to slaughter and eat him once their leader has awoken. Eventually, three bandit chiefs show up and the henchmen prepare to slaughter Song Jiang. Song Jiang laments his fate aloud, saying, "O wretched Song Jiang, your life must end here!"[38] When the bandit chiefs hear this name, they are shocked. They know him and his reputation in the rivers and lakes underworld well. One of the chiefs, the Brocade Tiger, cuts Song Jiang's bonds and wraps him in his own robes and all three kowtow to him. The Brocade Tiger declares that he should gouge his own eyes out for failing to recognize such a great man. When Song Jiang asks what he has done to deserve such high praise, the Brocade Tiger exclaims that his renowned throughout the world for his bravery and generosity.

After his release, Song Jiang stays on with the band for a time. One of the chiefs, Short Arse (following the Dent-Young translation), captures a woman who turns out to be the wife of the civil governor of Windy Fort. Hoping to keep in the good graces of the Windy Fort officials, Song frees her and swears to Short Arse that he will bring him another, better wife. She later lies about her release, saying that the troops sent to save her did so by force. When Song Jiang arrives at Windy Fort, he learns of a power struggle between the military and civil governors there; his move to save the civil governor's wife and play up to the local officials was for nought.

In the Yu Xiangdou edition, the potential subversive quality of the righteous release of Song Jiang remains constrained; the underworld values that are shared across the normative constraints of the law are not praised, nor are they presented as the "social" versions of loyalty and righteousness that the paratextual Yu Xiangdou outlines in the preface. Rather, it is presented more in the commercial light of the "Discerning the *Water Margins*" note printed above the preface, promising that the edition would cater to readers' needs.

The first righteous release of Song Jiang occurs in a span of eight pages.[39] In this particular edition, the chapter is numbered twenty-one, but retains the same title. In addition to appearing in the main body of the text, the event is also narrated through the captioned images and Yu's evaluations in the upper registers.

A reader might read the main text and be helped along by the images and paratext; a reader already familiar with the story might also revisit the narrative by looking at the sequence of images and their captions, which form an outline of the events. This "illustrated narrative" does not line up precisely with the narrative in text below it. In the text, for example, the reader is left in suspense as to the identity of the figure Song Jiang encounters in Chai Jin's lair. The captions, however, reveal him to be the hero Wu Song a full two pages earlier. The relatively minor character Bullock Tang is also more prominently featured in the captions, appearing in three of the eight for the episode. More important, the captions do not refer to the actions of Zhu Tong and Lei Heng as a "righteous release" of Song Jiang as the chapter title does. Instead of that phrase, the caption for the relevant image merely says that Zhu Tong and Lei Heng "let Song Jiang go" (figure 4.2). These events and evaluations, experienced through the top register of the pages, are as follows:

The first page in the sequence features Bullock and Grandmother Yan sitting in front of the imposing magistrate:

Bullock and Grandmother Yan are hauled off to see the magistrate

An evaluation of Bullock: Note that Bullock hits Mother Yan to free Song Jiang not just because he'd been chased off by her the previous day. It certainly was not because he'd been insulted. Even had it been someone else who'd taken hold of Song Jiang, Bullock would still have risked his life . . .[40]

This comment is continued on the next page. The image shows the magistrate leaning forward, pointing a finger:

The magistrate questions Bullock Tang

. . . to save him. Note that Bullock can be compared to a benefactor. Consider that later Bullock is wrongfully blamed by an official and is punished—seeing this point later, one has a sigh of pity for Bullock.[41]

The image on the next page shows Sergeants Zhu Tong and Lei Heng arriving at the Song family compound, where they will first encounter Song Jiang's father, Squire Song. The evaluation, however, is of the magistrate, who is not pictured:

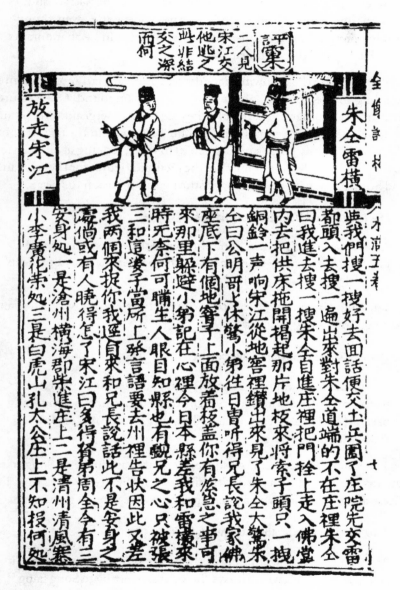

FIGURE 4.2. Yu Xiangdou edition, "Zhu Tong and Lei Heng Let Song Jiang Go."

Source: Reprinted from the Shanghai guji chubanshe edition of *Shuihu zhizhuan pinglin*, 208.

Runners arrive at the village and see Squire Song

An evaluation of the magistrate: Note that the magistrate shouts at the old woman and intends to save Song Jiang, even though Song Jiang clearly has killed someone. How could he abandon his official duties due to private reasons?[42]

The image on the following page depicts three similarly attired figures standing in the doorway of the Song family compound. One gestures away from the others. Presumably, they are the two sergeants and Squire Song; the gesturing figure should be Zhu Tong, who in the text went off alone to find Song Jiang's hiding spot. However, looking at the caption to the page, a reader might mistake the pictured figures for the sergeants and Song Jiang, with Song Jiang gesturing his intention to leave:

Zhu Tong and Lei Heng let Song Jiang go

An evaluation of Lei and Zhu: The two men see Song Jiang and allow him to slip away from them—if that is not the start of a deep friendship, then what is it?[43]

The following page returns to the magistrate's court, with an evaluation of Song Jiang's father:

The magistrate condemns Bullock Tang

An evaluation of Squire Song: The Squire uses wine to pay respects to the two officers and keep them from denouncing Song Jiang because of this one feast. In actuality, they already had strong relations with Song Jiang.[44]

The following page in the sequence features an image of Song Jiang and his brother, who has fled with him, paying their respects to Chai Jin. The evaluation remarks on a poem in the lower register of the same page:

Song Jiang and his brother see the high official Chai

An evaluation of the phrasing of the poem: Where it says "rouge," it is referring to Poxi; where it says "hero," it is referring to Song Jiang.[45]

Next, Song Jiang is depicted meeting Wu Song. Wu Song is named in the caption, though not in the main text of the lower register until two pages later. The evaluation comments on his reception by Chai Jin:

Song Jiang is grabbed by Wu Song

An evaluation of the reception: Song Jiang arriving here and receiving a warm reception from Chai Jin is good fortune in the midst of ill fortune.[46]

On the final page of the chapter, the image depicts Chai Jin alone, raising his hand in greeting. The evaluation remarks on a line of dialogue from Wu Song, who says of Song Jiang without recognizing him, "He takes no shortcuts in treating people. As soon as I am better, I'll go and join up with him!":

Chai Jin comes to see Song Jiang and Wu Song

An evaluation of the words on treating people: When he [Wu Song] says "[Song Jiang] takes no shortcuts [in treating people]," you can see the sincerity with which Song Jiang treats people.[47]

The second righteous release of Song Jiang figures much less prominently in the Yu Xiangdou *Thicket of Comments* edition of *The Water Margin* than in "full-recension" versions such as the Rongyu tang edition. It takes place in chapter 30 of the edition, which consists of material found in chapters 31 and 32 of the received, full-recension editions. The words *righteous release* are not to be found in the chapter title; instead, it is called "In Ducks and Drakes Tower the General's blood will spill; Pilgrim Wu travels Centipede Hill by night."[48] Nor does Yu Xiangdou use the term in the paratext concerning Song Jiang's release, which takes place over just three pages. They are as follows:

The image on the page depicts a single bandit reaching out to Song Jiang, who appears to be moving away from him. The evaluation comments on the bandit Short Arse, who is not pictured but who is introduced in the text of the lower register:

Song Jiang is captured and taken up to the mountainous lair

An evaluation of Short Arse: The phrasing in the lines of the poem below presents Short Arse as a lustful figure who has an imposing presence. He is at once admirable and detestable. The critical term for this is "one-up one-down" phrasing method.[49]

On the next page, the image depicts a seated bandit king looking on as an underling stands sword in hand before a kneeling Song Jiang. The caption mentions Short Arse, though in the text another bandit, Yan Shun the "Brocade Tiger," is seated alone first:

Song Jiang is tied up and presented to Short Arse Wang

An evaluation of "water splashing the heart": For an explanation of the splashing of water onto the chest, it is because people's hearts have hot blood within them. Using cold water to disperse the hot blood makes the organ easier to remove.[50]

The final page in the sequence appears to depict Yan Shun assisting Song Jiang to a seat next to Short Arse. In the text in the lower register below, Yan refers to Song Jiang as a "benevolent older brother":

Yan Shun assists Song Jiang to a seat

An evaluation of calling "benevolent older brother": Note how Yan Shun uses the title "benevolent older brother" to refer to Song Jiang. This is because he'd long heard of Song's reputation and on this day had the opportunity to meet him—the utmost in luck.[51]

In sum, the paratextual character of Yu Xiangdou plays down the potentially subversive elements of the righteous releases of Song Jiang. He does not frame these two events in terms of wider social significance; they are not made out to be examples of the "loyalty" or "righteousness" of the underworld. Instead, Yu emphasizes the more commonplace values of friendship and human relations, expressed in terms such as "having a relationship," "treating" or "receiving" people, and addressing people with proper terms. Such values may be loosely conceptually related to those like loyalty and righteousness, but they do not present a challenge to the established social order in a way that needs the sort of justifications found in the preface. Yu even appears to side with the supposedly corrupt authorities when he gently criticizes the magistrate for shirking his official duties by not pursuing Song Jiang.

Friendships and personal relations, in Yu's paratextual explanation, are built on reciprocity. We might see the "start of a deep friendship," and characters might have "strong relations" with one another, but these relationships are not explicitly built on shared values, nor do they have broader social implications for "the country" and "the people." Yu asks us to sigh for Bullock Tang, who assisted in Song Jiang's escape and ended up a collateral victim, but he does not depict him as acting out of any shared sense of righteousness; Bullock Tang can be "compared to a benefactor." Random chance also plays a role: Yu presents Song Jiang's encounters with Chai Jin and Yan Shun as "good fortune in the midst of ill fortune" and "the utmost in luck," rather than the natural consequence of membership in a fraternity based on shared values.

It is also notable that the paratextual Yu provides the reader with some minor assistance in comprehending the poem and some literary technique in the text. This suggests a readership that requires some guidance through the text but at the same time sees itself as connoisseurs who appreciate the craft of the writing they read. These promises were also made in the front of the book—again, in the "Discerning the *Water Margins*" advertisement rather than the preface on values. Yu presents the righteous releases of Song Jiang in a manner that is commercial and somewhat literary, but only minimally subversive.

Let us now revisit these same incidents in the plot of the novel accompanied not by the paratextual character Yu Xiangdou, but Li Zhuowu. Whereas the former appeared in a dedicated top register of each page, the latter appears only occasionally throughout the pages of the novel in the form of occasional "eyebrow comments" (*meipi*) in the upper margin or in smaller print mixed in with the main text. Each chapter is preceded by two lavish, full-page illustrations, and concluded with a final comment by Li Zhuowu. Since the paratextual materials are not afforded a dedicated place in the design of the page, one could not as easily reconstruct the narrative through the images and paratextual comments by browsing through it; the commentary thus seems more tightly intertwined with the text of the novel.

The first righteous release of Song Jiang, by the sergeant Zhu Tong, takes place in chapter 22 of the edition.[52] Preceding the chapter are two full-page illustrations, each with a line in the couplet of the chapters title: "Grandmother Yan raises havoc in Yuncheng County" and "Zhu Tong righteously releases Song Jiang" (figure 4.3). The first is a more lavish courtroom scene, similar to those of the Yu Xiangdou edition but more finely cut. The second depicts Song Jiang emerging from his hiding place in the family compound's Buddhist altar, hands in a gesture of gratefulness, as Zhu Tong points the way to freedom.

The text of chapter 22 is twenty-five pages long in the edition, with eyebrow comments on eight pages, interlinear comments on five, and the final chapter-closing comment on the last. Though the Li Zhuowu preface, discussed above, emphasizes the importance—and the threat—of loyalty and righteousness, the comments to chapter 22 do not mention them specifically. The only one that touches on those values is one

Figure 4.3. Rongyu tang "Li Zhuowu" edition, "Zhu Quan Righteously Releases Song Gongming."
Source: Reprinted from the Shanghai guji chubanshe edition of *Li Zhuowu ping Shuihu zhuan*, 664.

in reference to a poem that opens the chapter. A line of the poem reads, "The world's heroes are generous in their thoughts; talk of loyalty and righteousness moves officials"; the comment, over the second part of the line, reads simply, "A fine line" (*jiaju*).[53]

The comments do, however, echo the Yu Xiangdou evaluations that emphasize human relationships. Yet Li Zhuowu radicalizes these relationships in a way that Yu did not: he mocks official duties and the rule of law, and praises giving free rein to personal emotions. In particular, he praises the magistrate who is reluctant to prosecute Song Jiang due to their personal relationship. At the point in the text where it mentions that he and Song Jiang are "on excellent terms" and how he "would have dearly liked to get him off," an interlinear comment reads, "What a good magistrate" (*hao zhixian*)![54] An eyebrow comment above the passage continues along the same lines, saying, "What a good magistrate who understands fairness" (*hao yige mingbai gongdao de zhixian*)![55]

By contrast, Zhang Wenyuan—Yan Poxi's lover who pushes to have Song Jiang prosecuted for her murder—is mocked on the next page for his allegiance to the law. Above the passage in which Zhang submits that the evidence points to Song Jiang and demands that he be brought in for questioning, an eyebrow comment reads, "People only know that Zhang Wenyuan is covetous and lustful; they don't know that he is actually enforcing the law" (*ren dan zhi Zhang Wenyuan duse, bu zhi shi zhifa*)![56]

Meanwhile, when it comes to the actual righteous release, Li Zhuowu again does not couch it in terms of "loyalty" and "righteousness." In the text, Zhu Tong has found Song Jiang in his hiding place and is conferring with him about where he should run to take refuge. Li Zhuowu's eyebrow comment above the passage reads, "What a good sergeant—he's only concerned with doing personal favors. When you've done personal favors, what is the rule of law" (*haoge dutou, zhiguan zuo zijia renqing; dou zuole renqing, ru wangfa he?*)[57] (figure 4.4).

Song Jiang makes his way to Chai Jin's lair, and the chapter concludes. Li Zhuowu closes the chapter with the following comment, reiterating his subversive reading: "Elder Baldy Li says: Zhu Tong, Lei Heng, and Chai Jin pay no mind to the rule of law. They are only concerned with personal emotions/favors (*renqing*), so they are bandits to the core. Someone like Zhang Wenyuan, on the other hand, who enforces the law, is a 'good citizen.' One might ask, 'The magistrate also did personal favors; why doesn't he become a bandit?' I answer: 'Are you saying that the magistrate is not a bandit?'"[58]

好個都頭只管做自家人情都做了人情如王法何

知投何處去好朱仝道兄長可以作急尋思當行即行今
晩便可動身勿請遲延自悞宋江道上下官司之事全望
兄長維持金帛使用只顧來取朱仝道這事放心都在我
身上兄長只顧安排去路宋江謝了朱仝再入地窨子去
朱仝依舊把地板蓋上還將供牀壓了開門拿朴刀出來
說道眞箇沒在莊裏叫道雷都頭我們只拏了宋太公去
如何雷橫見說要拿宋太公去尋思朱仝那人和宋江最
好地怎地顚倒要拏宋太公這話以定是反說他若再提
起我落得做人情朱仝雷橫叫攏土兵都入草堂上來宋
太公慌忙置酒管待衆人朱仝道休要安排酒食且請太
公和四郎同到本縣裡走一遭雷橫道四郎如何不見宋

李卓吾批評水滸傳 卷之二十二

Figure 4.4. Rongyu tang “Li Zhuowu” edition, “What a Good Sergeant.”
Source: Reprinted from the Shanghai guji chubanshe edition of *Li Zhuowu ping Shuihu zhuan*, 675.

The second righteous release of Song Jiang, this time at the hands of the Brocade Tiger and his band of minor bandits, occurs in chapter 32 of the edition. Again, the chapter is preceded by two elaborate, full-page images, one for each part of the chapter title couplet: "Pilgrim Wu drunkenly beats Kong Liang" and "The Brocade Tiger righteously releases Song Jiang."[59] In the latter image, Song Jiang is shown gesturing in gratitude to the three bandit kings, who kowtow before him. In the foreground of the image, two underlings stand near a stake; on the ground are a rope and a knife. The chapter is forty-one pages long, with eleven eyebrow comments and six interlinear ones.

Much of the chapter is on Wu Song; for our purposes here we will concentrate on the portion of the chapter relating Song Jiang's righteous release. Here, again, the paratextual Li Zhuowu casts a cynical eye on society. When the bandits learn Song Jiang's identity and fall to the ground kowtowing to him, the Brocade Tiger exclaims that he should use the knife that cut the ropes binding Song Jiang to gouge out his own eyes for not recognizing the great figure in front of him. Above the passage, Li's eyebrow comment reads, "If people of today were all to gouge out their eyes like this, it would be a blind world" (*ruo jinren dou ruci wanqi yanjing lai, dang cheng yipian gu shijie*).[60]

Li Zhuowu takes an interest in the bandit Short Arse's attempt to capture the official's wife and force her to be his wife. Song Jiang thinks to himself that he must save her because she must be the wife of a colleague of Colonel Hua of Windy Fort; above the passage, Li Zhuowu simply agrees, "Yes" (*shi*).[61] Song Jiang tries to talk Short Arse into letting her go, and Short Arse complains that all the women are snatched up by "high and mighty officials"; an interlinear comment reads, "Well said" (*haohua*), and an eyebrow comment reads, "What if the 'high and mighty officials' could hear that" (*da toujin tingzhi heru*)?[62] But when on the same page Song Jiang promises to bring him a better wife at a later time, Li Zhuowu scoffs in an interlinear comment, "Which one would be willing to marry a bandit" (*nage ken jia qiangdao*)? Two pages later, the woman herself becomes the target of mockery when she lies and tells the troops sent to save her that the bandits released her due to the authority of her husband's name. Li's eyebrow comment reads, "One who speaks inaccurately like that wouldn't be a good wife" (*kou buzhun, bian bushi hao furen le*).[63] The troops beg her to report that their rescue mission was a success so they will escape punishment. When on the next page she follows their request and gives a false report, an eyebrow comment reads, "A wife like this may as well be a bandit's old lady" (*ruci furen, zhihao zuo qiangdao pozi*)![64]

Li Zhuowu closes the chapter with the following comment: "Li the Monk says, 'People nowadays only read the events that follow this and say that Song Jiang should not have saved Liu Gao's wife. Little do they realize that, had Song Jiang not done so, he would have been with Short Arse for a lifetime. How would he have gone on to accomplish so many great things? How would he have been able to serve as elder brother to those other 107 of the band?' "[65]

The paratextual character Li Zhuowu's treatment of the two righteous releases of Song Jiang illustrates the evasive nature of his commentary. Like Yu Xiangdou, he too praises reciprocal relationships and "personal favors." Yet Li Zhuowu is willing to allow them to throw the social order into disarray—magistrates are bandits, the lustful are upholders of laws, and personal considerations trump the rule of law. At the same time, however, the figure of the bandit is not lionized for its own sake—only the worst of women would be a partner for one. Li's subversiveness reaches the extent that he casts doubt on the world's ability to recognize the qualities of those around them.

The connection between Li Zhuowu the commentator and the empirical Li Zhi whose style name he bears is tenuous at best, and such Li Zhuowu fiction commentaries are often considered in terms of "authenticity." But here, such questions aside, the commentary does provide a provocative literary experience that is similar to that found in the more "canonical" writings of Li Zhi. In a recent study, Rivi Handler-Spitz has used Barbara C. Bowen's term "bluff" to capture Li Zhi's evasive qualities.[66] "Bluff," here, refers to provocative and open-ended statements intended to shock or otherwise disorient readers into reconsidering their own thoughts. "Li Zhuowu," in these passages, does the same. Handler-Spitz also ties this quality of "bluff" to the age in which Li Zhi lived (and Li Zhuowu commentaries appeared), when both moral and monetary values were increasingly difficult to distinguish.

Turning away from the aesthetic qualities of the commercial, the subversive, and the literary, and turning instead to another concept from Sianne Ngai's work, it is easy to portray "paratextual characters" such as Yu Xiangdou and Li Zhuowu as mere "gimmicks." They seem to have been offering readers of their era some sort of hermeneutical shortcut, allowing them to take a book like *The Water Margin* and digest it in readymade ways that appeal to their preexisting sensibilities. This is especially the case since these editions of *The Water Margin* appeared at a time of rapid expansion of the commercial book market in late Ming China—which spurred the growth of the vernacular novel genre.

Commercial publishing is often seen through the lens of social class; books lent respectability to a rising "gentry" class that lacked the traditional status of the literati despite their literacy. Yu Xiangdou himself is taken as a literal image of the class anxiety of the gentry, through the portrait of himself at leisure in his garden included in his *Orthodox Instructions for Ten Thousand Uses* mentioned above.

On these terms, we could see the two editions of *The Water Margin* under discussion in this chapter as pitches to two different subsegments of this gentry class, perhaps with one targeting more highly educated members than the other, but with neither targeting traditional literati. However, here it is important to keep in mind the warnings of Bruno Latour about the subtle distinction between what he calls "intermediaries" on the one hand and "mediators" on the other. An intermediary "is what transports meaning or force without transformation," while a mediator can "transform, translate, distort, and modify the meaning or the elements they are supposed to carry."[67] When we treat the commercial imprints of the late Ming merely as functions of social class dynamics, they become intermediaries; the class distinctions of gentry, literati, etc. are projected on rather than transformed by them. If we treat these editions as mediators, on the other hand, rather than as mere gimmicks, we might consider how they harnessed these class distinctions in subtle ways, feeding them into the commercial, the subversive, and the literary.

Ultimately, it is hard to say if the commercial became a vector for the spread of the subversive, if the subversive was a contributing factor to the commercial appeal, or if the literary was aligned with one or the other of these qualities. It is also impossible to gauge the extent to which any particular paratextual character shaped the reception of *The Water Margin* in the popular imagination as the commercial print industry expanded. However, it is apparent that there was a wide range of possibilities, as these two figures represent. It is also apparent that, once *The Water Margin* did find these wider audiences, it took on a more subversive air. In fact, it began to inspire real-life bandits, some of whom gathered at the real Mount Liang to emulate their heroes from the novel. In 1642, just over one hundred years from the fire in the imperial ancestral hall that led to the end of the careers of Guo Xun, Wang Tingxiang, and Li Kaixian, a memorial was presented at the court of the Chongzhen emperor, calling for a ban on *The Water Margin*. It warned that the book was teaching how to rally people, sack towns, commit murder and arson, and even discuss terms of surrender. In the era of commercial printing, what had once been seen by literati elites as a work rivaled only by the *Record of the Grand Historian* had become, in the eyes of officialdom, a manual for banditry and subversion.[68]

Within two months of this memorial, an order banning *The Water Margin* was issued. In a particularly ironic turn of events, the agency tasked with overseeing the ban was none other than the Censorate, the agency that decades earlier was among the first to print the novel.

CHAPTER 5

"The Art of Subtle Phrasing Has Been Extinguished"
The Jin Shengtan Edition

By 1642, the year that the Censorate was called on to enforce a ban on *The Water Margin*, that novel had existed in print for more than a century. It had taken on several different forms, from a token of status for the consumption of elite connoisseurs to a commodity in a growing marketplace for books. Editor-commentators had introduced to its pages various paratextual characters, heightening its literary, subversive, or commercial qualities in different combinations in order to best capture particular targeted readerships. Finally—in the eyes of the authorities, at least—it had become a textbook for banditry that needed to be removed from circulation.

An Unsuccessful Ban

The official ban on *The Water Margin* could not have been very successful or long-lasting, however, as around the same time came the most influential edition of the novel yet: that of the great editor-commentator Jin Shengtan. The precise date of its appearance is unknown; a preface included in the edition is dated 1641, while other sources state that the edition was published in 1644.[1] Regardless, it appeared soon after the purported ban on the novel, as the dynasty was collapsing. The Jin edition then became the dominant edition of the novel for more than a century and a half, until reformers of the early Republican era published a modern, typeset edition.

This historical backdrop may have been the impetus behind one of Jin Shengtan's greatest editorial decisions that set his edition apart from all of its predecessors. Previous editions saw the complete band of outlaws finally assemble in a newly christened Hall of Loyalty and Righteousness for a great ceremonial feast in chapter 71. A divine tablet appears, with the names of the heroes inscribed on it in mystical script that a Daoist adept must read for the heroes. The proceedings are soon darkened by dissension in the ranks when the leader Song Jiang—whom we have seen held up as a model of loyalty and righteousness by previous commentators—continually brings up his desire for an official amnesty. In those earlier editions, the amnesty does come, and the outlaw heroes spend most of the remainder of the novel—thirty to fifty chapters, depending on the edition—fighting campaigns on behalf of the Song dynasty against the Liao kingdom and various rebels. Jin's edition, by contrast, ends immediately after the feast. In its wake, the second in command of the band, Lu Junyi, dreams that he and the others are captured and executed by the authorities, who announce that they would never accept the surrender of such criminals. Lu Junyi is startled awake, only to see a banner before him that reads "Great Peace under Heaven" (*Tianxia taiping*).

While this editorial decision may have been motivated by politics, the commentary of the Jin Shengtan highlights instead the fact that the novel begins and (now) ends with mystical stelae. It began with an arrogant official opening a sealed chamber, seeing a tablet, and releasing the thirty-six Heavenly Spirits (*Tiangang*) and seventy-two Earthly Demons (*Disha*); now, the incarnations of those one hundred and eight have gathered together and are memorialized for posterity on a new tablet. Jin comments several times on how "wondrous" (*miao*) this writing is, and what authorial genius it reflects.

Biographical details of the empirical Jin Shengtan's life may have given the politicized understanding of his *Water Margin* some further traction. In the wake of the death of the Qing Shunzhi emperor in 1661, Jin took part in a memorial observance that turned into a protest against the local magistrate. He was later arrested for treason and—in circumstances eerily similar to Lu Junyi's dream with which Jin's edition of *The Water Margin* concludes—executed by decapitation along with more than a hundred others. Especially in the turbulent early years of the People's Republic of China, scholars went to great lengths to discern the political implications of Jin Shengtan and his work.

The more lasting image of Jin, however, comes from the other aspect of Jin's commentary, the interest in the formal and structural elements of the novel that brought him to remark on the parallels between the work's opening and its closing. The paratextual character of Jin Sheng-tan, who emerges throughout the edition via its extensive commentary and prefatory materials, is indeed greatly occupied with such "literary" matters. Western-trained scholars have even drawn comparisons between this aspect of the Jin Shengtan commentary and the "close read-ing" methodology of the British and American New Critics of the mid- to late twentieth century. Indeed, scholars frequently point to Jin's com-ments on the structure of the novel, the fineness of its prose, and the evi-dent genius of its author as evidence that Jin "elevated" the status of the "lowly" or even "despised" genre of the novel to the level of the classics.[2]

However, Jin's work on *The Water Margin* was not completely unprec-edented in taking the novel seriously; as previous chapters have shown, readers and editors had been drawing comparisons between *The Water Margin* and classic works of literature for over a century by the time the Jin Shengtan edition appeared. It is true that much of Jin Shengtan's commentary on *The Water Margin* is concerned with the characters of the novel and how they are depicted; Jin details the techniques used by the purported author in creating detailed portraits of the heroes, and literary scholars have used such comments as evidence that Jin was working to "elevate" the purportedly lowly genre to the level of the clas-sics. However, Jin's discussions are not limited to the literary. They are also intimately tied with what might be termed the "character of char-acters"—that is, the moral qualities that the figures in the novel exhibit and exemplify. These discussions go deeper than the rather superficial ones about the loyalty and righteousness of the novel's heroes seen in earlier-stage commentaries, which were couched in commercial or sub-versive terms or apologetically explained as literary contrivances. At the same time, they remain a collection of recurring themes rather than a systematic philosophical statement—after all, they remain bound, however loosely, to the novel itself and inevitably return to it. However, even as tangential points, they often steal the spotlight from the novel itself. Jin's comments do more than point out the genius of the text's author. That proclaimed genius is only intermediary; it is used to depict the character of the characters in sharp relief. This first character—the moral qualities exhibited by individual heroes—often takes precedence over "literary" matters in his comments, and the discussions can be de-veloped in surprisingly intricate ways. That is to say, for Jin Shengtan, even a story of an untamed outlaw can become an occasion for an explication of the Neo-Confucian classics *The Highest Order of Cultivation* (*Daxue*) and *On the Practice of the Mean* (*Zhongyong*).[3]

The Jin Shengtan Edition

The Jin Shengtan edition of *The Water Margin*, titled *The Fifth Book of Genius: Shi Nai'an's Water Margin* (*Diwu caizi shu Shi Nai'an Shuihu zhuan*), features extensive front matter before the text of the novel begins.[4] First, there are three prefaces by Jin. The first of these prefaces is a long discussion of who has the authority (*quan*) to "author" (*zuo*) texts.[5] It ascribes the sages (*shengren*) of antiquity with the moral authority and the knowledge to author texts, with the result being the Confucian classics. Confucius lacked the position of a sage but was compelled to put together the *Spring and Autumn Annals*; the preface says that though he was justified in doing so, his actions inspired others without proper authority to author texts. Because of this, it goes on, the authoritarian Qin Shihuang was justified in burning of books though blameworthy for extending the burning to the classics. The subsequent Han dynasty, the preface claims, was likewise blameworthy for seeking out and collecting books that had escaped the fires of the Qin—with the result that there were even more unauthorized books in circulation than there had been before. The preface bemoans the deleterious effects of these books on the governance and the custom of the land. It then proposes another type of book that is justified not by the sagely authority of its author but rather by the author's "genius" (*cai*). Genius is unique to a particular individual, yet all authors of genius are able to enter into a meditative trance, exhaust their breath until their faces appear like a corpse's, and write. The text names six authors of genius: the proto-Daoist thinker Zhuangzi, author of the eponymous text; Qu Yuan, the poet who composed the lament "Encountering Sorrow" (*Lisao*); the great historian Sima Qian, author of *Records of the Grand Historian*; the Tang-dynasty master poet Du Fu; Shi Nai'an, to whom the preface credits the authorship of *The Water Margin*; and Dong Jieyuan, author of *Record of the Western Chamber* (*Xixiang ji*). The preface then laments that those not possessed of genius nonetheless proceed to author books without taking adequate stock of their meager abilities. As a mere commoner, Jin says, he is unable to issue a ban on such unauthorized books; however, he hopes that his exemplary edition of *The Water Margin* will help to rid the world of their pernicious influence.

The second preface is considerably shorter than the first, at around a quarter of the length.[6] It appears to be a veiled critique of Li Zhuowu, who is not mentioned by name, and of the addition of the words "The Loyal and Righteous" to the title *Water Margin* as seen in the Li Zhuowu Rongyu tang edition. The preface argues that "loyalty" is "the consummate virtue of serving those above" (*shishang zhi shengjie*), and "righteousness" is "the great canon of serving those below" (*shixia zhi dajing*). The "water margin," meanwhile is literally positioned at the margins of society rather than its center. To place such fine moral qualities at the margins would imply that they are not present at the center, and that the relations between ruler and minister, father and son, have broken down in the state. Therefore, the second preface claims, whoever would append the words "Loyal and Righteous" to *The Water Margin's* title resents their ruler and their father. Shi Nai'an's purpose in writing *The Water Margin*, the preface continues, was to correct the bad precedent set by the band of outlaws evading execution by the Song authorities; the book was meant to be read (in the translation of Naifei Ding) as "prohibitory" (*jie*) rather than as "exhortational" (*quan2*).[7] Incorrect readings of the latter type will cause those who are already bandits to feel proud, and those who are not yet bandits to become bandits.

The third preface takes the form of a letter from Jin to his son.[8] In it, Jin describes how as a child he was bored with his studies of the Confucian Four Books. When he left his studies due to illness and began reading for his own enjoyment, he discovered the *Lotus Sutra*, Qu Yuan's "Encountering Sorrow," Sima Qian's *Records of the Grand Historian*, and an "ancient edition" (*guben*) of *The Water Margin*. He gained a special attachment to the latter, and credits the experience with teaching him to read widely. He laments that some fathers and elder brothers would not allow young boys to read such books. No literary work, he exclaims, bests *The Water Margin*, and no "Gentleman" who conducts Neo-Confucian "investigation of things" (*gewu junzi*) bests Shi Nai'an. For these reasons, he advises his son to follow the same path he did. It was through the investigation of things that Shi Nai'an was able to depict the one hundred and eight heroes of the novel as unique individuals. The entry point to investigating things, he continues, is loyalty and reciprocity (*zhong shu*). In a seeming contradiction with the previous preface, he claims here that loyalty appears naturally in all things, even dogs, rats, and bandits, due to karmic mutually dependent origination (*yinyuan shengfa*); this shared quality is then the basis of reciprocity. He then uses language from *On the Practice of the Mean* to build a causal chain: loyalty and reciprocity allow for the investigation of things; the investigation of things allows for the complete understanding of people's character (*jin ren zhi xing*), assists in sustenance (*zan huayu*), and forms a trinity with Heaven and Earth (*san Tiandi*). Shi Nai'an used loyalty, reciprocity, and mutually dependent origination to craft *The Water Margin* as literature and as the depiction of individual characters, the preface claims; for these reasons, Jin copied out the "ancient edition" of the novel by hand when he found it in the Flower Garland Hall (*Guanhua tang*) at age twelve. Thus, he explains, he uncovered his method for reading all books and finding their internal structures. He recommends that his son also learn this method.

This third preface is dated the fifteenth day of the second month of Chongzhen 14, or March 25, 1641, by the Western calendar. It is the only preface that bears a date.

The three prefaces are followed by brief outlines of relevant Song history in two parts, the "Song History Guidelines" (*Songshi gang*)" and the "Song History Details" (*Songshi mu*).[9] Each of these is followed by comments by the "Historian Minister" (*shichen*). The comments explain why it is said that the bandit Song Jiang was "put down" (*xiang*) rather than "executed" (*zhu*), why his captor, the official Zhang Shuye, is referred to as a "magistrate" (*zhizhou*), and what the implications are for granting amnesty to bandits.

After the discussion of Song history comes a list of items under the title "How to Read the Fifth Book of Genius" (*Du diwu caizi shu fa*).[10] This list has often been mined for insights into Jin's purportedly "formalist" textual criticism, or even for the building blocks of a late imperial Chinese theory of fiction. However, of the sixty-nine items listed, only fifteen are definitions of formal techniques that Jin supposedly finds in the author Shi Nai'an's work. The majority of the items in the list are concerned with evaluating the characters in the novel, ranking them from "highest high" (*shangshang*) to "lowest low" (*xiaxia*). These rankings are based on the characters' personalities and moral qualities as well as the literary skill with which they are depicted. In all, he evaluates thirty-three of the novel's one hundred and eight heroes. The most elaborate evaluations are reserved for the band's leader Song Jiang, who is ranked as "lowest low," and the unrestrained Li Kui, who is ranked as "highest high."

Finally, there is a short preface that Jin claims to have copied from an "ancient edition" (*guben*) held in the Guanhua tang hall, signed by none other than Shi Nai'an himself.[11] In the preface, the author describes a carefree life filled with friendship and the simple pleasures of conversation. He describes how he would pen *The Water Margin* in idle evenings, after his friends had left, with no ambitions in his mind. It is likely written by Jin himself and reads as a tongue-in-cheek inversion of the "subversive," politicized rage of the Li Zhuowu preface.

What is in most editions chapter 1 is, in the Jin edition, made into a prologue (*xiezi*), and subsequent chapter numbers are then renumbered accordingly. As mentioned above, the Jin edition ends with the triumphant gathering of the predestined number of heroes in their lair and Jin's rewritten dream conclusion in chapter 70; the capitulation of the band to the authorities and their subsequent battles on behalf of the Song are excised. In addition to this major excision, which later critics morbidly termed his "cutting off at the waist" (*yaozhan*) of *The Water Margin*, Jin also made any number of finer incisions into the text. He cut out the poems and lyrics found throughout the novel and altered the phrasings of its prose.

Perhaps even more audacious than his editing handiwork, however, was the paratextual character he played in the body of the text. It includes introductory comments to each chapter, which are frequently quite lengthy and only tangentially related to the story itself. It also includes frequent eyebrow comments in the upper register of the page, and interlinear comments printed in half-width characters interrupting the story. The commentary plays a very prominent role in the edition, much larger than those of predecessors such as Yu Xiangdou and Li Zhuowu.

"Flower Garland Hall," the Market, and the Canon of Genius

The Jin Shengtan edition is often referred to as the "Guanhua tang," or "Flower Garland Hall," edition, after the name found on its title page and in the center of its woodblocks. Though the name Guanhua tang is reminiscent of those of for-profit publishers, such as Yu Xiangdou's Shuangfeng tang or the Rongyu tang that printed the Li Zhuowu edition of *The Water Margin,* and is often mistaken for one, the name in fact does not refer to such a firm. There is some uncertainty about its origins: "Guanhua" was the monastic name of a friend of Jin Shengtan's, and there may be some connection. It was also apparently the name of Jin's own private library. There are no other known imprints bearing the "Guanhua tang" name other than the first edition of Jin's *Water Margin,* casting further doubt on the idea that it was the name of a commercial publisher. Roland Altenberger has even speculated that the Jin may have hired woodblock carvers to carve his *Water Margin* edition at home, making it a "private edition" (*sike*).[12]

The Guanhua tang name is symbolic of the ambiguous relationship between the Jin edition and the marketplace. It was less concerned with the "commercial" and "subversive" qualities that typified much of the fiction that appeared around the turn of the seventeenth century, when novels proliferated along with the beginnings of the commercial printing boom. The Jin edition was very concerned, however, with the concept of the "literary," and it redefined that quality in a new way. David Rolston has referred to Jin as being representative of a new, third stage of fiction commentary, following a first stage in the last decades of the sixteenth century, typified by Yu Xiangdou, and a second stage in the first decades of the seventeenth century, "when the market was flooded with bogus Li Zhi commentaries."[13] Naifei Ding, meanwhile, has characterized the shift between the second and third phases as being a transition from a discourse of authenticity in texts to one of authorization to write and transmit texts. The preface to the Rongyu tang Li Zhuowu edition, Ding writes, is written from the perspective of a "loyal yet critical reader" of *The Water Margin* "within the physical and geopolitical empire of the Ming in a moment of internal crisis."[14] She also characterizes that preface as being "exhortational" and driven by political rage.[15] By contrast, Ding characterizes the three prefaces in the Jin Shengtan edition as being concerned not with the geopolitical Ming dynasty but a "textual empire" consisting of vernacular texts that are worthy of transmission due to "corrective readings and rewritings (reprintings)."[16] That is, Jin's edition portrays itself through its prefaces as an attempt to stem the tide of (commercially printed) books that have no right to be written or transmitted. This stance is at once counter to the market and enabled by it, a position that Ding attributes to Jin's particular circumstances as a commoner in Chongzhen-era (1627–44) Suzhou, a time and place where the commercial book market had already reached maturity.[17]

In some ways, Jin's conception of a flood of "unauthorized," commercially published books against which his own edition of *The Water Margin* would have to contend is reminiscent of what Janice Radway has called "the circulating book."[18] In a previous chapter, we have used Radway's work to discuss the targeted publishing activity of Guo Xun, Marquis of Wuding, which was intended to create cultural capital. In contrast with those early fine editions, the circulating book was cheaply made and meant for leisure reading or for accomplishing a particular task rather than becoming an heirloom or part of a permanent collection. It was a commodity, and when demand outstripped the amount of texts available to print, a new type of writer, the "hack," arose to fill it. Hacks could write "very quickly, regularly, and according to the specifications of another."[19] Hacks, therefore, did not maintain authorial presences of their own; rather, they often worked under corporate names supplied by publishers for particular series about recurring characters. Such writers and their works did not, and often still do not, receive literary respect.

Though Radway was describing eighteenth-century American book culture and the eventual rise of the commercial phenomenon of the Book of the Month Club, the parallels with late-Ming China are again striking and clear. The commercial publisher Xiong Damu, as we have seen, pieced together "new" works of historical fiction in the hopes of duplicating the success of *The Water Margin* and *Romance of the Three Kingdoms*. Yu Xiangdou reshaped texts with the desires of his potential readers in mind. "Li Zhuowu" as the name of a paratextual character was adopted by multiple writers and, capitalizing on the notoriety of the empirical Li Zhi, indicated something of a certain "brand" of commentary.

The parallels are less immediately clear, however, for what might stand in opposition to the "circulating book" of the late Ming commercial printing boom. Radway juxtaposes this commodified "circulating book" against the "literary book," which "was conceived of as the emanation of an author, as serious, as a classic, and as a permanent and precious possession."[20] Unlike the utilitarian and ephemeral circulating book, it was to be appreciated for the intrinsic value of its text and its material form. In the case of the late Ming, one might think that the equivalent to Radway's "literary book" would be the Confucian classics that were the basis of the examination system and thus the focus of serious scholarly attention. Or, such books might be fine editions of classic literature such as Tang poetry, printed from Song-era woodblocks. However, the paratextual Jin Shengtan who emanates from the prefaces includes a canon of his own creation into which *The Water Margin* is to enter. These are his six "Books of Genius," which are mentioned in Jin's first preface and discussed above.

This "Books for Genius" program is notable for the heterogeneous nature of the texts included. What brings them together is not their generic features but the assumption of "genius" on the part of their (assumed) authors. Those authors include very familiar figures as well as the more shadowy—and more recent—Shi Nai'an and Dong Jieyuan. In those latter cases, the lack of knowledge about these figures provides Jin Shengtan the opportunity to interpret and even craft them at will within his prefaces and commentaries.

Throughout the Jin *Water Margin* commentary, he refers to fiction or "unofficial history" (*baishi* or *baiguan*) several times. The opening comment for chapter 1, for example, plays on the entrance of the character Shi Jin (literally, "history enters") to claim that "unofficial history" is still a type of history; it records the opinions of the people when the Way is not present in the world and official history does not reflect those opinions.[21] In the comment for chapter 2, Jin says that the vigorous depiction of the unrestrained Lu Da will make readers feel as if they have not fully lived their lives; quoting Confucius's famed statement from the *Analects* that the *Classic of Poetry* (*Shijing*) can "stimulate" (*xing*), Jin says, "I say the same of unofficial history" (*wu yu baiguan yi yun yi*).[22] He states several times that unofficial history is important and can tackle weighty issues just as the classics do (see comments for chapters 13, 18, and 41). He also states several times that unofficial history reprimands and exhorts its readers (chapters 16 and 60), and that it is written with a similar "praise-and-blame" methodology as the classic *Spring and Autumn Annals* (chapter 35). Unofficial history requires a skillful reader (chapters 5 and 14), and is written by a skillful author (chapters 5, 49, and 59). However, these statements never form a cohesive defense of a genre as a whole; they are, rather, often made in tandem with statements about the skill of this particular author, Shi Nai'an (chapter 5, 21, 51, and 59). To Jin, Shi Nai'an was an author who possessed genius, a quality that transcends genre. Meanwhile, Jin disparages two of the most beloved works of fiction, *Journey to the West* and *Romance of the Three Kingdoms*. In the "How to Read" list, he complains that the former work is "too fantastic" and disjointed "like setting off fireworks on New Year's Eve."[23] The latter is too constrained by the sheer number of characters and events of its historical basis; the fiction ends up "like an official sending a message through his attendant."[24] For Jin, it seems that it is *The Water Margin* alone that fulfills the potential of the "unofficial history."

Evaluating Characters

Though the Jin Shengtan edition of *The Water Margin* appears radically different from those that came before it, with its major cuts and its elaborate paratextual materials, it was not completely unprecedented. It bears some parallels with editions of the novel from both before and after the imperial ancestral temple fire. As with the Wuding and Censorate editions, it is situated within a set of works that transcend any single generic classification or literary register. Guo Xun, the Marquis of Wuding, used publishing to bolster his position within elite society, and the Censorate appears to have targeted similar—if not the very same—audiences for its publications. Their publishing output freely mixed *The Water Margin* and *Romance of the Three Kingdoms* with Tang poetry anthologies, *Records of the Grand Historian*, and many other books of widely varying genres. Jin's projected "Six Books of Genius" commentary set was never completed—only *The Water Margin* and *Record of the Western Chamber* commentaries were published in Jin's lifetime—but he similarly conceptualized *The Water Margin* as part of a canon of his own creation. Comparison between Jin and the early reader of *The Water Margin* Li Kaixian is also instructive; both Li and Jin saw *The Water Margin* as a carefully constructed literary work, and both used *Records of the Grand Historian* as a point of comparison. Additionally, both Li and Jin used *The Water Margin* as a starting point for their own writing, albeit in very different ways: Li was inspired by the novel to write his drama *Record of the Precious Sword*, while Jin was inspired by it to write his extended commentary. Both the drama and the commentary are attempts to recast or control the meaning of the "parent" novel.

Publishers of the turn-of-the-century commercial printing boom such as Yu Xiangdou, meanwhile, would seem to be the primary target of the scorn in Jin Shengtan's *Water Margin* prefaces. These are the figures who produced an unprecedented number of the "unauthorized" books that Jin sees fit to be put to the torch. Yet, at the same time, to a certain extent Jin could be said to be following in Yu's footsteps. The Yu edition features evaluations of characters in the upper register of nearly every page. The commentary in the Jin edition is not so confined on the page and tends to go on at much greater length, but it shares with the Yu edition a strong interest in the characters of the novel and their values. As for the Li Zhuowu editions, as mentioned above, Jin criticized their appending of the words "Loyal and Righteous" to the title of a novel about outlaws at the literal margins of society. Yet at the same time, the Li Zhuowu editions are an obvious influence on Jin as well. As in the Li Zhuowu preface, the Jin prefaces look beyond the mimetic level of the fictional characters in their Song-dynasty setting and justify the novel as a work of written expression. Like the Li Zhuowu commentary, the Jin commentary also deliberately prods complacent readers into more careful reading through provocative and even outrageous statements.

Though Jin is frequently portrayed as a champion or savior of vernacular fiction who elevated the genre to the level of the classics, we have seen how *The Water Margin* had already drawn comparison to classics for over a century by the time of the Jin edition's appearance. Among elites such as Li Kaixian and for-profit publishers like Yu Xiangdou alike, favorable comparisons with *Records of the Grand Historian* and even the *Spring and Autumn Annals* were common. Granted, some such comparisons were undoubtedly made for commercial reasons or in order to provoke readers, but this is true in the case of Jin Shengtan as well. However, all of these types of claims, no matter from elite or commercial entities, are woven within larger discourses that point toward something other than mere bad faith.

For Jin, as we have seen in the prefaces discussed above, the literariness of *The Water Margin* stems from the genius of its purported author, Shi Nai'an. Jin has established genius as a quality that transcends time and genre, and which invests writers with the authority to write despite their position as commoners rather than sages. Jin has also insisted that *The Water Margin* was not written out of anger but rather leisurely contemplation; it was meant to warn rather than incite the reader. The genius of the author's literary skill allowed him to craft fine depictions of the novel's characters, and those fine depictions in turn allowed for the characters' moral qualities to make themselves clear. Throughout his commentary, Jin keeps these aspects intertwined; for him, writing of genius is not an end in itself.

In order to condemn the banditry of the novel without condemning it as a whole, Jin points to Song Jiang as a hypocrite and an untrustworthy schemer. By scapegoating Song Jiang, Jin is then free to praise positive qualities of other members of the outlaw band. In the aforementioned prefatorial "How to Read" list, several characters rank as "highest high" in contrast to Song Jiang's "lowest low"; however, none receives as much attention in the commentary as Li Kui. To Jin, Li Kui is the polar opposite of Song Jiang, the embodiment of spontaneous integrity to Song Jiang's hypocrisy. The literary genius of the author, Jin claims, allowed for such a fine depiction.

Tigers, Filial Piety, and the Doubling of Li Kui

Were the Jin commentary only concerned with literary features, it would have much material in chapter 42, a chapter featuring recurring figures and themes that suggest intentional thematic and structural design (figure 5.1).[25] In the chapter, the "Black Whirlwind" Li Kui decides that he must return home, fetch his mother, and bring her back to the bandits' lair where he resides. The previous chapter of the novel had depicted Song Jiang, the band's leader, unsuccessfully attempting to return home for his father and Gongsun Sheng going off for his mother. These acts had stirred filial emotions in Li Kui, who despite his rough exterior always wears his heart on his sleeve.

Knowing that Li Kui is liable to fly into a rage at the slightest provocation, Song Jiang sets conditions before agreeing to let Li Kui depart. He must promise to go straight to his mother's home and back. He must avoid drinking alcohol for the entire journey. And, he must leave his trademark twin battle axes behind. But almost immediately, Li Kui finds trouble when he is stopped by a highwayman who claims to be none other than Li Kui. The true Li Kui reveals his identity to his doppelgänger, who knows he is no match and can do nothing but apologize and beg for his life. He introduces himself as Li Gui, and says that killing him would be killing two people since he is responsible for caring for his aging mother. Li Kui is moved by what he takes to be a fellow filial son and lets him go, even providing his doppelgänger with some silver to use in starting a reputable business. The two then go on their separate ways.

Eventually, Li Kui becomes hungry and stops at a nearby house to ask for food. The woman living there says she has no meat or alcohol to provide but offers to cook some rice for him. As he waits, he overhears the woman's husband return through the back door. It ends up that it is his doppelgänger, Li Gui. Li Kui overhears Li Gui tell his wife of the previous encounter, and how he invented a story about caring for his elderly mother to save himself from imminent danger. Enraged, Li Kui kills Li Gui as the wife runs away. His bloodlust sated, Li turns to the rice that has been prepared and wishes he had some meat to accompany it. He then remembers the body of Li Gui and, in a grotesque parody of stories of filial children offering their flesh to their sick or starving parents, Li Kui slices two pieces from Li Gui's leg and cooks and eats them.

Li Kui makes it to his mother's house, where he discovers she's gone blind by crying over him. He fetches her and, on the journey back to the

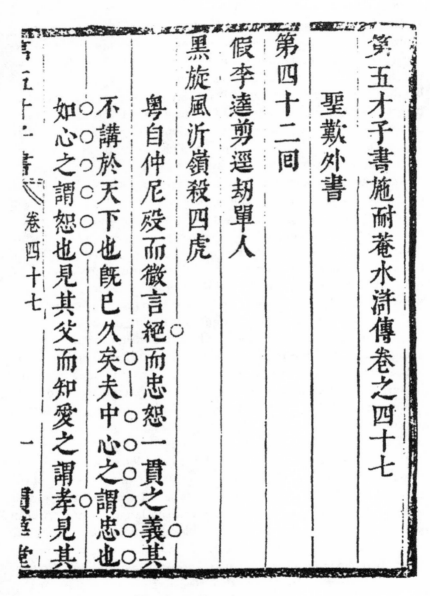

FIGURE 5.1. Jin Shengtan edition, chapter 42 opening.
Source: Reprinted from *Diwu caizi shu Shi Nai'an Shuihu zhuan*, 5.1.

bandits' lair, as they climb the steep Yiling Heights pass, she tells him she is thirsty. He sets her down and goes in search of water. When he returns, his mother is nowhere to be found; only blood tracks are to be seen. He follows the tracks to the mouth of a cave, where he sees two tiger cubs playing with a severed human leg. He kills one and follows the other into the cave, where the tiger mother awaits. He kills the other cub and begins to battle the mother. When the mother attempts to swipe at him with her tail, he thrusts his knife into her anus and slices her through to her stomach, killing her. The male tiger returns and Li Kui kills it as well.

Afterward, locals discover that Li Kui has rid their area of these dreaded "great pests" and wish to reward him. He hides his identity, saying his name is "Gutsy Zhang." The wife of Li Gui, however, recognizes him and reports him to the authorities as her husband's killer. The authorities drug his drink during a celebration and subdue him. The governor orders for him to be brought to the county seat. Li Kui's bandit brothers catch word of this, and devise a plan to intercept the procession. They prepare drugged food and drink to offer the guards escorting Li Kui. The plan works, and as the procession is held up, Li Kui escapes his bonds. He goes on a murderous rampage, first killing his captors and Li Gui's wife and then parties of hunters and soldiers.

Chapter 42 is a dense web of irony and self-parody. Themes of filial piety and personal identity recur throughout. The hero, filled with love for his mother, finds himself slaughtering a mother tiger and its cubs. He comes across his doppelgänger and ends up feasting on his leg, only to end up seeing a tiger feasting on his mother's leg. Enraged by a man using his name, he ends up using a hastily invented alias himself. This web of irony extends beyond the chapter, as well, enmeshing it with events from elsewhere in the novel. Li Kui, after all, is not the most renowned tiger killer of *The Water Margin*; Wu Song takes that honor. Li Kui's tiger killing is a raucous, ironic undercutting of Wu Song's: Wu Song's club has broken and he faces down the tiger head-on, beating it to death with his fists. Li Kui, by contrast, manages to keep his weapon—a knife—and thrusts it into the tiger's anus. Wu Song is feted for his deed; Li Kui gives a false name to avoid the attention of the authorities. The story appears to be purposely woven into the structure of the novel as an ironic inversion, as well: The two stories appear exactly twenty chapters apart, and as Andrew Plaks and others have argued, the ten-chapter "decade" is one of the structural hallmarks of the "masterworks" of the

Ming novel.[26] The two similar tiger-killing stories occur two "decades" apart, in what could be interpreted as conscious design.

Past Ironies

The multiple parallels and ironies of chapter 42 did not escape the eye of previous commentators. The Rongyu tang Li Zhuowu commentary, for instance, compares Li Kui's filial piety not only to that of Song Jiang but that of Gongsun Sheng as well: Song Jiang's retrieval of his father, it says, had "a bit of a pedantic air" (*youxie daoxue qiwei*) and was calculating, while Gongsun Sheng's thoughts of his mother were a "complete fraud" (*yituan jianzha*).[27] Only Li Kui's thoughts, it concludes, were naturally filial and focused on his mother's happiness. At the end of the chapter, the Rongyu tang Li Zhuowu also remarks on Li Kui and his doppelgänger: "With a false Li Kui, never again is there Li Kui's falsehood" (*zhiyou jia Li Kui, zai wu Li Kui jia*).[28] The remark continues on to praise Li Kui's bravery in killing the four tigers.

Another "Li Zhuowu" commentary edition—the one published by Yuan Wuyai in 1614—goes a step further. It uses verse to make frequently ironic references to the parallels between Li Kui, his double, and the tigers. When Li Kui believes Li Gui's story about having a mother to care for and consequently lets him go, a poem interjects:

> Li Kui greets his mother but encounters harm;
> When did Li Gui ever care for his mom?
> But it is apparent that of instances of loyalty and filiality in the world
> Actions as well as words are worth keeping tabs on.[29]

At the point in the story when Li Kui finds the tiger gnawing on his mother's leg, another poem draws an ironic parallel to Li Kui's earlier consumption of Li Gui's leg:

> The False Black Whirlwind [i.e. Li Gui] really played pranks;
> In life, a treacherous heart; in death a roasted shank.
> Who was to know a mother's leg would also come to harm?
> Hungry tigers, hungry men—for food, all will hanker![30]

Finally, another poem points out the irony in the fact that Li Kui, who is himself the victim of identity theft at the hands of Li Gui, gives the false name "Gutsy Zhang" later in the chapter:

> People speak only of the false Li Kui;
> Of Li Kui's falsehood it is never spoken.

How a Li assumed the name Zhang,[31]
Who's false and who's true? They're all joking![32]

Though the Yuan Wuyai edition of *The Water Margin* is frequently assumed to be the basis for Jin's own, Jin's edition excises all of these poems.

Jin Shengtan's Li Kui, Neo-Confucian Outlaw

Jin Shengtan gained a posthumous reputation in the twentieth century as a "formalist" critic who elevated the status of fiction. However, in the opening comment to chapter 42, Jin forgoes the many opportunities to elucidate the parallels between Li Kui and Li Gui, the multiple slayings of tigers, or the unfortunate demises of mothers that predecessor editions of *The Water Margin* exploited in their commentaries or verse. Instead, he uses the tale of Li Kui's journey home and subsequent encounter with his doppelgänger as an occasion for an extended discussion of self-cultivation and the virtues of spontaneity and authenticity, the core of which is based on *The Highest Order of Cultivation* (*Daxue*) and *On the Practice of the Mean* (*Zhongyong*). The comment weaves together several of the strands of thought that are seen in the prefatorial materials. It seems wildly tangential to the narrative of the novel itself, but it is tied to it in two ways. First, Jin claims that the true message of Confucianism has long been lost and that, in the current age, vernacular novels or "unofficial history" might carry it. Second, he claims that the characters in the novel embody the virtues he outlines, by both positive and negative example. It is in this second aspect that Jin touches on literary technique; however, it is important to him not merely for its own sake but because it allows the characters to be more clearly defined and therefore more clearly represent the moral values that they embody.

The evaluation of characters and the values they represent—the "character of characters"—is one of the major concerns of Jin's paratextual materials. It features most prominently in the "How to Read" list at the beginning of the edition. Although the "How to Read" list has been mined for clues toward a late imperial Chinese theory of fiction, only fifteen of the sixty-nine items in the list are definitions of formal techniques that Jin claims the purported author, Shi Nai'an, used in the work. Furthermore, many of those fifteen items are themselves mutually contradictory to the point that one might wonder if Jin had tongue firmly in cheek while listing them: For example, the "method of extreme narrative frugality" (*ji sheng fa*) is praiseworthy, as is its opposite, the "method of extreme avoidance of narrative frugality" (*ji busheng fa*).[33]

The remaining items on the "How to Read" list consists of the evaluation of characters in the novel. Jin ranks thirty-three of the bandit heroes based on their personalities and moral qualities as well as the literary skill by which they are depicted. Lu Da is example of a character rated by his character. He rates as "highest high" because "he is shown to have an honest heart and an imposing physique."[34] The comparatively minor character Shi Jin, on the other hand, is rated according to the literary quality of his part of the tale: Jin ranks him as "middle high" "because the second part of his story is not well-done."[35]

Li Kui's evaluation as "highest high" rank is due to his character as well as his literary depiction. Jin sees Li Kui's character as being one of utter guilelessness and simplicity, and remarks that Li Kui would not be impressed by any of the other outlaws of Mount Liang. Jin goes so far as to apply Mencius's definition of a "great man" (*da zhangfu*) to Li Kui: "He cannot be led into excesses when wealthy and honored or deflected from his purpose when poor and obscure, nor can he be made to bow before superior force."[36] Jin then describes the literary skill with which Li Kui is depicted, emphasizing that these two factors are related. He states that outstanding writing must have a reason or motive (*yuangu*) behind it, and such a motive is what compels an author to write. Without one, any prose an author would be able to produce would be dull and tasteless. The skillfully depicted guilelessness of Li Kui, it is implied, is a result of the author's motivation to write of such a quality.

According to Jin, values lead to motives, and motives lead to good writing. Li Kui's character is depicted so well because of the importance of guilelessness. To draw that quality in finer detail, Jin claims, the author of *The Water Margin* has placed Li Kui into contrast with Song Jiang. As seen in a previous chapter of this book, previous commentators from Yu Xiangdou to Li Zhuowu took the character of Song Jiang at face value, as a depiction of righteous anger at a corrupt age. Jin Shengtan, on the other hand, rates him here as a "lowest low" character, the only one to be ranked as such other than the minor character Shi Qian, a petty thief.[37] Jin casts Song Jiang in opposition to Li Kui; whereas Li Kui is praised for his guilelessness, Song Jiang is condemned as one who manipulates the other outlaws without their knowledge. Jin condemns Song Jiang at the very beginning of the "How to Read" list, remarking that the novel's author had contempt for the character and depicted him as so lowly that even dogs and swine would not eat him. Jin claims that the author's contempt stemmed from the fact that

Song Jiang came to be the head of the band of outlaws; by condemning the head, the other members of the band are blameless.[38] Jin returns to Song Jiang while discussing Li Kui, claiming that episodes featuring Li Kui tend to follow ones featuring Song Jiang in order to highlight this contrast between their characters.[39]

With his emphasis on the quality of guilelessness over that of cunning, as embodied by the character Li Kui over the character Song Jiang, Jin Shengtan deemphasizes many of the literary parallels in chapter 42 in his introductory comment. His main point of comparison for Li Kui is not Wu Song, the most famous of tiger killers in the novel, or Li Gui, his doppelgänger, but Song Jiang. That is to say, for Jin, pairing by character wins out over the pairing by formal features of the text.

Jin's introductory comment to chapter 42 itself is some two thousand characters in length.[40] The majority of the comment is a discussion of values couched in the language of the classics; it is only in the final quarter of its text that Jin turns to Li Kui, positing him as the incarnation of the values he has discussed and drawing the contrast between him and Song Jiang. It is worth examining the comment at length, both for its discussion of values and for the rhetorical practices by which it does so. It begins:

> Much time has passed since Confucius left this world and the art of "subtle phrasing" was extinguished, and the world no longer takes pains to understand the meaning of the single thread of loyalty (*zhong*) and empathy (*shu*) that ran through his teachings.

These opening words echo Ban Gu's "Treatise on Arts and Letters" (*Yiwen zhi*) from the official history of the Han about the confusion over the values in the wake of the death of Confucius. They then allude to *Analects* 4:15, in which Master Zeng defines loyalty and empathy as the "single thread" running through all of Confucius's teachings. Jin's comment then continues to define these two qualities by breaking down the constituent parts of those two characters. The character for loyalty is comprised of the element for "center" (*zhong2*) above that for "mind" (*xin*), the comment reminds us, so "loyalty" is the quality of having a centered or balanced mind. That for empathy, meanwhile, is comprised of the element for "similar" or "like" (*ru*) above "mind," so "empathy" is being of like mind.

It is notable that the comment frames its discussion in terms of loyalty and empathy, the "single thread" that runs through Confucian teachings, rather than loyalty and righteousness, as usually found in discourse around *The Water Margin* and its bandit protagonists. The preface of the earlier Yu Xiangdou edition, it will be recalled, framed discussion of the bandits in terms of the latter pair; Yu even provided similar paronomastic glosses when he defined those qualities as exhausting one's abilities in fulfilling one's duties to the nation and the people. Li Zhuowu's preface also discussed the bandits as the embodiments of those qualities, as Jin's prefaces vehemently object. Furthermore, Jin's definition of loyalty, as we will see, tends more toward other nuances of the term; it might be better understood as remaining true not to a person but to an ideal or truth. This sense of the word *zhong* might even be translated as "fidelity," though for the sake of consistency I will continue to use "loyalty" here.

In the next passage, Jin describes how the "centered mind" of loyalty spontaneously gives rise to two other qualities, "filiality" (*xiao*) and "respect" (*jing2*) at the sight of one's father and ruler, respectively. No conscious effort needs to be made to feel these. To emphasize this point about spontaneous feelings, he crafts a sentence from fragments of *The Highest Order of Cultivation* and *On the Practice of the Mean*:[41]

> "Just as spontaneously as one feels distaste for a distasteful smell, or takes delight in a delightful sight,"[42] one obtains "a state of centered balance with no striving."[43] "This is what is meant by the expression 'being at ease with oneself.' "[44]

One who acts spontaneously by maintaining loyalty, he continues, can therefore feel all emotions naturally without the need to inhibit them. One need not be a sage to feel emotions; common people, newborn babies, and even birds and insects can feel them. This he defines as the Way, and again employs a quotation from *On the Practice of the Mean* to further explain the concept: "What we take to be 'the Way' does not admit the slightest separation therefrom, even for an instant."[45]

He then glosses this sentence in terms of the Confucian concept of "paying heed to one's individual core" (*shendu*), found in both the *Highest Order of Cultivation* and *On the Practice of the Mean*. "The Way," he declares, is "one's individual core" (*du*), and "not admitting the slightest separation even for an instant" is "paying heed" (*shen*). He develops this concept of unmediated spontaneity with a pastiche of several more phrases from these two classics, including most notably "coming to rest in the fullest attainment of the good" (*zhiyu zhishan*) from *The Highest Order of Cultivation*. For Jin, this "coming to rest" is critical.

After a discussion on the meaning of "coming to rest," Jin arrives at an explanation of what can be achieved through reaching this state. One can, as *The Highest Order of Cultivation* says, "shine forth one's bright virtue" (*ming mingde*). Doing so then enables one to move through two different chains of conditions drawn from the first two passages of *The Highest Order of Cultivation* the allow one to achieve particular goals. The first chain begins with knowing the point of rest (*zhizhi*) and proceeds through reaching a state of unwavering stability (*ding*), attaining quietude (*jing*), achieving inner calm (*an*), exercising the capacity to deliberate clearly (*lü*), and finally, achieving moral attainment (*de*). The second chain begins with the investigation of things (*gewu*), expanding one's range of comprehension (*zhizhi2*), bringing one's consciousness to a state of wholeness (*yicheng*), setting straight one's faculties (*xinzheng*), cultivating one's character (*shenxiu*), putting one's family into proper balance (*jiaqi*), bringing one's kingdom into a state of orderly rule (*guozhi*), and finally allowing the world to enjoy peace (*tianxia taiping*). Jin combines these two chains of conditions into one: after one comes to rest in the fullest attainment of the good, shines forth one's bright virtue, and eliminates misunderstandings, one can "reach a state of unwavering stability; one expands one's range of comprehension thus one's innermost consciousness can be brought to a state of wholeness," and so on until one achieves moral attainment and the world enjoys peace. Jin insists that this chain, from its beginnings in understanding to its ultimate end in bringing peace to the world, leaves nothing out.

Finally, this discussion comes back around to the paronomastic gloss on the character for loyalty. This time, however, the elements of the character—"center" and "mind"—are redefined with quotations from *On the Practice of the Mean*:

> Now, the word "loyalty" means a centered heart. When "joy, wrath, grief, and delight have yet to emerge,"[46] this is called "centered." When they emerge and are manifested as "joy, wrath, grief, and delight in balance and due proportion,"[47] this is called "mind." The phenomena that are of themselves authentic internally and manifested externally as the joy, wrath, grief, and delight that command one's self are called "loyalty."

"Loyalty" is now fully redefined as being true to one's authentic emotions rather than any external factor; Jin then states that to feel authentic emotions and express them outwardly in an unmediated way is to "extend to all things the correct conceptual grid" (*gewu*).[48] Doing so, it follows, will lead to peace in the world. Jin then ends this long intervention into the concept of "loyalty" by returning to the subject of the lost art of "subtle phrasing" after the death of Confucius. No one, he opines, has expounded on loyalty and empathy for three thousand years; he claims he would like to do so himself but fears that that would be immodest. Instead, he claims he finds that "unofficial histories" will occasionally reach such a level of discourse.

It is only now, after this long discussion of loyalty and empathy in the world after Confucius, that Jin finally turns to the characters of *The Water Margin*. Loyalty and empathy go hand in hand, and they are both exemplified by the cannibalistic outlaw Li Kui. Li Kui is spontaneous and unmediated, and is thus an embodiment of the values of loyalty and empathy as defined through quotations from the canonical *On the Practice of the Mean* and *The Highest Order of Cultivation*. Jin then returns to the theme of Li Kui and Song Jiang as polar opposites that he has already laid out in the "How to Read" list at the beginning of the edition. He makes a list of twelve contrasts between the "evil" Song Jiang and the "good" Li Kui—Song Jiang went to retrieve his father and met a goddess, while Li Kui went to retrieve his mother and met a "demon" (*gui*), and so on. He refers to these contrasts as "couplets" (*lian*), as if they were rhyming lines, and praises each of them. Only in the final lines of the comment, after the "couplets," does Jin mention the similarity between Li Kui's killing of tigers and that of Wu Song twenty chapters earlier. Jin remarks on the differences between them rather than the similarities, and notes that these are the ultimate height of skillful writing.

Conclusion: Replaced by Punctuation?

Jin's edition of *The Water Margin* remained widely influential throughout the Qing dynasty. His work on the novel inspired others to pen similar commentaries that also vied with their parent novels for their readers' attention: just as Jin's edition became the most prominent version of *The Water Margin*, so did Mao Zonggang's commentary edition of *Romance of the Three Kingdoms* and Zhang Zhupo's of *Jin Ping Mei*.[49] Jin's commentary also directly influenced later writers of fiction, most notably Chen Chen's sequel to *The Water Margin* and the "autocommentary" appended to it by the author himself.[50] Jin's influence spread to Edo Japan as well, where his *Water Margin* commentary inspired Kyokutei Bakin (1767-1848) and others.[51] However, the Jin

Shengtan *Water Margin* edition fell from prominence in the early twentieth century. In 1921, the Oriental Book Company of Shanghai printed a new edition of *The Water Margin* that purported to be the first such "old" text to be printed in typeset characters, with modern punctuation. It was to be the inaugural publication of a new series of modernized editions of Ming and Qing fiction, and it featured a preface by Hu Shih heralding its arrival.[52]

In his preface, Hu Shih praised the editors for their decision to excise Jin Shengtan's commentary. With the advent of modern typesetting and punctuation, Hu announced, readers could parse the text of the novel on their own. They no longer needed Jin's markings to discern where sentences ended, and they would be able to tell when sections concluded by paragraph breaks. Furthermore, Hu claimed, Jin's frequent comments detracted from the reading experience. Readers no longer needed such an intermediary; Jin Shengtan's commentary was considered obsolete.

Hu did offer limited praise for Jin, however. Jin, he wrote, was an "eccentric talent" who was ahead of his time in pronouncing that *The Water Margin* was on the same literary level as classical texts such as *Records of the Grand Historian* or *Intrigues of the Warring States* (*Zhanguo ce*). To do so in the seventeenth century, according to Hu, took a rare sort of bravery and vision. However, in Hu's estimation, Jin was ultimately a man of his times, affected adversely by the Confucian pedantry and eight-legged essay form of the day. Hu blamed such influences for giving Jin's criticism a mechanical, unthinking air, leading Jin to count the usage of particular words or to list off the techniques supposedly used by the author.

The other major fault that Hu found in Jin's work extended beyond Jin's particular era—the purported inability of Chinese to escape from *Spring and Autumn Annals*-style hermeneutics of traditional historiography. Traditional scholars combed the *Spring and Autumn Annals* for the "praise and blame" judgments encoded by Confucius in the phrasing of its text, and Jin applied such methods to *The Water Margin*. Echoing Jin's own wording to the opening of the chapter 42 comment, which itself echoed the "Treatise on Arts and Letters" of the *Book of the Han*, Hu criticized Jin for seeking the "subtle phrasings and great meanings" (*weiyan dayi*) of the *Spring and Autumn Annals* in *The Water Margin*. This approach, according to Hu, led Jin to make absurd and far-fetched remarks; for an example of such remarks, Hu pointed to Jin's treatment of Song Jiang throughout the novel.

Jin Shengtan could not be completely replaced by punctuation and paragraph breaks, however. As his chapter 42 commentary shows, Jin was interested in much more than championing the literary worth of "vernacular" writing. He was also interested in its moral worth and its ability to express values. Rather than courageously operating in opposition to the elite sphere and its classical texts, he was engaging the same moral concerns as they were. Yet he was doing so while remaining free of the elite power structure. Jin did not hold office, and his *Water Margin* was printed commercially, not officially. Unmoored from the official orthodoxy, *The Water Margin* was a space in which Jin was free to discuss cultivation on his own terms, even when those terms were lodged in the novel's images of banditry, cannibalism, and frenzied violence. This space was opened by figures like Yu Xiangdou and developed by the literary name Li Zhuowu. Jin expanded the space further, making it allow for elaborate discussion of weighty matters.

Using *The Water Margin* as a rhetorical space to comment on self-cultivation might seem so outré that one wonders whether Jin was sincere in his message, or if he was merely trying to provoke or shock his readers with outrageous comments. Here, comparison with Li Zhuowu once again proves instructive. In her study of Li, Rivi Handler-Spitz demonstrates the contradictions to be found in his writing. On the one hand, Li lamented what he saw as a latter-day slippage of meaning in language. Yet on the other hand, Li himself employed any manner of ironic, dissembling language in his own writing.[53] This was not, Handler-Spitz argues, merely evidence of imprecise thinking on Li's part. Rather, it was a deliberate strategy employed to shock readers into interpreting texts—all texts, including his own—for themselves without recourse to external authorities. Borrowing from Barbara C. Bowen's study of Rabelais and Montaigne, she terms this strategy "bluff." Bowen defines this term not in its conventional sense or that used in betting, but to mean "the act of disconcerting," the aim of which "is to make us stop and think, either about the subject under discussion or about the literary techniques being used."[54]

Is Jin also "bluffing"? Much discussion of Jin's rhetorical strategy has centered around his creation of the heretofore largely ignored authorial figure of Shi Nai'an. Jin, as Martin Huang and others have argued, appropriated the figure of Shi Nai'an, using it as a source of authority over the text in a way that had not been seen before. Jin's rhetorical move, this argument goes, created a cover from behind which Jin could operate for his own purposes. Martin Huang, for example, has written of the seemingly paradoxical role Jin played in "authorizing" *The Water Margin* at the same time he privileged his own reading of it. Jin, Huang argues, was positioning himself as one who uniquely "knew the tone" (*zhiyin*) of Shi Nai'an and was thus able to speak of its meaning.[55] Huang argues that Jin challenged the author's control of a text, transferring it not as one might expect to the reader but instead to the commentator, "who became the ultimate agent of the author or the 'authorized' reader."[56] Similarly, Roland Altenburger has argued that Jin's "argumentation was in the exclusive service of vindicating the shifting of textual authority from any original or primary author of the past to the secondary author of the present, that is, to the ingenious author as whom he considered himself."[57]

The primary site for this move is the preface signed "Shi Nai'an" but obviously written by Jin himself. In it, Shi Nai'an presents himself as a carefree recluse writing *The Water Margin* in idle hours, drawn to the material because of its potential for expression. This is an obvious contrast with the image of the author found in Li Zhuowu's preface to *The Water Margin*, which states that the authors were men of the Yuan dynasty still full of resentment at the humiliating weakness of the Song. They channeled their anger, Li stated, into the writing of *The Water Margin* just as previous historical figures had. Writing without anger, Li declared, would be like moaning without being ill—one could do it, but what would be the point?

If Jin is "bluffing," perhaps he is doing so in the more conventional sense of the word—pretending that he has unique access to the mind of the author, even as his tongue remains in his cheek.

The interaction of Jin Shengtan and the other commentators with the text of *The Water Margin* and with each other again challenges the definition of what a single "work" is in this context, and how the "reception" of that work might be understood. Reception theory, as mentioned in the introduction of this book, imagines a new work of literature appearing on a continuum of previous works—a "horizon of expectations"—answering formal and moral questions posed by its predecessors. Readers have knowingly or unknowingly been conditioned by those very same predecessors and read the new work from that same perspective. In the case of *The Water Margin*, is there an essential version, free of commentary, that could be extracted from the Jin edition by the Oriental Book Company? Does Jin's *Water Margin* edition represent a single "work"—that is, a variant of that previously existing novel? Or does the variant of the novel that it contains represent one work, and Jin's commentary and other paratextual materials another separate, albeit intertwined, work? The same questions could be applied to the preceding editions such as those purportedly by Li Zhuowu or Yu Xiangdou, to which Jin was at least partially responding. However, no matter how one chooses to answer those questions, it is clear that the continuum on which editions of the novel appear includes other readings of the very same novel, as well as iterations of the novel itself. The reception of *The Water Margin* resembles not so much a "horizon" but a hall of mirrors.

Into that hall of mirrors, Jin Shengtan introduced the Neo-Confucian texts *The Highest Order of Cultivation* and *On the Practice of the Mean*. This can be seen in the terms of reception theory as the "social function" of literature; this hall of mirrors became a site where not only the "formal" problems of the nascent vernacular novel genre but also the "moral" problems of the time could be discussed. There, these problems were free of the examination system curriculum and its expectations of orthodoxy. Jin did, to an extent, discuss formal problems, as can be seen from the number of critics who have pointed to him as a champion of vernacular fiction. Though these critics exaggerate the degree to which vernacular fiction was disparaged by the literati, they were not entirely wrong. Jin did expend much effort in pointing out textual features. Yet as the chapter commentary under discussion here demonstrates, Jin was perfectly willing to pass up discussion of those sorts of problems in order to take the opportunity to discuss problems of authenticity and integrity in their place, in his own terms. There, as long as their intentions are unmediated, the sage and the fool are equals, and the rampaging tiger killer is a model of Confucian virtue.

Conclusion
Bandits in Print

In episode 21 of the 2011 television adaptation of *The Water Margin* titled "All Men Are Brothers" in English, the character Song Jiang, played by Zhang Hanyu, pays a visit to his father after his slaying of Yan Poxi. Filled with regret, he reports to his father that he has committed a terrible crime, but he does not wish to go on the run. His father asks why he has come if he does not intend to evade the authorities, to which Song Jiang answers that he wishes to pay his father this one last visit. His father warns him that he will surely be put to death if he turns himself in. Song Jiang replies, "Your son has been an official for my life up to this point, responsible for the land and the people. I've carried out my duties with the utmost loyalty (*jinzhong zhishou*). I didn't wish to commit a bloody crime and bring harm to the innocent, but now it's too late to repent! Even nine deaths would not atone for it!" Zhu Tong and Lei Heng appear and offer Song Jiang the chance to escape, making a great show of being unable to "find" him while he is standing before them, but Song Jiang refuses. He insists on returning with them to the yamen, where he is tortured and tattooed as a criminal, a martyr to his own belief in law and order.

One can only wonder what the readers and commentators of traditional print editions would make of such a scene, had they been able to view it. Would Li Kaixian and the social circles that read *The Water*

Margin in the time before the imperial ancestral hall fire have been moved by Song Jiang's unwavering principles and dedication to his official position, or would they have been left unimpressed by the director's techniques for "narrating history"? Would Yu Xiangdou have been relieved to see that his version was actually a closer match to the values espoused in his preface? Or would he update his "Discerning the *Margins*" pitch for the twenty-first century and proclaim that this too was inferior to his own edition? The "Li Zhuowu" of the Rongyu tang edition would certainly have much to criticize in this scene, with its conventional values. Jin Shengtan, too, would surely find it hard to take Song Jiang, whom he deemed "lowest low" in character, referring to himself as "carrying out official duties in with the utmost loyalty." It is easy to imagine Jin taking issue with the straightforward direction as well. At heart, however, this television adaptation of *The Water Margin* shares something with the editions that traditional editor-commenters created—though its media is video rather than the woodblock print, it too is *The Water Margin* reshaped in speculation of the needs, desires, and values of particular audiences.

The broad familiarity of works like *The Water Margin* to the general public today, whether through new media adaptations and reimaginings or the "original" received texts, belies the genre's roots as a printed phenomenon of the elite. We have seen how the earliest known editions of *The Water Margin* appeared in the circles around the Jiajing emperor, printed by Guo Xun and the Censorate, likely around the tenure of Wang Tingxiang as Chief Censor. It was accompanied at that stage by *Romance of the Three Kingdoms* and possibly an edition of *Record of the Heroes and Martyrs* commissioned by Guo Xun, but surprisingly no other, similar titles.

After the ancestral temple fire of 1541, *The Water Margin* began to take a different turn. Within two decades, it was widely printed commercially, and its success inspired for-profit publishers like Xiong Damu to create further works emulating it and *Romance of the Three Kingdoms*. At the same time as it took this more "popular" turn, the burgeoning genre of the novel was also injected with a modicum of socially critical attitude, both through the inspiration of Li Kaixian's *Water Margin* adaptation *Record of the Precious Sword*, fragments of which ended up interpolated into the *Jin Ping Mei*, and also in slightly later commentaries by such paratextual characters as "Li Zhuowu." The novel became a vector for wider transmission of iconoclastic literary ideas. This transformation culminated in the elaborate commentary edition of Jin Shengtan.

Jin's edition in turn influenced the further writing of both commentaries and novels themselves.

The Water Margin both before and after the fire was continually reshaped by print, across the sectors of "official," "commercial," and "private" into which scholars of the Chinese book have traditionally divided publishing activity. As it moved back and forth across these boundaries, it maintained qualities typically associated with each sector. The Water Margin also played a critical role in the development of the genre as one of the first of its kind to appear in print, as the first to become the object of commentary, and as the inspiration for further works. It is no coincidence that when the Oriental Book Company began their project of attempting to wrest the traditional novel from its traditional woodblock print format, The Water Margin was the first to be treated.

The role of print in shaping The Water Margin and the early modern Chinese novel genre more widely is obscured by the seemingly "oral" quality of these texts. Led along by language such as "it is told that . . ." (hua shuo) and "you must listen to the next chapter to understand" (ting xiahui fenjie) on virtually every page, readers might well imagine themselves in a Ming-dynasty teahouse, listening to a professional storyteller give an evening's performance—and inviting them to the next evening's, presumably after taking collections in appreciation of his efforts. Some scholars have even assumed that hypothetical oral storytellers' promptbooks served as antecedents to the novel.

In fact, however, such novels are highly "written" texts that employ such storyteller rhetoric for effect. They are also notoriously long. It could even be said that their very length is one of the defining features of the genre, setting it apart from other related types of narrative such as huaben short stories. A modern, typeset edition of The Water Margin published by Taiwan's Linking Publishing Company, for a representative example, runs to nearly fifteen hundred pages. To memorize and recite a work such as The Water Margin verbatim would be an extremely impressive mnemonic feat, to say the least. Ironically, texts that more readily lend themselves to memorization and recitation are more terse and, therefore, "literary" in the language they use. Scholars have even suggested recently that many classical works circulated as oral bodies of knowledge committed to memory by experts before being canonized in written form.[1]

Even setting aside questions of its text and its authorship, we are left with many questions about the history of The Water Margin. What, precisely, did Guo Xun's "Wuding edition" of the novel look like? What was the relationship between Guo Xun and Wang Tingxiang of the Censorate, and did they collaborate in some fashion in printing the several titles that are associated with both entities? Could theirs have been the edition read in the capital by Li Kaixian and his literati coterie? What were the commercial editions of *The Water Margin*, now apparently lost, that inspired Xiong Damu to create his own historical narratives through the "Xiong Damu mode" of editing? How many copies of the Yu Xiangdou, Rongyu tang, and Jin Shengtan editions were sold? How, if at all, was the "ban" on the novel carried out? Barring the unearthing of new evidence, these questions are destined to remain unanswered.

Nevertheless, by returning *The Water Margin* to the circumstances surrounding the publication of particular editions, we have seen in the aggregate a truer picture of the novel genre and its meaning. It has become clear how *The Water Margin* is not simply a product of popular culture with oral roots, nor is it only a self-conscious literati inversion of such products. Rather, it is a hybrid of both that could be reconfigured by editor-publishers for their own purposes in crafting an edition. It could always be presented at surface value as an exciting collection of adventure tales, or as embodying sophisticated narrative techniques and provocative philosophical positions. Its history in print imbued it with both possibilities—from the earliest known editions, which circulated among the Jiajing court elite, to the variety of commercial editions that sprang up soon afterward. *The Water Margin*, a phenomenon of print, in turn broke the path for other works in the genre to follow.

SELECTED LIST OF CHARACTERS

Table 1 Selected list of characters

PINYIN	CHINESE
an	安
ba yi	八懿
Bai Juyi	白居易
Bai Letian wenji	白樂天文集
Bai Xiangshan shiji	白香山詩集
Baichuan shuzhi	百川書志
baifan	稗販
baiguan	稗官
baishi	稗史
Baohua lou	寶華樓
Baojian ji	寶劍記
Baowen tang	寶文堂
bian	編
Bian Gong	邊貢
buzhizhe	不知者
cai	才
Cai Zhengsun	蔡正孫
Cantong qi	叁同契
ce	冊
cehai	測海
Chang Yuchun	常遇春
Chao Li	晁瑮
Chen Chen	陳忱
Chen Jin	陳金
Chen Jiru	陳繼儒
Chen Shu	陳束
Chen Youliang	陳友諒
Chengdi	成帝
chongke	重刻
chuanqi	傳奇
chuanshuo gongjin, dongren tingwen	傳說宮禁，動人聽聞

(Continued)

Table 1 (Continued)

PINYIN	CHINESE
Cilin zhaiyan	詞林摘艷
Cixue	詞謔
Cui Xian	崔銑
Da Liyi	大禮議
Da Song zhongxing yanyi	大宋中興演義
da toujin tingzhi heru	大頭巾聽之何如?
da zhangfu	大丈夫
Daben xiansheng	大本先生
dapu	打譜
Daxue	大學
de	得
ding	定
Ding Bing	丁丙
Dingtao	定陶
Dingxiang	定襄
dingzi	訂梓
Disha	地煞
Diwu caizi shu Shi Nai'an Shuihu zhuan	第五才子書施耐庵水滸傳
Dong Jieyuan	董解元
Dongchang	東廠
du	獨
Du Cui gong Houqu xu Yang Zi zhezhong	讀崔公後渠敍楊子折衷
Du diwu caizi shu fa	讀第五才子書法
Du Nan	杜枏
Du shi jijie	杜詩集註
Du Yangang ji	杜研岡集
Duan Chaoyong	段朝用
Ducha yuan	都察院
dunshou jilu	頓首輯錄
duo guqu	多古趣
fanke	翻刻
Fei Hong	費宏
Feng shi	馮氏
Gao Ru	高儒
Gao Shusi	高叔嗣
Geng Chun	耿純
gewu	格物
gewu junzi	格物君子
Guangyun	廣韻
Guanhua tang	貫華堂
guanxi	關係

PINYIN	CHINESE
guban	古板
guben	古本
gui	鬼
Gui E	桂萼
Gujin shuke	古今書刻
Gun Xun	郭勛
Guo Cong	郭聰
Guo Deng	郭登
Guo Liang	郭良
Guo Ming	郭銘
Guo shi jia zhuan	郭氏家傳
Guo Ying	郭英
Guo Ying yijian sheng shiwan shi, qigong he kedang ye	郭英一箭勝十萬師，其攻何可當也
Guo Zhen	郭珍
guo zhi du	國之毒
guozhi	國治
haipian	海篇
hao yige mingbai gongdao de zhixian	好一個明白公道的知縣
hao zhixian	好知縣
haoge dutou, zhiguan zuo zijia renqing; dou zuole renqing, ru wangfa he	好個都頭，只管做自家人情。都做了人情，如王法何？
haohua	好話
He Jingming	何景明
Houqu	后渠
Hu Yinglin	胡應麟
hua shuo	話說
huaben	話本
hui	回
ji	集
ji busheng fa	極不省法
Ji qianjia zhu fenlei Du Gongbu shi ershi juan	集千家注分類杜工部詩二十卷
ji sheng fa	極省法
Jiajing ba caizi	嘉靖八才子
jiaju	佳句
Jiangdong xueya laoren	江東雪厓老人
Jiangnan sanren	江南散人
jianzipu	減字譜
jiaqi	家齊
jie	戒
jin ren zhi xing	盡人之性
Jin Shengtan	金聖嘆
jing	靜

Table 1 (Continued)

PINYIN	CHINESE
jing2	敬
Jingben zengbu quanxiang jiaozheng Zhongyi Shuihu zhizhuan pinglin	京本增補全像校正忠義水滸志傳評林
Jintai	金台
Jinyan	今言
Jinyi wei	錦衣衛
jinzhong zhishou	盡忠職守
Jiuzhang bilei suanfa daquan	九章比類算法大全
jiwai xushi zhi yaolan	紀外敘事之要覽
juan	卷
Kang Hai	康海
kanxing	刊行
Ke Weixong	柯維熊
kou buzhun, bian bushi hao furen le	口不准，便不是好婦人了。
kuaizhi renkou	膾炙人口
Lanke jing	爛柯經
lei	類
Li Danian	李大年
Li Fuda	李福達
Li Kaixian	李開先
Li Mengyang	李夢陽
Li Ye	李冶
Li Yinghong	栗應宏
Li Zhi	李贄
Li Zhuowu	李卓吾
lian	聯
Lisao	離騷
Liushi zi shi	六十子詩
lü	慮
Lu Rong	陸容
Lu shi	魯氏
Mao Zonggang	毛宗崗
meipi	眉批
miao	妙
min zhi zei	民之賊
ming mingde	明明德
Mingshi jishi benmo	明史紀事本末
Mu Ying	沐英
nage ken jia qiangdao	那個肯嫁強盜？
Nanbei Song zhizhuan	南北宋志傳
Piaojing	嫖經

PINYIN	CHINESE
ping	評
pingdian	評點
pitu	披圖
Pitu cehai	披圖測海
qi zheng	七政
Qi zheng lu	七政曆
Qian qizi	前七子
Qianfu lun	潛夫論
Qianjia zhu Su shi	千家註蘇詩
Qianjin baoyao	千金寶要
Qiezhong ji	篋中集
qiji	奇計
qijia suochuan	其家所傳
qing dan	輕誕
Qingbai tang	清江堂
Qingjiang tang	清白堂
Qinyun qimeng	琴韻啟蒙
quan	權
Quan Han zhizhuan	全漢志傳
quan2	勸
Quxian shenqi mipu	臞仙神奇密譜
ren dan zhi Zhang Wenyuan duse, bu zhi shi shi zhifa	人但知張文遠妒色，不知實是執法。
renqing	人情
Renzong	仁宗
Riji gushi	日記故事
Rongyu tang	容與堂
ru	如
Ru jiang	儒將
ru zuo Yu ting	如坐虞廷
ruci furen, zhihao zuo qiangdao pozi	如此婦人，只好做強盜婆子。
ruo jinren dou ruci wanqi yanjing lai, dang cheng yipian gu shijie	若今人都如此剜起眼睛來，當成一片瞽世界。
ruo you qi	若有契
san Tiandi	參天地
Sanguo zhi yanyi	三國志演藝
Sanjia shidian	三家世典
Santai guan	三台館
Shanben shushi cangshu zhi	善本書室藏書志
shangshang	上上
shen	慎
Shen Defu	沈德符

(Continued)

Table 1 (Continued)

PINYIN	CHINESE
shendu	慎獨
shengren	聖人
Shengshi xinsheng	盛世新聲
shenxiu	身修
shi	是
Shi ji	史記
shichen	史臣
shidafu yixia	士大夫以下
Shidui yayun	詩對押韻
Shilin guangji	詩林廣記
Shiqing lu	適情錄
shishang zhi shengjie	事上之盛節
shiwai chuanxin zhi yaodian	史外傳心之要典
shixia zhi dajing	使下之大經
Shiyun shiyi	詩韻釋義
shu	恕
Shuangfeng tang	雙峰堂
Shuihu bian	水滸辯
Shuihu zhuan	水滸傳
shuochang cihua	說唱詞話
Shuzhai manlu	樗齋漫錄
Shuzhuang ji	書莊記
sike	私刻
Siku quanshu	四庫全書
Silijian	司禮監
Songshi gang	宋史綱
Songshi mu	宋史目
Suanfa daquan	算法大全
Sui Tang zhizhuan	隋唐志傳
Sun Pu	孫樸
taibao	太保
Taigu yiyin	太古遺音
Taihe zhengyin pu	太和正音譜
Taihe zhuan	太和傳
Taiping yuefu	太平樂府
taishi	太師
Taizu	太祖
Tang Long	唐龍
Tang shu zhizhuan	唐書志傳
Tang Shunzhi	唐順之

PINYIN	CHINESE
Tang yin	唐音
Tiandu waichen	天都外臣
Tiangang	天罡
Tianwei shensuan suozhi, chen hegong yi	天威神算所至，臣何功矣
Tianxia taiping	天下太平
tianyuan shu	天元術
ting xiahui fenjie	聽下回分解
Tongjian gangmu	通鑑綱目
Tongxin shuo	童心說
tuanying	團營
tuanyuan	團圓
Wang Daokun	汪道昆
Wang Jiusi	王九思
Wang Liang	汪諒
Wang Shenzhong	王慎中
Wang shi cangji	王氏藏集
Wang Tingxiang	王廷相
Wang Yan	王言
Wang Zan	王瓚
Wang Zhi	王質
Wanhua xuanji	萬化玄機
Wanyong zhengzong	萬用正宗
weiyan dayi	微言大義
weizao jizhuan yu youli yan	則偽造紀傳，與有力焉
wenji	文集
Wenxuan	文選
wu er haowen	武而好文
wu yu baiguan yi yun yi	吾於稗官亦云矣
Wuding	武定
Wuding Guo gong Ying	武定郭公英
Wujing zhijie	武經直解
Wumu wang jingzhong lu	武穆王精忠錄
Wuzhen pian	悟真篇
xian Ru	先儒
xiang	降
xiao	孝
Xiaojing zhushu	孝經註疏
xiaoshu yibu	小書一部
xiaxia	下下
Xie Zhaozhe	謝肇淛
xiezi	楔子

(Continued)

Table 1 (Continued)

PINYIN	CHINESE
xin	心
xing	興
Xingli daquan	性理大全
xinzheng	心正
Xiong Damu	熊大木
Xiong Guo	熊過
Xiong Zhonggu	熊鍾谷
Xiuranzi	修髯子
Xixiang ji	西廂記
Xu Da	徐達
Xu Zhenqing	徐禎卿
Xu Zichang	許自昌
Xuantian shangdi	玄天上帝
Xun huchong, po jiaozi	勛怙寵，頗驕恣
Xun jiexia you zhishu, po she shushi	勛桀黠有智數，頗涉書史
xunfu	巡撫
xunyi	勳懿
Yan shi	晏氏
Yang Chaoying	楊朝英
Yang Shen	楊慎
Yang Shihong	楊士弘
Yang Su	楊素
Yang Tinghe	楊廷和
Yang Yiqing	楊一清
Yang Zi zhezhong	楊子折衷
Yangchun baixue	陽春白雪
yaozhan	腰斬
yicheng	意誠
Yifeng	儀封
Yiguo gong	翊國公
Yingguo gong	營國公
Yinglie zhuan	英烈傳
yinyuan shengfa	因緣生法
yishi	義釋
yituan jianzha	一團奸詐
Yiwen zhi	藝文志
Yongjia	永嘉
Yongquan	湧泉
Yongshun tang	永順堂
Yongxi yuefu	雍熙樂府

PINYIN	CHINESE
You Mao	尤袤
youji	遊記
youxie daoxue qiwei	有些道學氣味
Yu Shaoyu	余邵魚
Yu Xiangdou	余象斗
Yu Zhangde	余彰德
Yuan Cishan wenji	元次山文集
Yuan Hongdao	袁宏道
Yuan Jie	元結
Yuan Junzhe	袁均哲
Yuan Wuyai	袁無涯
Yuan Zhongdao	袁中道
yuangu	緣故
Yue jia	岳家
yuefu	樂府
yuewei neizhu	約為內助
Yuji weiyi	玉機微義
Yumu xingxin bian	娛目醒心編
yuqing	毓慶
Yuqing xunyi ji	毓慶勳懿集
yushi dafu	御史大夫
Yushi tai	御史台
Yuyin haipian	玉音海篇
zan huayu	贊化育
ze	則
Zhan Ruoshui	湛若水
Zhang Boyuan	張伯顏
Zhang Cong	張璁
Zhang Shicheng	張士誠
Zhang Shuye	張叔夜
Zhang Zhupo	張竹坡
Zhanguo ce	戰國策
zheng xiang tenglu	爭相謄錄
Zheng Xiao	鄭曉
Zhengde	正德
zhenglang Shi jun	正郎石君
zhenshou	鎮守
Zhenwu	真武
zhiyin	知音
zhiyou jia Li Kui, zai wu Li Kui jia	只有假李逵，再無李逵假
zhiyu zhishan	止於至善

(Continued)

Table 1 (Continued)

PINYIN	CHINESE
zhizhi	知止
zhizhi2	知至
zhizhou	知州
zhong	忠
zhong shu	忠恕
Zhong Xing	鐘惺
zhong yi	忠義
zhong2	中
Zhongqing liji	鍾情麗集
Zhongyong	中庸
Zhongyuan yinyun	中原音韻
Zhongzheng tang	中正堂
Zhou Deqing	周德清
Zhou Hongzu	周弘祖
Zhou Nan	周南
zhu	誅
Zhu Yuanzhang	朱元璋
zhuyi wenmo yu Rujia chen tong	注意文墨與儒家臣同
zishu	字書
ziza	子雜
zongmu	總目
zuo	作
zuo zhuguo	左柱國
zuoci shifa	作詞十法

Notes

Introduction

1. For a nuanced social history of the development of copyright and related practices in modern China, see Fei-Hsien Wang, *Pirates and Publishers: A Social History of Copyright in Modern China* (Princeton, NJ: Princeton University Press, 2019). On the relations between authors and copyright holders in Europe, see Mark Rose, *Authors and Owners: The Invention of Copyright* (Cambridge, MA: Harvard University Press, 1993); Adrian Johns, *Piracy: The Intellectual Property Wars From Gutenberg to Gates* (Chicago: University of Chicago Press, 2009).

2. The brief comments about Luo Guanzhong are found in the *Lugui bu xubian*, reprinted in Zhu Yixuan and Liu Yuchen, *Shuihu zhuan ziliao huibian* (Tianjin: Baihua wenyi chubanshe, 1981), 117. For a fuller discussion of these early sources, see Ge Liangyan, *Out of the Margins: The Rise of Chinese Vernacular Fiction* (Honolulu: University of Hawai'i Press, 2001), 101–4.

3. Andrew H. Plaks, *The Four Masterworks of the Ming Novel: Ssu Ta Ch'i-shu* (Princeton, NJ: Princeton University Press, 1987), 309.

4. Chen Jianping, *Shuihu xi yu Zhongguo xiayi wenhua* (Beijing: Wenhua yishu chubanshe, 2008), 29–61, for a discussion and catalogue of *Shuihu* plays that predate the novel. See also Xie Bixia, *Shuihu xiqu ershi zhong yanjiu* (Taipei: Taiwan daxue chuban weiyuanhui, 1981), passim.

5. For an overview of such oral traditions and the story of Wu Song battling a tiger, see Vibeke Børdahl, *Wu Song Fights the Tiger: The Interaction of Oral and Written Traditions in the Chinese Novel, Drama and Storytelling* (Copenhagen: NIAS Press, 2013).

6. For a discussion of the various theories concerning why Song Jiang's postamnesty career is not discussed in the official historiography, see Richard Gregg Irwin, *The Evolution of a Chinese Novel: Shui-Hu-chuan.* (Cambridge: Harvard University Press, 1953), 13.

7. For a translation of the *Xuanhe yishi*, see William O. Hennessey, *Proclaiming Harmony* (Ann Arbor: Center for Chinese Studies, University of Michigan, 1981).

8. On editions of *Three Kingdoms*, see Anne E. McLaren, "Ming Audiences and Vernacular Hermeneutics: The Uses of 'The Romance of the Three Kingdoms,'" *T'oung Pao* second series 81, no. 1/3 (1995): 51–80; Anne E. McLaren, "Constructing New Reading Publics in Late Ming China," in *Printing and Book Culture in Late Imperial China*, edited by Cynthia Brokaw and Kai-wing Chow (Berkeley: University of California Press, 2005), 152–83.

9. Imre Galambos, *Orthography of Early Chinese Writing: Evidence From Newly Excavated Manuscripts* (Budapest: Department of East Asian Studies, Eötvös Loránd University, 2006), 2.

10. The traditional Confucian hermeneutics of poetry and personality are discussed in Steven Jay Van Zoeren's classic study, *Poetry and Personality: Reading, Exegesis, and Hermeneutics in Traditional China* (Stanford, CA: Stanford University Press, 1991).

11. Xiaofei Tian, *Tao Yuanming and Manuscript Culture: The Record of a Dusty Table* (Seattle: University of Washington Press, 2005), 31.

12. Book-length studies on the continual redefinition of the poetic personality include E. Shan Chou, *Reconsidering Tu Fu: Literary Greatness and Cultural Context* (Cambridge: Cambridge University Press, 1995) on Du Fu, and Paula M. Varsano, *Tracking the Banished Immortal: The Poetry of Li Bo and its Critical Reception* (Honolulu: University of Hawai'i Press, 2003) on Li Bai.

13. Tian, *Tao Yuanming and Manuscript Culture*, 7.

14. Christopher M. B. Nugent, *Manifest in Words, Written on Paper: Producing and Circulating Poetry in Tang Dynasty China* (Cambridge, MA: Harvard University Asia Center, 2010).

15. Susan Cherniack, "Book Culture and Textual Transmission in Sung China," *Harvard Journal of Asiatic Studies* 54, no. 1 (1994): 19.

16. Cherniack, "Book Culture," 21.

17. Suyoung Son, *Writing for Print: Publishing and the Making of Textual Authority in Late Imperial China* (Cambridge, MA: Harvard University Asia Center, 2018), 32–42.

18. David Scott Kastan, *Shakespeare and the Book* (Cambridge: Cambridge University Press, 2001), 16. For a complete discussion, see 14–44.

19. Kastan, *Shakespeare and the Book*, 20.

20. Kastan, *Shakespeare and the Book*, 117. See also Roger Chartier, *The Author's Hand and the Printer's Mind* (Malden, MA: Polity Press, 2014), 159.

21. Chartier, *The Author's Hand and the Printer's Mind*, 130.

22. See Chartier, *The Author's Hand*, 150–57.

23. On *"Water Margin* fever" (*Shuihu zhuan re*) in the Ming, see Chen Songbo, *Shuihu zhuan yuan kaolun* (Beijing: Renmin wenxue chubanshe, 2006), 29.

24. Hans Robert Jauss, *Toward an Aesthetic of Reception* (Minneapolis: University of Minnesota Press, 1981), 32.

1. "Falsifying a Biography Brought Him Power"

1. Brief outlines of Guo Xun's life can be found in Lienche Tu Fang, "Kuo Hsun," entry in L. Carrington Goodrich and Zhaoying Fang, eds. *Dictionary of Ming Biography, 1368–1644* (New York: Columbia University Press, 1976): 770-773; Ma Shutian, "Kanke Shuihu zhuan de Guo Xun," *Wenshi zhishi* 12 (1983): 75–78. Political ramifications of Guo's publishing are discussed in Hu Jixun, "Guo Xun kanshu kaolun: jiazu shi yanyi kanbu yu Ming zhongye zhengzhi de hudong," *Zhonghua wenshi luncong* 117 (2015): 368–89. The Censorate, Wang Tingxiang, and Li Kaixian are the subjects of subsequent chapters.

2. For an overview of the growth of the commercial print industry in Fujian and the Jiangnan region, see Lucille Chia, *Printing for Profit: The Commercial Publishers of Jianyang, Fujian (11th-17th Centuries)* (Cambridge, MA: Harvard University Asia Center, 2002). and Yasushi Ōki, *Minmatsu Kōnan No Shuppan Bunka* (Tokyo: Kenbun Shuppan, 2004). On the editing practices of the late Ming, see Yuming He, *Home and the World: Editing the "Glorious Ming" in Woodblock-Printed Books of the Sixteenth and Seventeenth Centuries* (Cambridge, MA: Harvard University Asia Center, 2013).

3. On popular song collections, see Kathryn A. Lowry, *The Tapestry of Popular Songs in 16th- and 17th-Century China: Reading, Imitation, and Desire* (Leiden; Boston: Brill, 2005). On chantefables, see Anne E. McLaren, *Chinese Popular Culture and Ming Chantefables* (Leiden: Brill, 1998). The higher-end commercial publishers of Ming Beijing are discussed in the following chapter.

4. Chao Li, *Chao Shi Baowen Tang Shumu* (Shanghai: Gudian wenxue chubanshe, 1957), 108–9.

5. The 1589 date for the Tiandu waichen edition, however, has been questioned by Andrew Plaks. See Andrew H. Plaks, *The Four Masterworks of the Ming Novel: Ssu Ta Ch'i-Shu* (Princeton, NJ: Princeton University Press, 1987), 286–87. The preface is reprinted in Zhu Yixuan and Liu Yuchen, *Shuihu zhuan ziliao huibian* (Tianjin: Baihua wenyi chubanshe, 1981), 167–69.

6. Zhang Guoguang, "Shuihu zuben tankao: jian lun Shi Nai'an wei Guo Xun menke zhi tuoming," *Jianghan luntan* 1 (1982): 41–46.

7. See Yuan Shishuo. *Wenxue shixue de Ming Qing xiaoshuo yanjiu* (Jinan: Qi Lu shushe, 1999), 17–34.

8. For his claim, see his 1953 preface to *Shuihu quanzhuan*, a variorum edition of *The Water Margin* printed by the Renmin wenxue chubanshe. For a disputation of this claim, see Zhu Qing and Li Yongyu, "Guo Wuding ben wenti xinyi," *Wenxue yichan* 5 (1997): 81–92.

9. See Y. W. Ma, *Shuihu Erlun* (Taipei: Lianjing chubanshe, 2005), 69–110.

10. Hans Robert Jauss, *Toward an Aesthetic of Reception* (Minneapolis: University of Minnesota Press, 1981), 22.

11. Janice A. Radway, *A Feeling for Books: The Book-of-the-month Club, Literary Taste, and Middle-Class Desire* (Chapel Hill: University of North Carolina Press, 1997), 5.

12. The concept of a semiautonomous field of cultural production is delineated in Pierre Bourdieu, *The Field of Cultural Production: Essays on Art and Literature* (New York: Columbia University Press, 1993).

13. *Mingshi, juan* 130.

14. An account of the Li Fuda affair and its aftermath can be found in B. J. ter. Haar, *The White Lotus Teachings in Chinese Religious History* (Leiden: E. J. Brill, 1991), 155–66. In the Qianlong era of the Qing dynasty, a fictionalization of the Li Fuda case appeared in the collection *Stories to Delight the Eye and Awaken the Heart (Yumu xingxin bian)*.

15. Many such ranks did not survive the purges that followed in the wake of the Hu Weiyong affair of 1380. These include the Gongchang marquisate that was granted to Ying's son Zhen.

16. David McMullen, "Yuan Chieh" entry, in William H. Nienhauser, ed. *The Indiana Companion to Traditional Chinese Literature* (Bloomington: Indiana University Press, 1986), 952. On Yuan Jie, see also Owen, "The Cultural Tang (650–1020)," 315. In *The Cambridge History of Chinese Literature*, ed. Kang-i Sun Chang and Stephen Owen (Cambridge: Cambridge University Press, 2010), 286-380.

17. The original of Zhan Ruoshui's preface is found in the Sibu congkan edition of the *Yuan Cishan wenji.*

18. A copy of this edition is held by the National Library in Beijing.

19. This preface is from the rare edition held by the National Library of China.

20. James Geiss, "The Chia-ching Reign," 454. In *The Cambridge History of China: The Ming Dynasty*, edited by Denis Twitchett and Frederick Mote (Cambridge: Cambridge University Press, 1988), 440-510.

21. A copy of the 1531 edition of the *Yongxi yuefu* is held by the National Central Library, Taipei. It should be noted that the *Yongxi yuefu* is frequently incorrectly dated to 1566; that is the date of a later edition that was included in the Sibu congkan and is therefore the most widely available.

22. Chao Li, *Chao shi Baowen Tang shumu* (Shanghai: Gudian wenxue chubanshe, 1957), 108-9.

23. Reprinted in Zhu and Liu, *Shuihu zhuan ziliao huibian*, 167-69.

24. Shen Defu, *Wanli yehuo bian* (Beijing: Zhonghua shuju, 1959), 139-40.

25. For an example of discussion of these prefaces, see Anne E. McLaren, "Constructing New Reading Publics in Late Ming China," in *Printing and Book Culture in Late Imperial China*, ed. Cynthia Brokaw and Kai-wing Chow (Berkeley: University of California Press, 2005), 152-183.

26. In his dissertation, Andrew West has remarked as such concerning this edition and its tentative identification as a product of the Censorate. Andrew Christopher West, "Quest for the Urtext: The Textual Archaeology of the Three Kingdoms" (PhD diss., Princeton University, 1993), 79.

2. "One Freshly Slaughtered Pig, Two Flagons of Jinhua wine . . . and a Small Book"

1. Sophie Volpp, "The Gift of a Python Robe: The Circulation of Objects in 'Jin Ping Mei,'" *Harvard Journal of Asiatic Studies* 65, no. 1 (2005): 143.

2. This chapter is available in translation in David Tod Roy, *The Plum in the Golden Vase Or, Chin P'ing Mei Volume Three: The Aphrodisiac* (Princeton, NJ: Princeton University Press, 2011): 129–46.

3. Xiaoxiaosheng, *Jin Ping Mei*, 588. Modified translation from Roy, *The Plum in the Golden Vase or, Chin P'ing Mei Volume 3: The Aphrodisiac*, 176.

4. Xiaoxiaosheng, 628. Modified from Roy, *The Plum in the Golden Vase or, Chin P'ing Mei Volume 3: The Aphrodisiac*, 249.

5. Craig Clunas, *Superfluous Things: Material Culture and Social Status in Early Modern China* (Cambridge: Polity, 1991), 38.

6. Paraphrased from Lu Rong, *Shuyuan Zaji* (Beijing: Zhonghua shuju, 1985), *juan* 10, 128–29.

7. See Ning, *Mingdai juan*, 73.

8. Printed, along with Gao Ru's *Baichuan shuzhi*, in a typeset edition Gao Ru and Zhou Hongzu, *Baichuan Shuzhi Gujin Shuke* (Shanghai: Gudian wenxue chubanshe, 1957), for the Censorate list, see 325. For a publishing history of the *Gujin shuke*, see Chen Qinghui, "Gujin shuke banben kao," *Wenxian* 4 (2007): 161-168. While there are minor variations between editions, the *Shuihu zhuan* appears on the list of Censorate publications in all of them. As Chen points out, the later editions of *Gujin shuke* lack the listing for "Lanke jing" under *Du-cha yuan*, but feature *Da Ming lüli*. Yang Hongtao and Jia Erqiang have recently expressed skepticism that such an august agency would publish novels, which they assume to be of low culture. They raise the possibility of errors in the received list of Censorate publications, including that of a list of Guo Xun's publications becoming intermingled with the official ones. They do not, however, account for the relations between Guo and the Censor-in-Chief Wang Tingxiang, nor do they discuss the early reception of *The Water Margin* among elites such as Li Kaixian; both of these topics are discussed in detail in later chapters. See Yang Hongtao and Jia Erqiang, "Mingdai Duchayuan kanke *Sanguo zhi yanyi*, *Shuihu zhuan* chuyi," *Lishi wenxian* 42 (2019): 300–308. Li Yonghu, meanwhile, has speculated that the Censorate *Water Margin* was printed under the direction of Censor-in-Chief Hu Zongxian; as a renowned martial figure and a quasher of rebellions, Hu may have had a personal interest in the novel and wanted to present copies as gifts. Ultimately, however, this speculation cannot be proven. See Li Yonghu, "*Shuihu zhuan* santi," *Ming-Qing xiaoshuo yanjiu* 3 (2015): 19–35.

9. The translated titles as listed in this chart will be used in the discussion below.

10. Plaks makes a brief mention of the Censorate *Water Margin*: "One may well assume that this . . . would have been something more serious than a cheap commercial printing." Andrew H. Plaks, *The Four Masterworks of the Ming Novel: Ssu Ta Ch'i-Shu* (Princeton, NJ: Princeton University Press, 1987), 281.

11. For examples of such an identification, see Zheng Zhenduo, "*Shuihu zhuan* de yanhua" and Wang Chung-min, *A Descriptive Catalog of Rare Chinese Books*, as cited in Andrew Christopher West, *Quest for the Urtext: The Textual Archaeology of the Three Kingdoms* (PhD diss., Princeton University, 1993), 79; see also the preface to the 1975 Renmin wenxue chubanshe facsimile reprint of the edition. West notes that it is impossible to confirm that the edition is a Censorate imprint.

12. See, for example, Robert E. Hegel, *Reading Illustrated Fiction in Late Imperial China* (Stanford, CA: Stanford University Press, 1998), 161.

13. Both of these titles are available in the Princeton East Asian Library *hishi* collection.

14. For a biological sketch of Wang Tingxiang, see Fang, "Wang T'ing-hsiang," in *Dictionary of Ming Biography, 1368–1644*, ed. L. Carrington Goodrich and Zhaoying Fang (New York: Columbia University Press, 1976), 2:1431–34; on the diversity of his thought, and how it was perhaps out of step with that of his contemporaries, see Ong Chang Woei, "The Principles Are Many: Wang Tingxiang and Intellectual Transition in Mid-Ming China," *Harvard Journal of Asiatic Studies* 66, no. 2 (2006): 461–93.

15. The "Former Seven Masters," it should be acknowledged, is of course a retrospective categorization. On the establishment of this group, see Daniel Bryant, *The Great Recreation: Ho Ching-Ming (1483–1521) and His World* (Leiden: Brill, 2008), 641–58.

16. As the next chapter will show, Cui Xian and his acquaintance Li Kaixian were among the first admirers of *The Water Margin*.

17. W. L. Idema, *The Dramatic Oeuvre of Chu Yu-Tun (1379–1439)* (Leiden: Brill, 1985), 18, in reference to Zhu Youdun.

18. Tian Yuan Tan has discussed communities of discharged officials (including Li Kaixian) that formed around the qu genre. See Tian Yuan Tan, *Songs of Contentment and Transgression: Discharged Officials and Literati Communities in Sixteenth-Century North China* (Cambridge, MA: Harvard University Asia Center, 2010).

19. This copy is held by the Beijing National Library. It was reprinted in facsimile form by the Wenxue kanxing chubanshe in 1955.

20. Princeton microfilm 9101/1165.1 r.1009(4).

21. Reprinted in the 1955 Wenxue kanxing chubanshe edition, 7–8.

22. On this process of textualization, see Patricia Sieber, *Theaters of Desire: Authors, Readers, and the Reproduction of Early Chinese Song-Drama, 1300–2000* (New York: Palgrave Macmillan, 2003), passim.

23. Reprinted in Yang Chaoying, *Chaoye Xinsheng Taiping Yuefu* (Beijing: Zhonghua shuju, 1958), 3.

24. The geographical referent of the titular "Central Plains" is the subject of dispute. It has been interpreted by Wang Li and others as referring metaphorically to the Yuan capital, Dadu (Beijing). Wang Jiexin, on the other hand, has interpreted it as referring to Henan. See Wang Jiexin, *Zhongyuan Yinyun Xinkao* (Taipei: Taiwan shangwu yinshuguan, 1988), 37–114.

25. On the creation of a canonical song lyric scheme, see Sieber, *Theaters of Desire*, 47–51. Details of the phonological system of *Rhymes of the Central Plain* are to be found in Jerry Norman, *Chinese* (Cambridge: Cambridge University Press, 1987), 48–50; and Hu Qiguang, *Zhongguo xiaoxue shi* (Shanghai: Shanghai renmin chubanshe, 1987), 185–99. See also William Dolby's entry "Chung-yuan yin-yun" in *The Indiana Companion to Traditional Chinese Literature*, ed. William H. Nienhauser (Bloomington: Indiana University Press, 1986), 370–71.

26. Cai Zhengsun, *Gujin Mingxian Conghua Shilin guangji* (Taipei: Guangwen shuju, 1973), 10.

27. For a typeset edition of the *Shilin guangji*, see Cai Zhengsun, *Shilin guangji* (Beijing: Zhonghua shuju, 1982). This edition is based on the Hongzhi printing. The Zhang Nai in question is a Hongzhi-era graduate, not to be confused with the Wanli-era graduate or the Chongzhen-era rebel of the same name.

28. For a description of editions of the *Sounds of the Tang*, see Yang Shihong, *Tang Yin Pingzhu* (Baoding Shi: Hebei da xue chu ban she, 2006), 2–4.

29. See Ning Jifu, *Hanyu Yunshu Shi Mingdai Juan* (Shanghai: Shanghai renmin chubanshe, 2009), 437–40.

30. See Robert Hans van Gulik, *The Lore of the Chinese Lute: An Essay in the Ideology of the Ch'in* (Tokyo: Sophia University, 1969), 180.

31. The Jiajing edition of the *Secret Sourcebook* is reprinted in facsimile form in the 1963 compendium of qin handbooks *Qinqu jicheng*, the editors of which assume it to be a product of the Beijing publisher Jintai Wang Liang (to be discussed below). However, it bears no colophon or publisher's mark; the editors make no mention of a Censorate edition of the *Secret Sourcebook*. See Beijing guqin yanjiuhui, ed., *Qinqu jicheng* (Beijing: Zhonghua shuju, 1963), vol. 1a, 11. The Jiajing *Shenqi mipu* itself is reprinted in 69–144 of the same volume, based on an original held by the Capital Library, Beijing. (A later version of the *Qinqu jicheng* reproduces the Wanli edition of the *Secret Sourcebook* rather than the Jiajing edition.) The same compendium features the Jiajing-era Wang Liang edition of *Remnant Sounds* (31–68). This edition does feature a Wang Liang colophon. A bibliographical description of *Remnant Sounds* is also available in Tang Jianyuan, ed., *Qin Fu* (Taipei: Lianguan chubanshe, 1971), vol. 2a, endnotes pp. 7–9.

32. A scan is available at http://www.archive.org/details/02095112.cn (accessed April 24, 2019).

33. Hu Yinglin, *Shaoshi Shanfang Bicong* (Beijing: Zhonghua shuju, 1958), 55.

34. Xie Zhaozhe, *Wu zazu, juan* 13, reprinted in *Biji xiaoshuo daguan: ba bian* (Taipei: Xinxing shuju, 1975), 4233.

35. On this point, see also Qi Fukang, *Zhongguo Gudai Shufang Yanjiu* (Beijing: Shangwu yinshu guan, 2007), 191.

36. More precisely, Zhang Xiumin counts ninety-three, while Miao Yonghe counts ten more. See Zhang Xiumin, *Zhongguo Yinshua Shi* (Hangzhou: Zhejiang guji chubanshe, 2006), 243–47, Miao Yonghe, *Mingdai chuban shigao* (Nanjing: Jiangsu renmin chubanshe, 2000), 73–74. See also Qi, *Zhongguo gudai shufang yanji*, 174–97; Zhang, "Mingdai Beijing de keshu," in *Zhang Xiumin yinshua shi lunwen ji*, ed. Zhang Xiumin (Beijing: Yinshua gongye chubanshe, 1988), 151–61.

37. Miao, *Mingdai chuban shigao*.

38. The low figure is from Qu Mianliang, *Zhongguo gujii banke cidian* (Suzhou: Suzhou daxue chubanshe, 2009), while the high figure is from Du Xinfu, *Mingdai banke zonglu* (Yangzhou: Yangzhou guji shudian, 1983).

39. This advertisement is reprinted in Qi, *Zhongguo Gudai shufang yanjiu*, 250.

40. The title, in full as advertised, is "*Han Shi waizhuan*, one set in ten volumes, the Collection of Han Ying." Hightower translates *Han Shi waizhuan* as "Exoteric Commentary on the Han school text of the *Classic of Songs*": see Ying Han, *Han Shih Wai Chuan: Han Ying's Illustrations of the Didactic Application of the Classic of Songs*, trans. James Robert Hightower (Cambridge, MA: Harvard University Press, 1952).

41. *Fanke* are made by tracing the characters of an old edition, typically one from the Song or Yuan, and re-creating the edition by pasting the tracing onto blocks for carving. *Chongke* editions are printed from newly carved blocks that are based on the text, but not necessarily the design, of an older edition. See entries for *fanke ben* and *chongke ben* in Qu, *Zhongguo gujii banke cidian*, 432, 656.

42. Kathryn A. Lowry, *The Tapestry of Popular Songs in 16th- and 17th-Century China: Reading, Imitation, and Desire* (Leiden: Brill, 2005), 49–50, 90. (Lowry refers here not to Jintai Wang Liang but another "Jintai" publisher, Mr. Lu of Jintai.)

43. You Mao edited and printed a commentary edition of *Selections of Literature*. After its blocks were destroyed in a fire, the Yuan-era scholar Zhang Boyan created facsimile blocks based on the You edition and reprinted it in the Yuanyou era (1314–20). See Xiao Tong, *Wen Xuan, or, Selections of Refined Literature*, trans. David R. Knechtges (Princeton, NJ: Princeton University Press, 1982), 55.

44. Ding Bing, *Shanben shushi cangshu zhi* (Taipei: Guangwen shuju, 1967), *juan* 38, 1.

45. Ding, ibid., *juan* 24, 10. On Yuan editions of this title, see Lucille Chia, *Printing for Profit: The Commercial Publishers of Jianyang, Fujian (11th-17th Centuries)* (Cambridge, MA: Harvard University Asia Center, 2002), 88–93. According to Ye Dehui, Ding was slightly mistaken: Wang Liang acquired the woodblocks for the title from Guangqin tang, which had in turn acquired them from Qinyou tang and modified their colophon. The "thicker" strokes were due to flattening of the blocks through repeated use. See Ye Dehui, *Shulin qinghua: Fu Shulin yuhua* (Beijing: Xinhua shudian, 1957), 122–24. Chia, however, points out that the families owning the latter two firms may have been related by marriage. Ye does not, however, provide an explanation of why Wang Liang would advertise the Du Fu collection as a *fanke* facsimile reprint if it were actually printed from the original Yuan blocks. It is possible that the *fanke* implied to customers that the text was edited; Ke Weixiong's preface to the *fanke* edition of *Records of the Grand Historian*, for example, says he was asked to correct the text. A microfilm version of this Ke Weixiong edition is held by Princeton University's East Asian Library.

46. The overlapping titles of the Censorate and Jintai Wang Liang can be compared against other commercial printings from Beijing by consulting Du Xinfu, *Quan Ming fensheng fenxian keshu kao* (Beijing: Xianzhuang shuju, 2001).

47. The excavated Yongshun tang works were reprinted as a set of thread-bound volumes by the Shanghai wenwu baoguan weiyuanhui, 1973, under the title *Ming Chenghua shuochang cihua congkan*. For more on these volumes, their contents, and their discovery, see Anne E. McLaren, *Chinese Popular Culture and Ming Chantefables* (Leiden: Brill, 1998).

48. Richard G. Wang, *Ming Erotic Novellas: Genre, Consumption, and Religiosity in Cultural Practice* (Hong Kong: Chinese University Press, 2011), 14, and passim.

49. Ye, *Shulin qinghua: Fu Shulin yuhua, juan* 5.

50. See, for example, Zhang, *Zhongguo yinshua shi*, 252; Zhang Lian, *Mingdai zhongyang zhengfu chuban yu wenhua zhengce zhi yanjiu* (Taibei xian Yonghe shi: Hua Mulan wenhua chubanshe, 2006); Hegel, *Reading Illustrated Fiction in Late Imperial China*, 133; and Cynthia Brokaw, "On the History of the Book in China," in *Printing and Book Culture in Late Imperial China*, ed. Cynthia Brokaw and Kai-wing Chow (Berkeley: University of California Press, 2005), 17.

3. After the Fire

1. For a brief biography of Li Kaixian, see Lee Hwa-chou, "Li K'ai-hsien," in *Dictionary of Ming Biography, 1368–1644*, ed. L. Carrington Goodrich and Zhaoying Fang (New York: Columbia University Press, 1976), 835–37.

2. Li Kaixian, *Li Kaixian ji* (Shanghai: Zhonghua shuji, 1959), 945. Translation mine.

3. Li Kaixian's phrasing here about "veins" echoes Zhu Xi's preface to *On the Practice of the Mean*, which is also echoed in the Zhang Zhupo commentary to the *Jin Ping Mei*. See Andrew Schonebaum, *Novel Medicine: Healing, Literature, and Popular Knowledge in Early Modern China* (*Modern Language Initiative Books*) (Seattle: University of Washington Press, 2016), 59–60.

4. Yuan Hongdao, for example, famously wrote to the painter Dong Qichang to request the second part of the novel. See Tina Lu, "The Literary Culture of the Late Ming," in *The Cambridge History of Chinese Literature*, ed. Kang-i Sun Chang and Stephen Owen (Cambridge: Cambridge University Press, 2010), 105.

5. Li, *Li Kaixian ji*, 334; see also discussion in Patricia Sieber, *Theaters of Desire: Authors, Readers, and the Reproduction of Early Chinese Song-Drama, 1300–2000* (New York: Palgrave Macmillan, 2003), 49.

6. Reprinted in *Zhan Ruoshui nianpu* (Shanghai: Shanghai guji chubanshe, 2009).

7. Li, *Li Kaixian ji*, 220–21. Translations mine.

8. Li, *Li Kaixian ji*, 223.

9. Li, *Li Kaixian ji*, 229.

10. Li, *Li Kaixian ji*, 222.

11. Reprinted in Li, *Li Kaixian ji*, 749–853.

12. Li, *Li Kaixian ji*, 843. Translation mine.

13. Translation modified from David Roy's in Xiaoxiaosheng and David Tod Roy, *The Plum in the Golden Vase, Or, Chin P'ing Mei Volume 4: The Climax* (Princeton, NJ; Princeton University Press, 2011), 300–301, which also includes these songs verbatim.

14. Li, *Li Kaixian ji*, 844; translation mine.

15. Roy, "Introduction," in Xiaoxiaosheng and David Tod Roy, *The Plum in the Golden Vase, Or, Chin P'ing Mei Volume 1: The Gathering* (Princeton, NJ: Princeton University Press, 1993), xxxiv–xxxv.

16. Shang Wei, "The Making of the Everyday World: The *Jin Ping Mei Cihua* and Encyclopedias for Daily Use," in David Der-wei Wang and Shang Wei, eds. *Dynastic Crisis and Cultural Innovation: From the Late Ming to the Late Qing and Beyond*, (Cambridge, MA: Harvard University Press, 2005), 67.

17. Katherine Carlitz, *The Rhetoric of Chin P'ing Mei* (Bloomington: Indiana University Press, 1986), 125.

18. This scene takes place in chapter 70 of the *cihua* version; see Xiaoxiaosheng and Roy, *The Plum in the Golden Vase, or, Chin P'ing Mei Volume 4: The Climax*, 277–305.

19. For Wu Xiaoling's original claim, see Zhongguo shehui kexueyuan wenxue yanjiusuo, Zhongguo wenxue shi bianxie zu, *Zhongguo wenxue shi* (Beijing: Renmen wenxue chubanshe, 1962), 3:949. He develops the claim further in Wu Xiaoling, "*Jin Ping Mei* he Li Kaixian shiliu shi," *Jilin daxue shehui kexue xuebao* 2 (1989): 76–83. For Xu Shuofang's claim, see Xu Shuofang. "*Jin Ping Mei* de xieding zhe shi Li Kaixian," *Hangzhou daxue xuebao* 1 (1980): 78–85. Miao Huaiming has traced the claim of Li Kaixian's authorship of the Jin Ping Mei further back, to Sun Kaidi; see Miao Huaiming, "*Jin Ping Mei* zuozhe Li Kaixian shuo de shouchuang zhe dang wei Sun Kaidi," *Gudian wenxue zhishi* 6 (2003):

51-54. A complete account of such claims can be found in Bu Jian, *Jin Ping Mei zuozhe Li Kaixian kao* (Lanzhou: Gansu renmin chubanshe, 1988).

20. Also called *Tang shu yanyi* and *Tang shu zhizhuan tongsu yanyi* within the same edition; see Sun Kaidi, *Zhongguo tongsu xiaoshuo shumu* (Beijing: Zhonghua shuju, 2012), 38; Ōtsuka Hidetaka, ed., *Zōho Chūgoku Tsūzoku Shōsetsu Shomoku* (Tokyo: Kyūko Shoin, 1987), 204. Facsimile reprint *Tang shu zhizhuan tongsu yanyi* (Taipei: Tianyi chubanshe, 1985).

21. *Tang shu zhizhuan tongsu yanyi*, 3-4. Translation mine.

22. Miao Yonghe, *Mingdai chuban shigao* (Nanjing: Jiangsu renmin chuban-she, 2000), 527.

23. On the *Riji gushi* and moral exemplar tales, see Liu Ch'iung-yun, "Women keyi cong Mingdai daode gushi leishu zhong duchu shenme? Zhishi bianji, wenhua wangluo, yu tongsu zhongguan," *Xin shixue* 30, no. 3 (2019): 1-73.

24. Reprinted in Xiong Damu, *Da Song Zhongxing tongsu yanyi* (Shanghai guji chubanshe, 1990), 1-3. Translation mine.

25. See Chen Dakang, *Mingdai xiaoshuo shi* (Beijing: Renmin wenxue chuban-she, 2007), 229-56.

26. See introduction by Yuan Shishuo in the facsimile reprint Chen Jiru, *Nanbei Song zhizhuan* (Shanghai: Shanghai guji chubanshe, 1990), 1-2.

4. Characters in the Margins

1. Sianne Ngai, *Our Aesthetic Categories: Zany, Cute, Interesting* (Cambridge, MA: Harvard University Press, 2012).

2. Sianne Ngai, *Theory of the Gimmick: Aesthetic Judgment and Capitalist Form* (Cambridge, MA: The Belknap Press of Harvard University Press, 2020).

3. Yuming He, *Home and the World: Editing the "Glorious Ming" in Woodblock-Printed Books of the Sixteenth and Seventeenth Centuries* (Cambridge, MA: Harvard University Asia Center, 2013).

4. The "Classic of Whoring" is translated in He, *Home and the World*, 261-73.

5. On the Yu publishing clan and Jianyang printing, see Lucille Chia, *Printing for Profit: The Commercial Publishers of Jianyang, Fujian (11th-17th Centuries)* (Cambridge, MA: Harvard University Asia Center, 2002), 87-93. Chia has identified 20 Yu clan imprints from the Song, 43 from the Yuan, and 371 from the Ming. Of those 371, she counts 72 as being Yu Xiangdou's. See Chia, *Printing for Profit*, 155, 298-302, 364n24. For slightly higher estimates, see also Xiao Dongfa, "Mingdai xiaoshuojia, keshujia Yu Xiangdou," in *Ming Qing xiaoshuo luncong*, vol. 4 (Shenyang: Chunfang wenyi, 1984), 195-211.

6. This reconstructed chronology is detailed in Xiao, "Mingdai xiaoshuo-jia, keshujia Yu Xiangdou."

7. The *Records of the Grand Historian* preface is reprinted in Xiao, "Mingdai xiaoshuojia, keshujia Yu Xiangdou."

8. The court-case fiction collections, *Lianming qipan gong'an zhuan*, are re-printed in the Guben xiaoshuo jicheng series published by the Shanghai guji chubanshe. On the editing practices by which the cases were reshaped, see Wu Junqing, "Sex in the Cloister: Behind the Image of the 'Criminal Monk' in Ming Courtroom Tales," *T'oung Pao* 105, no. 5-6 (2020): 545-86; Lin Kuei-ju,

"Shuye yu yusong: Cong wan Ming chuban wenhua lun Yu Xiangdou gong'an xiaoshuo de bianzuan guocheng yu chuangzuo yitu," *Bulletin of the Institute of Chinese Literature and Philosophy* 39 (2011): 1–39.

9. See, for example, the 1522 edition of *Romance of the Three Kingdoms*.

10. See *Lianming qipan gong'an zhuan*. This preface is also reprinted and discussed in Lin, "Shuye yu yusong."

11. Wu, "Sex in the Cloister: Behind the Image of the "Criminal Monk" in Ming Courtroom Tales," 560.

12. Y. W. Ma, "The Textual Tradition of Ming Kung-an Fiction: A Study of the Lung-T'u Kung-an," *Harvard Journal of Asiatic Studies* 35 (1975), 196.

13. Wu, "Sex in the Cloister"; Lin, "Shuye yu yusong."

14. Gary Seaman, *Journey to the North: An Ethnohistorical Analysis and Annotated Translation of the Chinese Folk Novel Pei-Yu Chi* (Berkeley: University of California Press, 1987), 4.

15. Seaman, *Journey to the North*, 35–39.

16. Timothy Brook, *The Confusions of Pleasure: Commerce and Culture in Ming China* (Berkeley: University of California Press, 1998), 213.

17. Preface to *Baxian zhuan*, also known as *Journey to the East: Origins of the Eight Immortals* (*Baxian chuchu dongyou ji*), reprinted in *Baxian chuchu Dongyou ji* (Shanghai: Shanghai guji chubanshe, 1990), 1–2. Irwin saw this preface as an example of Yu's limited literary abilities and a "frank admission" of his single-minded pursuit of profit. See Richard Gregg Irwin, *The Evolution of a Chinese Novel: Shui-Hu-chuan* (Cambridge: Harvard University Press, 1953), 67.

18. On the development of the copyright system and its influence on literary creation in the West, see Mark Rose, *Authors and Owners: The Invention of Copyright* (Cambridge, MA: Harvard University Press, 1993); Adrian Johns, *Piracy: The Intellectual Property Wars From Gutenberg to Gates* (Chicago: University of Chicago Press, 2009).

19. For a discussion of Li Zhi's paradoxical thought, of which his appearance was symbolic, see Rivi Handler-Spitz, *Symptoms of an Unruly Age: Li Zhi and Cultures of Early Modernity* (Seattle: University of Washington Press, 2017). For a biography of Li Zhi, see K. C. Hsiao, "Li Chih," in *Dictionary of Ming Biography, 1368–1644*, ed. L. Carrington Goodrich and Zhaoying Fang (New York: Columbia University Press, 1976), 807–18.

20. For a bibliography of books with these attributions, see Lin Qixian, *Li Zhuowu shiji xinian* (Taipei: Wenjin chubanshe, 1988).

21. On Li Zhuowu as both a product and a victim of "mass communication society," see Ōki Yasushi, *Minmatsu Kōnan no shuppan bunka* (Tokyo: Kenbun Shuppan, 2004), 129–34.

22. For a newspaper report on the "Luther Blissett" phenomenon and the reaction of the real "Luther Blissett," an uninvolved footballer, see https://www.theguardian.com/uk/2003/aug/28/football.books1.

23. Robert E. Hegel, "Performing Li Zhi: Li Zhuowu and the Fiction Commentaries of a Fictional Commentator," in *The Objectionable Li Zhi: Fiction, Criticism, and Dissent in Late Ming China*, ed. Rivi Handler-Spitz, Pauline C. Lee, and Haun Saussy (Seattle: University of Washington Press, 2020), 200–203.

24. Li Zhi, *Fenshu Xu Fenshu* (Beijing: Zhonghua shuju, 2009).; also translated twice in Li Zhi et al., *A Book to Burn and a Book to Keep (Hidden): Selected Writings* (New York: Columbia University Press, 2016), 106–13. The first translation, by Lee and Handler-Spitz, is "more meticulously annotated" while the second, by Saussy, is in a "freer style."

25. On Li Zhuowu's relationship with Yuan Zhongdao and his brothers, see Chih-p'ing Chou, *Yuan Hung-Tao and the Kung-an School* (Cambridge: Cambridge University Press, 1988), 21–26.

26. The Zhonghua shuju has printed a paginated facsimile reprint edition: *Shuihu zhizhuan pinglin* (Shanghai: Shanghai guji chubanshe, 1990), hereafter SHZZPL.

27. A facsimile reprint of the Rongyu tang edition is included in the Shanghai guji chubanshe's *Guben xiaoshuo jicheng* series: *Li Zhuowu Piping Zhongyi Shuihu zhuan* (Shanghai: Shanghai guji chubanshe, 1991). Hereafter referred to as RYTSHZ for pagination.

28. Xu Zichang is likely an alias of Ye Zhou, a "shadowy figure" who has been identified as the actual author of some "Li Zhi" commentaries. See Rolston, "The Li Chih Commentaries," in *How to Read the Chinese Novel*, ed. David L. Rolston and Shuen-fu Lin (Princeton, NJ: Princeton University Press, 1990), 356–63; and David L. Rolston, *Traditional Chinese Fiction and Fiction Commentary: Reading and Writing Between the Lines* (Stanford, CA: Stanford University Press, 1997), 2–3. For a full description of the editions, see the descriptive bibliography of *Water Margin* editions in Rolston, *How to Read the Chinese Novel*, 404–30.

29. Chou, *Yuan Hung-Tao and the Kung-an School*, 68–69.

30. Rolston and Lin, *How to Read the Chinese Novel*, 405.

31. Hegel, "Performing Li Zhi," 189.

32. This preface is reprinted in Zhu Yixuan, *Shuihu zhuan ziliao huibian* (Tianjin: Nankai daxue chubanshe, 2002), 192–93; erroneously attributed there to "Tian Haicang" (from the stamp in the Japanese original reading "From the collection of [the monk] Tenkai").

33. RYTSHZ vol. 5, supplement, 1–17. Also reprinted in Zhu, *Shuihu zhuan ziliao huibian*, 171–72.

34. Plaks has suggested that this "climactic watershed" served as a model for the structures of other, later novels. See Andrew H. Plaks, *The Four Masterworks of the Ming Novel: Ssu Ta Ch'i-Shu* (Princeton, NJ: Princeton University Press, 1987), 380–81.

35. Chapter numbers here are according to the received "full-recension" (*fanben*) editions. Chapter numbering, as will be seen below, varies by edition. Chapter divisions of the Yu Xiangdou edition will be discussed below. Also notable is that chapters in the Jin Shengtan edition, which will be discussed in the following chapter, differ by one. Translations of these chapters can be found in volumes 1 and 2 of the Dent-Young translation, Shi Nai'an and Luo Guanzhong, *The Broken Seals: Part One of the Marshes of Mount Liang*, trans. John Dent-Young and Alex Dent-Young (Hong Kong: The Chinese University Press, 1994); and Shi Nai'an and Luo Guanzhong, *The Tiger Killers: Part Two of the Marshes of Mount Liang*, trans. John Dent-Young and Alex Dent-Young (Hong Kong: Chinese University Press, 1997).

36. Translated in Dent-Young as "The old woman shelves her grievance when they pay; Sergeant Zhu allows Song Jiang to get away!" Shi and Luo, *The Broken Seals*, 415.

37. Translated in Dent-Young as "Wu Song gets drunk and beats Red Star; The Dandy treats Song Jiang with honor!" Shi and Luo, *The Tiger Killers*, 185.

38. Shi and Luo, *The Tiger Killers*, 202.

39. SHZZPL, 209–16.

40. SHZZPL, 209.

41. SHZZPL, 210.

42. SHZZPL, 211.

43. SHZZPL, 212.

44. SHZZPL, 213.

45. SHZZPL, 214.

46. SHZZPL, 215.

47. SHZZPL, 216.

48. SHZZPL, 281.

49. SHZZPL, 301.

50. SHZZPL, 302.

51. SHZZPL, 303.

52. The chapter and its illustrations are found in RYTSHZ, 663–89.

53. RYTSHZ, 665.

54. RYTSHZ, 667. For a translation of this passage of the novel, see Shi and Luo, *The Broken Seals*, 416.

55. RYTSHZ, 667.

56. RYTSHZ, 668.

57. RYTSHZ, 675.

58. RYTSHZ, 689.

59. The chapter and its preceding images are found in RYTSHZ, 997–1039.

60. RYTSHZ, 1029.

61. RYTSHZ, 1033.

62. RYTSHZ, 1034. The corresponding translation of this passage of the novel can be found in Shi and Luo, *The Tiger Killers*, 206.

63. RYTSHZ, 1036.

64. RYTSHZ, 1037.

65. RYTSHZ, 1039.

66. Handler-Spitz, *Symptoms of an Unruly Age*, 44–68.

67. Bruno Latour, *Reassembling the Social: An Introduction to Actor-Network-Theory* (Oxford: Oxford University Press, 2005), 39.

68. For this memorial and subsequent order, see Wang Liqi, *Yuan Ming Qing sandai jinhui xiaoshuo xiqu shiliao* (Beijing: Zuojia chubanshe, 1958), 16–18.

5. "The Art of Subtle Phrasing Has Been Extinguished"

1. The *Cambridge History of Chinese Literature*, for example, provides the 1641 date of the preface and adds, "published in 1644?" with the question mark but no further explanation. See Wai-Yee Li, "Early Qing to 1723," in *Cambridge History of Chinese Literature*, ed. Kang-i Sun Chang and Stephen Owen (Cambridge:

Cambridge University Press, 2010), 2:211. Fang Chao-ying's entry on Jin in *Eminent Chinese of the Ch'ing Period* claims that Jin's *Water Margin* commentaries were written "about 1641" and "were printed in 1644 by Han Chu, whose studio was named Kuan-hua t'ang." See "Chin Jen-jui" in *Eminent Chinese of Ch'ing Period (1644-1912)*, ed. Arthur W. Hummel (Washington: United States Government Printing Office, 1943), 164-66. Lu Lin, the editor of Jin's collected works, tends to agree with the earlier date. See Lu Lin, *Jin Shengtan shishi yanjiu* (Beijing: Renmin wenxue chubanshe, 2015), 663-64.

2. John Wang pioneered this comparison with the New Critics in his pathbreaking study on Jin; see John C. Y. Wang, *Chin Sheng-t'an* (New York: Twayne Publishers, 1972). For a more recent example of such comparison—a testament to Wang's lasting influence—see Wu Zilin, *Jingdian zai shengchan: Jin Shengtan xiaoshuo pingdian de wenhua toushi* (Beijing: Beijing daxue chubanshe, 2009).

3. For these texts (including their titles), I follow the translation by Andrew Plaks. See Andrew H. Plaks and Xinzhong Yao, *Ta Hsüeh and Chung Yung: The Highest Order of Cultivation, and on the Practice of the Mean* (New York: Penguin, 2003).

4. The prefaces of the edition are reprinted in Zhu Yixuan, *Shuihu zhuan ziliao huibian* (Tianjin: Nankai daxue chubanshe, 2002), 206-26. A facsimile reprint of the edition was printed as *Diwu caizi shu Shi Nai'an Shuihu zhuan*, by Zhonghua shuju in 1975.

5. Zhu, *Shuihu zhuan ziliao huibian*, 205-11.

6. Zhu, *Shuihu zhuan ziliao huibian*, 211-12.

7. Naifei Ding, *Obscene Things: Sexual Politics in Jin Ping Mei* (Durham, NC: Duke University Press, 2002), 65, 258-59n55.

8. Zhu, *Shuihu zhuan ziliao huibian*, 212-15.

9. Zhu, *Shuihu zhuan ziliao huibian*, 215-18.

10. Zhu, *Shuihu zhuan ziliao huibian*, 218-25. A translation by John Wang is available in David L. Rolston and Shuen-fu Lin, eds. *How to Read the Chinese Novel* (Princeton, NJ: Princeton University Press, 1990), 140-45.

11. Zhu, *Shuihu zhuan ziliao huibian*, 225-26.

12. See Roland Altenburger, "Appropriating Genius: Jin Shengtan's Construction of Textual Authority and Authorship in His Commented Edition of *Shuihu zhuan* (the *Water Margin* Saga)," in *That Wonderful Composite Called Author: Authorship in East Asian Literatures From the Beginnings to the Seventeenth Century*, ed. Christian Schwermann and Raji C. Steineck (Leiden: Brill, 2014), 171-73.

13. David L. Rolston, *Traditional Chinese Fiction and Fiction Commentary: Reading and Writing Between the Lines* (Stanford, CA: Stanford University Press, 1997), 3.

14. Ding, *Obscene Things: Sexual Politics in Jin Ping Mei*, 51.

15. Ding, *Obscene Things: Sexual Politics in Jin Ping Mei*, 65.

16. Ding, *Obscene Things: Sexual Politics in Jin Ping Mei*, 51.

17. Ding, *Obscene Things: Sexual Politics in Jin Ping Mei*, 73.

18. Janice A. Radway, *A Feeling for Books: The Book-of-the-Month Club, Literary Taste, and Middle-Class Desire* (Chapel Hill: University of North Carolina Press, 1997), 129.

19. Radway, *A Feeling for Books*, 132.

20. Radway, *A Feeling for Books*, 137.

21. Zhu, *Shuihu zhuan ziliao huibian*, 227–28.

22. Zhu, *Shuihu zhuan ziliao huibian*, 229.

23. Rolston and Lin, *How to Read the Chinese Novel*, 133.

24. Rolston and Lin, *How to Read the Chinese Novel*, 132.

25. For an English translation, see Shi Nai'an and Luo Guanzhong, *The Tiger Killers: Part Two of the Marshes of Mount Liang,* trans. John Dent-Young and Alex Dent-Young (Hong Kong: Chinese University Press, 1997), 419–43.

26. On the ten-chapter unit as a "standard generic feature" of the "literati novel form," see Andrew H. Plaks, *The Four Masterworks of the Ming Novel: Ssu Ta Ch'i-Shu* (Princeton, NJ: Princeton University Press, 1987), 72–75. For another argument for the intricacy of structural design in a Ming novel, see also Roy's introduction to his translation of the *Jin Ping Mei*, Xiaoxiaosheng. and David Tod Roy, *The Plum in the Golden Vase, Or, Chin P'ing Mei Volume 1: The Gathering* (Princeton, NJ: Princeton University Press, 1993); on ten-chapter units, see xxxv.

27. *Li Zhuowu Piping Zhongyi Shuihu zhuan* (Shanghai: Shanghai guji chubanshe, 1991), 1390.

28. *Li Zhuowu Piping Zhongyi Shuihu zhuan*, 1430.

29. Original in *Shuihu quanzhuan* (Chengdu: Sichuan wenyi chubanshe, 1986), 487. Translation mine; compare with Shi and Luo, *The Tiger Killers*, 425.

30. *Shuihu quanzhuan*, p. 491. Translation mine; compare with Shi and Luo, *The Tiger Killers*, 431.

31. This poem plays on the standard hypothetical names in Chinese, "Zhang the Third and Li the Fourth"; since Li Kui gives his name as "Zhang," the phrase fits.

32. Original in *Shuihu quanzhuan*, 493. Translation adopted from Shi and Luo, *The Tiger Killers*, 435.

33. Rolston and Lin, *How to Read the Chinese Novel*, 144.

34. Rolston and Lin, *How to Read the Chinese Novel*, 136.

35. Rolston and Lin, *How to Read the Chinese Novel*, 139.

36. The reference is to Mencius IIIB2; see Mencius, *Mencius,* trans. D. C. Lau (Harmondsworth: Penguin, 1970), 107. The equivalent passage in the "How to Read" list, with slightly different wording, is found in Rolston and Lin, *How to Read the Chinese Novel*, 136–37.

37. Rolston and Lin, *How to Read the Chinese Novel*, 136.

38. Rolston and Lin, *How to Read the Chinese Novel*, 132.

39. Rolston and Lin, *How to Read the Chinese Novel*, 137.

40. Zhu, *Shuihu zhuan ziliao huibian*, 270–73. Translations below are mine, except where noted.

41. Phrases here from *The Highest Order of Cultivation* and *On the Practice of the Mean* are translated following Plaks; I have placed them in quotation marks and provided page numbers for the corresponding place in Plaks's translation. Of course, these phrases are unmarked in Jin's original; an educated reader would recognize them without prompting. I mark them in this way to convey Jin's rhetorical practices and tone as much as his meaning.

42. Plaks and Yao, *Highest Order*, 11.

43. Plaks and Yao, *Mean*, 42.

44. Plaks and Yao, *Highest Order*, 11.

45. Plaks and Yao, *Mean*, 25.

46. Plaks and Yao, *Mean*, 25.

47. Plaks and Yao, *Mean*, 25.

48. For Plaks's explanation of this translation of *gewu*, see Plaks and Yao, *Ta Hsüeh and Chung Yung*, 110–11.

49. See Rolston, *Traditional Chinese Fiction*; Rolston and Lin, *How to Read the Chinese Novel*.

50. On Jin's influence on the writing of the sequel to *The Water Margin*, see Ellen Widmer, *The Margins of Utopia: Shui-Hu Hou-Chuan and the Literature of Ming Loyalism* (Cambridge, MA: Council on East Asian Studies, 1987). On "auto-commentary" and commentator-narrators, see also Rolston, *Traditional Chinese Fiction*, 269–348.

51. William C. Hedberg, *The Japanese Discovery of Chinese Fiction: The Water Margin and the Making of a National Canon* (New York: Columbia University Press, 2020).

52. Hu Shi, "Shuihu kaozheng," in *Shuihu zhuan*, ed. Wang Yuanfang (Shanghai: Oriental Book Company, 1920), 1-9.

53. Rivi Handler-Spitz, *Symptoms of an Unruly Age: Li Zhi and Cultures of Early Modernity* (Seattle: University of Washington Press, 2017).

54. Barbara C. Bowen, *The Age of Bluff; Paradox and Ambiguity in Rabelais and Montaigne* (Urbana: University of Illinois Press, 1972), 6; for Handler-Spitz's adaptation of the term, see Handler-Spitz, *Symptoms of an Unruly Age*, 44–68.

55. Martin W. Huang, "Author(ity) and Reader in Traditional Chinese Xiaoshuo Commentary," *Chinese Literature: Essays, Articles, Reviews (CLEAR)* 16 (1994): 67–41.

56. Huang, "Author(ity) and Reader in Traditional Chinese Xiaoshuo Commentary," 45.

57. Altenburger, "Appropriating Genius," 190.

Conclusion

1. See, for example, Michael Hunter's discussion of the *Shijing* as a "fluid repertoire" of orally transmitted songs and his "middle-distance" reading of the text. Michael Hunter, *The Poetics of Early Chinese Thought: How the* Shijing *Shaped the Chinese Philosophical Tradition* (New York: Columbia University Press, 2021).

BIBLIOGRAPHY

Altenburger, Roland. "Appropriating Genius: Jin Shengtan's Construction of Textual Authority and Authorship in His Commented Edition of Shuihu zhuan (the Water Margin Saga)." In *That Wonderful Composite Called Author: Authorship in East Asian Literatures From the Beginnings to the Seventeenth Century*, edited by Christian Schwermann and Raji C. Steineck, 163–94. Leiden: Brill, 2014.

Baxian chuchu Dongyou ji. Shanghai: Shanghai guji chubanshe, 1990.

Beijing guqin yanjiuhui, ed. *Qinqu jicheng* Beijing: Zhonghua shuju, 1963.

Biji xiaoshuo daguan: ba bian. Taipei: Xinxing shuju, 1975.

Børdahl, Vibeke. *Wu Song Fights the Tiger: The Interaction of Oral and Written Traditions in the Chinese Novel, Drama and Storytelling*. Copenhagen: NIAS Press, 2013.

Bourdieu, Pierre. *The Field of Cultural Production: Essays on Art and Literature*. New York: Columbia University Press, 1993.

Bowen, Barbara C. *The Age of Bluff: Paradox and Ambiguity in Rabelais and Montaigne*. Urbana: University of Illinois Press, 1972.

Brokaw, Cynthia. "On the History of the Book in China." In *Printing and Book Culture in Late Imperial China*, edited by Cynthia Brokaw and Kai-wing Chow, 3-54. Berkeley: University of California Press, 2005.

Brook, Timothy. *The Confusions of Pleasure: Commerce and Culture in Ming China*. Berkeley: University of California Press, 1998.

Bryant, Daniel. *The Great Recreation: Ho Ching-Ming (1483–1521) and His World*. Leiden; Boston: Brill, 2008.

Bu Jian. *Jin Ping Mei zuozhe Li Kaixian kao*. Lanzhou: Gansu renmin chubanshe, 1988.

Cai Zhengsun. *Gujin mingxian conghua Shilin guangji*. Taipei: Guangwen shuju, 1973.

Cai Zhengsun. *Shilin guangji*. Beijing: Zhonghua shuju, 1982.

Carlitz, Katherine. *The Rhetoric of Chin P'ing Mei*. Bloomington: Indiana University Press, 1986.

Chang, Kang-i Sun and Stephen Owen, eds. *The Cambridge History of Chinese Literature*. Cambridge: Cambridge University Press, 2010.

Chao Li. *Chao shi Baowen Tang shumu*. Shanghai: Gudian wenxue chubanshe, 1957.

Chartier, Roger. *The Author's Hand and the Printer's Mind*. Malden, MA: Polity Press, 2014.

Chen Dakang. *Mingdai xiaoshuo shi*. Beijing: Renmin wenxue chubanshe, 2007.

Chen Jianping. *Shuihu xi yu Zhongguo xiayi wenhua*. Beijing: Wenhua yishu chubanshe, 2008.

Chen Jiru. *Nanbei Song zhizhuan*. Shanghai: Shanghai guji chubanshe, 1990.

Chen Qinghui. "Gujin shuke banben kao." *Wenxian* 4 (2007): 161-168.

Chen Songbo. *Shuihu zhuan yuan kaolun*. Beijing: Renmin wenxue chubanshe, 2006.

Cherniack, Susan. "Book Culture and Textual Transmission in Sung China." *Harvard Journal of Asiatic Studies* 54, no. 1 (1994): 125-25.

Chia, Lucille. *Printing for Profit: The Commercial Publishers of Jianyang, Fujian (11th–17th Centuries)*. Cambridge, MA: Harvard University Asia Center, 2002.

Chou, Chih-p'ing. *Yuan Hung-Tao and the Kung-an School*. Cambridge: Cambridge University Press, 1988.

Chou, E. Shan. *Reconsidering Tu Fu: Literary Greatness and Cultural Context*. Cambridge: Cambridge University Press, 1995.

Clunas, Craig. *Superfluous Things: Material Culture and Social Status in Early Modern China*. Cambridge: Polity, 1991.

Ding Bing. *Shanben shushi cangshu zhi*. Taipei: Guangwen shuju, 1967.

Ding, Naifei. *Obscene Things: Sexual Politics in Jin Ping Mei*. Durham, NC: Duke University Press, 2002.

Diwu caizi shu Shi Nai'an Shuihu zhuan. Beijing: Zhonghua shuju, 1975.

Du Xinfu. *Mingdai banke zonglu* Yangzhou: Yangzhou guji shudian, 1983.

Du Xinfu. *Quan Ming fensheng fenxian keshu kao*. Beijing: Xianzhuang shuju, 2001.

Fang, Lienche Tu. "Kuo Hsun." In *Dictionary of Ming Biography, 1368–1644*, edited by L. Carrington Goodrich and Zhaoying Fang, 770-773. New York: Columbia University Press, 1976.

Galambos, Imre. *Orthography of Early Chinese Writing: Evidence from Newly Excavated Manuscripts*. Budapest: Department of East Asian Studies, Eötvös Loránd University, 2006.

Gao Ru and Zhou Hongzu. *Baichuan shuzhi gujin shuke*. Shanghai: Gudian wenxue chu ban she, 1957.

Ge, Liangyan. *Out of the Margins: The Rise of Chinese Vernacular Fiction*. Honolulu: University of Hawai'i Press, 2001.

Geiss, James. "The Chia-ching Reign." In *The Cambridge History of China: The Ming Dynasty*, edited by Denis Twitchett and Frederick Mote, 7:440-510. Cambridge: Cambridge University Press, 1988.

Goodrich, L. Carrington, and Zhaoying Fang, eds. *Dictionary of Ming Biography, 1368–1644*. New York: Columbia University Press, 1976.

Gulik, Robert Hans van. *The Lore of the Chinese Lute: An Essay in the Ideology of the Ch'in*. Tokyo: Sophia University Press, 1969.

Haar, B. J. ter. *The White Lotus Teachings in Chinese Religious History*. Leiden: E. J. Brill, 1991.

Han Ying. *Han Shih Wai Chuan: Han Ying's Illustrations of the Didactic Application of the Classic of Songs*. Translated by James Robert Hightower. Cambridge, MA: Harvard University Press, 1952.

Handler-Spitz, Rivi. *Symptoms of an Unruly Age: Li Zhi and Cultures of Early Modernity*. Seattle: University of Washington Press, 2017.

He, Yuming. *Home and the World: Editing the "Glorious Ming" in Woodblock-Printed Books of the Sixteenth and Seventeenth Centuries*. Cambridge, MA: Harvard University Asia Center, 2013.

Hedberg, William C. *The Japanese Discovery of Chinese Fiction: The Water Margin and the Making of a National Canon*. New York: Columbia University Press, 2020.

Hegel, Robert E. *Reading Illustrated Fiction in Late Imperial China*. Stanford, CA: Stanford University Press, 1998.

Hegel, Robert E. "Performing Li Zhi: Li Zhuowu and the Fiction Commentaries of a Fictional Commentator." In *The Objectionable Li Zhi: Fiction, Criticism, and Dissent in Late Ming China*, edited by Rivi Handler-Spitz, Pauline C. Lee, and Haun Saussy, 187-208. Seattle: University of Washington Press, 2020.

Hennessey, William O. *Proclaiming Harmony*. Ann Arbor: University of Michigan, Center for Chinese Studies, 1981.

Hu Jixun, "Guo Xun kanshu kaolun: jiazu shi yanyi kanbu yu Ming zhongye zhengzhi de hudong." *Zhonghua wenshi luncong* 117 (2015): 368-89.

Hu Qiguang. *Zhongguo xiaoxue shi*. Shanghai: Shanghai renmin chubanshe, 1987.

Hu Shi. "*Shuihu* kaozheng." In *Shuihu zhuan*, edited by Wang Yuanfang, 1-9. Shanghai: Oriental Book Company, 1920.

Hu Yinglin. *Shaoshi Shanfang Bicong*. Beijing: Zhonghua shuju, 1958.

Huang, Martin W. "Author(ity) and Reader in Traditional Chinese Xiaoshuo Commentary." *Chinese Literature: Essays, Articles, Reviews (CLEAR)* 16 (1994): 67-41.

Hummel, Arthur W., ed. *Eminent Chinese of Ch'ing Period (1644–1912)*. Washington: United States Government Printing Office, 1943.

Hunter, Michael. *The Poetics of Early Chinese Thought: How the Shijing Shaped the Chinese Philosophical Tradition*. New York: Columbia University Press, 2021.

Idema, W. L. *The Dramatic Oeuvre of Chu Yu-Tun (1379–1439)*. Leiden: Brill, 1985.

Irwin, Richard Gregg. *The Evolution of a Chinese Novel: Shui-hu-chuan*. Cambridge, MA: Harvard University Press, 1953.

Jauss, Hans Robert. *Toward an Aesthetic of Reception*. Minneapolis: University of Minnesota Press, 1981.

Johns, Adrian. *Piracy: The Intellectual Property Wars From Gutenberg to Gates*. Chicago: University of Chicago Press, 2009.

Kastan, David Scott. *Shakespeare and the Book*. Cambridge: Cambridge University Press, 2001.

Latour, Bruno. *Reassembling the Social: An Introduction to Actor-Network-Theory*. Oxford: Oxford University Press, 2005.

Li Kaixian. *Li Kaixian ji*. Shanghai: Zhonghua shuji, 1959.

Li, Wai-Yee. "Early Qing to 1723." In *The Cambridge History of Chinese Literature*, edited by Chang and Owen, 2:152 - 244. Cambridge: Cambridge University Press, 2010.

Li Yeming. *Zhan Ruoshui nianpu*. Shanghai: Shanghai guji chubanshe, 2009.

Li Yonghu, "*Shuihu zhuan* santi." *Ming-Qing xiaoshuo yanjiu* 3 (2015).

Li Zhi. *Fenshu Xu Fenshu*. Beijing: Zhonghua shuju, 2009.

Li Zhi, Rivi Handler-Spitz, Pauline C. Lee, and Haun Saussy. *A Book to Burn and a Book to Keep (Hidden): Selected Writings*. New York: Columbia University Press, 2016.

Li Zhuowu Piping Zhongyi Shuihu zhuan. Shanghai: Shanghai guji chubanshe, 1991.

Lin Kuei-ju. "Shuye yu yusong: Cong wan Ming chuban wenhua lun Yu Xiang-dou gong'an xiaoshuo de bianzuan guocheng yu chuangzuo yitu." *Bulletin of the Institute of Chinese Literature and Philosophy* 39 (2011): 1–39.

Lin Qixian. *Li Zhuowu Shiji Xinian*. Taipei: Wenjin chubanshe, 1988.

Liu Ch'iung-yun, "Women keyi cong Mingdai daode gushi leishu zhong duchu shenme? Zhishi bianji, wenhua wangluo, yu tongsu zhongguan." *Xin shixue* 30, no. 3 (2019: 1–73.

Lowry, Kathryn A. *The Tapestry of Popular Songs in 16th- and 17th-Century China: Reading, Imitation, and Desire*. Leiden: Brill, 2005.

Lu Lin. *Jin Shengtan shishi yanjiu*. Beijing: Renmin wenxue chubanshe, 2015.

Lu Rong. *Shuyuan zaji*. Beijing: Zhonghua shuju, 1985.

Lu, Tina. "The Literary Culture of the Late Ming." In *The Cambridge History of Chinese Literature*, edited by Chang and Owen, 2:63-151. Cambridge: Cambridge University Press, 2010.

Ma Shutian, "Kanke *Shuihu zhuan* de Guo Xun." *Wenshi zhishi* 12 (1983): 75–78.

Ma, Y. W. "The Textual Tradition of Ming Kung-an Fiction: A Study of the *Lung-T'u Kung-an*." *Harvard Journal of Asiatic Studies* 35 (1975): 190–220.

Ma, Y. W. *Shuihu Erlun*. Taipei: Lianjing chubanshe, 2005.

McLaren, Anne E. "Ming Audiences and Vernacular Hermeneutics: The Uses of 'The Romance of the Three Kingdoms.'" *T'oung Pao* second series 81, no. 1/3 (1995): 51–80.

McLaren, Anne E. *Chinese Popular Culture and Ming Chantefables*. Leiden: Brill, 1998.

McLaren, Anne E. "Constructing New Reading Publics in Late Ming China." In *Printing and Book Culture in Late Imperial China*, edited by Cynthia Brokaw and Kai-wing Chow, 152–83. Berkeley: University of California Press, 2005.

McMullen, David. "Yuan Chieh." In *The Indiana Companion to Traditional Chinese Literature*, edited by William H. Nienhauser, 952. Bloomington: Indiana University Press, 1986: 952.

Mencius. *Mencius*. Translated by D. C. Lau. Harmondsworth: Penguin, 1970.

Miao Huaiming. "*Jin Ping Mei* zuozhe Li Kaixian shuo de shouchuang zhe dang wei Sun Kaidi." *Gudian wenxue zhishi* 6 (2003): 51–54.

Miao Yonghe. *Mingdai chuban shigao*. Nanjing: Jiangsu renmin chubanshe, 2000.

Ngai, Sianne. *Our Aesthetic Categories: Zany, Cute, Interesting*. Cambridge, MA: Harvard University Press, 2012.

Ngai, Sianne. *Theory of the Gimmick: Aesthetic Judgment and Capitalist Form*. Cambridge, MA: The Belknap Press of Harvard University Press, 2020.

Nienhauser, William H., ed. *The Indiana Companion to Traditional Chinese Literature*. Bloomington: Indiana University Press, 1986.

Ning Jifu. *Hanyu yunshu shi Mingdai juan*. Shanghai: Shanghai renmin chubanshe, 2009.

Norman, Jerry. *Chinese*. Cambridge: Cambridge University Press, 1987.

Nugent, Christopher M. B. *Manifest in Words, Written on Paper: Producing and Circulating Poetry in Tang Dynasty China*. Cambridge, MA: Harvard University Asia Center, 2010.

Ōki Yasushi. *Minmatsu Kōnan no shuppan bunka*. Tokyo: Kenbun Shuppan, 2004.

Ong, Chang Woei. "The Principles Are Many: Wang Tingxiang and Intellectual Transition in Mid-Ming China." *Harvard Journal of Asiatic Studies* 66, no. 2 (2006): 461–93.

Ōtsuka Hidetaka, ed. *Zōho Chūgoku tsūzoku shōsetsu shomoku*. Tokyo: Kyūko Shoin, 1987.

Owen, Stephen. "The Cultural Tang (650–1020)," in *The Cambridge History of Chinese Literature*, ed. Kang-i Sun Chang and Stephen Owen (Cambridge: Cambridge University Press, 2010), 286-380.

Plaks, Andrew H. *The Four Masterworks of the Ming Novel: Ssu Ta Ch'i-Shu*. Princeton, NJ: Princeton University Press, 1987.

Plaks, Andrew H., and Xinzhong Yao. *Ta Hsüeh and Chung Yung: The Highest Order of Cultivation, and on the Practice of the Mean*. New York: Penguin, 2003.

Qi Fukang. *Zhongguo Gudai Shufang Yanjiu*. Beijing: Shangwu yinshu guan, 2007.

Qu Mianliang. *Zhongguo guji banke cidian*. Suzhou: Suzhou daxue chubanshe, 2009.

Radway, Janice A. *A Feeling for Books: The Book-of-the-month Club, Literary Taste, and Middle-Class Desire*. Chapel Hill: University of North Carolina Press, 1997.

Rolston, David L., and Shuen-fu Lin, eds. *How to Read the Chinese Novel*. Princeton, NJ: Princeton University Press, 1990.

Rolston, David L. *Traditional Chinese Fiction and Fiction Commentary: Reading and Writing Between the Lines*. Stanford, Calif.: Stanford University Press, 1997.

Rose, Mark. *Authors and Owners: The Invention of Copyright*. Cambridge, MA: Harvard University Press, 1993.

Roy, David Tod. *The Plum in the Golden Vase Or, Chin P'ing Mei Volume 3: The Aphrodisiac*. Princeton, NJ: Princeton University Press, 2011.

Schonebaum, Andrew. *Novel Medicine: Healing, Literature, and Popular Knowledge in Early Modern China*. Seattle: University of Washington Press, 2016.

Seaman, Gary. *Journey to the North: An Ethnohistorical Analysis and Annotated Translation of the Chinese Folk Novel Pei-Yu Chi*. Berkeley: University of California Press, 1987.

Shang Wei. "The Making of the Everyday World: The Jin Ping Mei Cihua and Encyclopedias for Daily Use." In *Dynastic Crisis and Cultural Innovation: From the Late Ming to the Late Qing and Beyond*, edited by David Der-wei Wang and Shang Wei, 63–92. Cambridge, MA: Harvard University Press, 2005.

Shen Defu. *Wanli yehuo bian*. Beijing: Zhonghua shuju, 1959.

Shi Nai'an and Luo Guanzhong. *The Broken Seals: Part One of the Marshes of Mount Liang*. Translated by John Dent-Young and Alex Dent-Young. Hong Kong: The Chinese University Press, 1994.

Shi Nai'an and Luo Guanzhong. *The Tiger Killers: Part Two of the Marshes of Mount Liang*. Translated by John Dent-Young and Alex Dent-Young. Hong Kong: Chinese University Press, 1997.

Shuihu quanzhuan. Beijing: Renmin wenxue chubanshe, 1954.

Shuihu quanzhuan. Chengdu: Sichuan wenyi chubanshe, 1986.

Shuihu zhizhuan pinglin. Shanghai: Shanghai guji chubanshe, 1990.

Sieber, Patricia. *Theaters of Desire: Authors, Readers, and the Reproduction of Early Chinese Song-Drama, 1300–2000.* New York: Palgrave Macmillan, 2003.

Son, Suyoung. *Writing for Print: Publishing and the Making of Textual Authority in Late Imperial China.* Cambridge, MA: Harvard University Asia Center, 2018.

Sun Kaidi. *Zhongguo tongsu xiaoshuo shumu.* Beijing: Zhonghua shuju, 2012.

Tan, Tian Yuan. *Songs of Contentment and Transgression: Discharged Officials and Literati Communities in Sixteenth-Century North China.* Cambridge, MA: Harvard University Asia Center, 2010.

Tang Jianyuan, ed. *Qin Fu.* Taipei: Lianguan chubanshe, 1971.

Tang shu zhizhuan tongsu yanyi. Taipei: Tianyi chubanshe, 1985.

Tian, Xiaofei. *Tao Yuanming & Manuscript Culture: The Record of a Dusty Table.* Seattle: University of Washington Press, 2005.

Van Zoeren, Steven Jay. *Poetry and Personality: Reading, Exegesis, and Hermeneutics in Traditional China.* Stanford, CA: Stanford University Press, 1991.

Varsano, Paula M. *Tracking the Banished Immortal: The Poetry of Li Bo and Its Critical Reception.* Honolulu: University of Hawai'i Press, 2003.

Volpp, Sophie. "The Gift of a Python Robe: The Circulation of Objects in 'Jin Ping Mei.'" *Harvard Journal of Asiatic Studies* 65, no. 1 (2005): 133–58.

Wang, Fei-Hsien. *Pirates and Publishers: A Social History of Copyright in Modern China.* Princeton, NJ: Princeton University Press, 2019.

Wang Jiexin. *Zhongyuan Yinyun Xinkao.* Taibei Shi: Taiwan shang wu yin shu guan, 1988.

Wang, John C. Y. *Chin Sheng-t'an.* New York: Twayne Publishers, 1972.

Wang Liqi. *Yuan Ming Qing sandai jinhui xiaoshuo xiqu shiliao.* Beijing: Zuojia chubanshe, 1958.

Wang, Richard G. *Ming Erotic Novellas: Genre, Consumption, and Religiosity in Cultural Practice.* Hong Kong: Chinese University Press, 2011.

West, Andrew Christopher. "Quest for the Urtext: The Textual Archaeology of the Three Kingdoms." PhD diss., Princeton University, 1993.

Widmer, Ellen. *The Margins of Utopia: Shui-Hu Hou-Chuan and the Literature of Ming Loyalism.* Cambridge, MA: Harvard University Press, 1987.

Wu, Junqing. "Sex in the Cloister: Behind the Image of the 'Criminal Monk' in Ming Courtroom Tales." *T'oung Pao* 105, no. 5–6 (2020): 545–86.

Wu Xiaoling. "*Jin Ping Mei* he Li Kaixian shiliu shi." *Jilin daxue shehui kexue xuebao* 2 (1989): 76–83.

Wu Zilin. *Jingdian zai shengchan: Jin Shengtan xiaoshuo pingdian de wenhua toushi.* Beijing: Beijing daxue chubanshe, 2009.

Xiao Dongfa. "Mingdai xiaoshuojia, keshujia Yu Xiangdou." *Ming Qing Xiaoshuo Luncong* 4:195–211. Shenyang: Chunfang wenyi, 1984.

Xiao Tong. *Wen Xuan, Or, Selections of Refined Literature.* Translated by David R. Knechtges. Princeton, NJ: Princeton University Press, 1982.

Xiaoxiaosheng and David Tod Roy. *The Plum in the Golden Vase, Or, Chin P'ing Mei Volume 1: The Gathering.* Princeton, NJ: Princeton University Press, 1993.

Xiaoxiaosheng and David Tod Roy. *The Plum in the Golden Vase, Or, Chin P'ing Mei Volume 4: The Climax.* Princeton, NJ: Princeton University Press, 2011.

Xie Bixia. *Shuihu xiqu ershi zhong yanjiu.* Taipei: Taiwan daxue chuban weiyuanhui, 1981.

Xiong Damu. *Da Song Zhongxing tongsu yanyi.* Shanghai guji chubanshe, 1990.

Xu Shuofang. *"Jin Ping Mei de xieding zhe shi Li Kaixian." Hangzhou daxue xuebao* 1 (1980): 78–85.

Yang Chaoying. *Chaoye xinsheng Taiping yuefu.* Beijing: Zhonghua shuju, 1958.

Yang Hongtao and Jia Erqiang, "Mingdai Duchayuan kanke *Sanguo zhi yanyi, Shuihu zhuan* chuyi." *Lishi wenxian* 42 (2019): 300-308.

Yang Shihong. *Tang yin pingzhu.* Baoding Shi: Hebei da xue chu ban she, 2006.

Ye Dehui. *Shulin qinghua: Fu Shulin yuhua.* Beijing: Xinhua shudian, 1957.

Yuan Shishuo. *Wenxue shixue de Ming Qing xiaoshuo yanjiu.* Jinan: Qi Lu shushe, 1999.

Zhang Guoguang. *"Shuihu* zuben tankao: jian lun Shi Nai'an wei Guo Xun menke zhi tuoming." *Jianghan luntan* 1 (1982): 41–46.

Zhang Lian. *Mingdai Zhongyang zhengfu chuban yu wenhua zhengce zhi yanjiu.* Taibei Xian Yonghe Shi: Hua Mulan wenhua chubanshe, 2006.

Zhang Xiumin. *Zhang Xiumin yinshua shi lunwen ji.* Beijing: Yinshua gongye chubanshe, 1988.

Zhang Xiumin. *Zhongguo yinshua shi.* Hangzhou: Zhejiang guji chubanshe, 2006.

Zhongguo shehui kexueyuan wenxue yanjiusuo. *Zhongguo wenxue shi bianxie zu, Zhongguo wenxue shi.* Beijing: Renmen wenxue chubanshe, 1962.

Zhu Qing and Li Yongyu. "Guo Wuding ben wenti xinyi." *Wenxue yichan* 5 (1997): 81–92.

Zhu Yixuan. *Shuihu zhuan ziliao huibian.* Tianjin: Nankai daxue chubanshe, 2002.

Zhu Yixuan. *Sanguo yanyi ziliao huibian.* Tianjin: Nankai daxue chubanshe, 2012.

Zhu Yixuan and Liu Yuchen. *Shuihu zhuan ziliao huibian.* Tianjin: Baihua wenyi chubanshe, 1981.

INDEX

CPSIA information can be obtained
at www.ICGtesting.com
Printed in the USA
LVHW041304240323
742403LV00004B/521